# EXPLAINING THE HOLOCAUST

# EXPLAINING THE HOLOCAUST

## How and Why It Happened

Mordecai Schreiber

Foreword by Mordecai Paldiel

 CASCADE *Books* • Eugene, Oregon

EXPLAINING THE HOLOCAUST
How and Why It Happened

Copyright © 2015 Mordecai Schreiber. All rights reserved. Except for brief quotations in critical publications or reviews, no part of this book may be reproduced in any manner without prior written permission from the publisher. Write: Permissions, Wipf and Stock Publishers, 199 W. 8th Ave., Suite 3, Eugene, OR 97401.

Cascade Books
An Imprint of Wipf and Stock Publishers
199 W. 8th Ave., Suite 3
Eugene, OR 97401

www.wipfandstock.com

ISBN 13: 978-1-4982-1991-4

*Cataloging-in-Publication data:*

Schreiber, Mordecai.

   Explaining the Holocaust : how and why it happened / Mordecai Schreiber ; foreword by Mordecai Paldiel.

   xx + 200 p. 23 cm—Bibliographical references and illustrations.

   ISBN 13: 978-1-4982-1991-4

   1. Holocaust, Jewish (1939–1945). 2. Holocaust—Jewish (1939–1945)—Causes. 3. Holocaust, Jewish (1939–1945)—Religious aspects—Judaism. 4. Holocaust, Jewish (1939–1945)—Religious aspects—Christianity. 5. Righteous Gentiles in the Holocaust. I. Paldiel, Mordecai. II. Title.

D804.348 S32 2015

Manufactured in the U.S.A.                    04/14/2015

Cover photo courtesy of Rhodes Jewish Historical Foundation

This book is dedicated to the little boy in the 1943 photo on the cover of this book. His name is Haim Angel. I first saw this photo over twenty years ago in the tiny Holocaust museum in the back of the synagogue on the island of Rhodes, and it has haunted me ever since. The boy is posing with the yellow star as a symbol of pride. In 1943, as the Germans were losing the war, they deported him to Auschwitz, where he perished along with hundreds of members of the small centuries-old Jewish community of the island.

When in the shadow of gallows our children were crying
The world's rage had turned to silence.
For You have chosen us from among all nations,
You loved us, You called us beloved.
For You have chosen us from among all nations,
Norwegians, and Czech, and British,
And as our children were marched to the gallows,
Jewish children, wise children,
They knew their blood didn't count in this world,
They only told their mother: *Kuk nisht*, don't look.
And as the hatchet consumed by day and by night,
The Holy Father in Rome
Did not go out with the Redeemer's sign
To witness the pogrom.
To stand only once, one single day,
In the place where for years,
Like a lamb,
Stands an unknown little boy,
A Jew.

(FROM *FROM AMONG ALL THE NATIONS* BY NATAN ALTERMAN, TRANSLATED FROM THE HEBREW BY MORDECAI SCHREIBER.)

# Contents

*Foreword by Mordecai Paldiel* | ix
*Preface* | xv
*Acknowledgments* | xix

## Part 1: Bottomless Evil | 1

**1** Not Just Another Genocide | 5

**2** How It All Started | 11

**3** Germany and Europe after World War I | 18

**4** Satan's Prophet: The Rise of Hitler | 25

**5** The World according to Hitler | 31

**6** The Complicity of the World: A Tale of Two Conferences | 37

**7** Those Who Did the Dirty Work | 45

**8** The Evolution of the Holocaust | 71

**9** The *Judenrat* Dilemma | 92

**10** Jewish Inaction during the Holocaust | 98

**11** Righteous Gentiles | 111

## Part 2: The Problem of Faith | 125

**12** A Brief History of Jewish Martyrdom | 129

**13** A New Language of Faith | 142

**14** Christianity and the Holocaust | 157

**15** The Problem of Jewish Victimhood | 168

**16** The State of Israel as Sign and Wonder | 171

**17** The Universality of Faith | 177

**18** The Possibility of Faith after the Holocaust | 182

**19** The Way Back | 187

*Conclusion* | 193
*Bibliography* | 195

# Foreword

One morning in 1953 I was sitting in a yeshiva (Talmudic academy) classroom, listening to the teacher, an elderly man with a long white beard, expound a difficult Talmudic discussion. As I lost track of the hairsplitting opinions of the different rabbinic scholars, I furtively opened a book on Polish Jewry that was tucked in my table drawer and that I had borrowed from the public library. Quickly flipping through the pages, I stopped to read that in the summer months of 1942, some two hundred fifty thousand Jews from the Warsaw Ghetto were delivered to the gas chambers in the Treblinka camp, and their remains turned into ashes. I remember sitting on my chair dumbfounded at this horrific event that took place quite recently, only eleven years ago, and that there was no mention at all and no reference to this ghastly deed in the yeshiva courses that I was attending. I wondered why this silence? Why this total educational neglect in a very traditional Jewish school? I also kept thinking what relevance the ancient Talmudic text has to that more recent catastrophe? Back at home, the story of that terrible *churban* ("devastation")—the term *Holocaust* had not yet come into vogue—was also not discussed, though it was confirmed to have happened; this omission was also experienced by my cousin in Israel, the author of this book.

This deliberate unwillingness to deal with the most shattering event in Jewish history, an event that almost succeeded in obliterating the Jewish people or its most creative part, kept nagging in the back of my mind, and when many years later the Jewish community finally awoke from this long slumber, we all realized we had a tremendous problem on our hands of how to make sense of that watershed event. Laymen and scholars tried to advance answers from their respective disciplines to a host of questions: How was it possible for it to happen? Why did it happen? How did the Jewish community and the civilized world respond to it, and what are the lessons for the future? All the explanations advanced, and the library is full of them, fall short of providing satisfactory answers to these disturbing questions. But try we must, for once an event of this magnitude happens, defying all imagination and boggling the mind, it can happen again, and we must remain vigilant for signs of such a recurrence. Yet the more I have immersed myself in studying and understanding the Holocaust over several decades of working as an employee of Yad Vashem, and currently in teaching this subject, the more I am resigned to the thought that we will never arrive at a full explanation of how such a horrific event took place on a continent and amid people steeped in the longest tradition of civilized life and religious teachings. We will always remain at a loss, but try we must.

In 1976, while in Philadelphia, I attended a public lecture by Professors Franklin Littell and Yehuda Bauer on the Holocaust, and suddenly something inside me burst forth, and a longtime subconscious urge to come to grips with the Holocaust took hold of me. When I further learned that Littell was giving a post-graduate course on the Holocaust at Temple University in Philadelphia, I decided to stay put and resume my studies on a post-graduate level, with an emphasis on the Shoah. I had earlier graduated from the Hebrew University with a BA degree in economics and political science and had forsaken further studies in these two important subjects. After graduating from Temple in 1982 with a PhD degree in Holocaust Studies, I returned to Israel and was appointed by Yad Vashem to head a department I had never heard about before: the Righteous among the Nations. It dealt with non-Jews who risked their lives to save Jews from the Nazis. For the next twenty-four years, I was immersed in that uplifting and inspiring work, and was instrumental in adding thousands of names to this unique honor roll presented by the Jewish people and by the State of Israel (Yad Vashem having been established by legislation as a government institution). I was also able to rediscover the French Catholic cleric Father Simon Gallay, who had helped my family to cross over into Switzerland, in September 1943, and he too was honored by Yad Vashem. At the same time, in my thinking and lectures, I tried to keep a balance between the inspiring behavior of the Righteous and the horrific deeds of the perpetrators and the nonchalant attitude of the bystanders, and I am still puzzled and perplexed, and still struggling to find the correct and proper balance between these two extreme types of behavior. Hence, my personal attempt at explaining and interpreting the Shoah is to be taken with some caution.

To properly gauge the nature of the Nazi movement and its leader, Adolf Hitler, one cannot simply regard it as an extreme form of fascism, or the display of brute force for its own sake, with total disregard for those who were not part of the Aryan community. And as far as the Jews are concerned, one cannot look upon it as just the most extreme manifestation of old-time anti-Semitism, of plain and simple hatred of Jews leading to the attempt to remove them from the face of the globe, if that could be possible. It was in truth more than that.

Anti-Semitism was not only one of several elements of Nazism, but its pivotal core and the epicenter of its worldview—its *Weltanschauung*—that represented a perverted and secular manifestation of an apocalyptic and messianic crusade. By this I mean that traditional forms of religious apocalyptic ideas were transformed, transmuted, and debased into metaphorical models of a secular-religious movement, which strove to establish the ultimate good society, but in a most perverted form. Nazism came forth with an explanation of all the ills afflicting the world; it had the world divided into the Sons of Light (the Aryans) and the Sons of Darkness (the Jews); it adhered to an extreme form of social Darwinism and a fall belief, of original sin—miscegenation, or the mixing of races; it had a semidivine messianic figure in the form of a Führer; a belief that in order to establish a "new heaven and new earth" an apocalyptic struggle had to take place with the satanic force represented by the Jews, and they had to be eliminated—lock, stock, and barrel, and without any regard to compassion (itself a Jewish principle), in order to inaugurate the thousand-year Reich, in itself a quasi-religious vision that would follow the killing of the Antichrist.

Anyone reading Hitler's words, be it *Mein Kampf*, his speeches, or his Political Testament, cannot walk away without realizing that Hitler was a man consumed with images and metaphors having no correlation with reality but taken from misguided religious teachings, distorted and perverted into a deadly secular messianic ideology. Hitler and a small clique of dedicated followers truly believed that in exterminating the Jews, and by implication undoing the Jewish ethical teachings embedded in the Bible, the world would be a better place to live in: a world based on extreme forms of social Darwinian and racist thinking. Tragically, many, or most, in German society were ready to follow blindly in the footsteps of this false messianic pied piper, to their ultimate doom. Thus, one may come closer to understanding how the Holocaust took place; closer, but not fully.

Now comes the next and equally difficulty problem of how to explain this tragic phenomenon from a Jewish religious perspective. Some have tried, and a host of the most reputable theologians have sincerely struggled to explain God's permissiveness in allowing such an event to take place; or, in one way or another, to absolve God from any responsibility, and thus to take us back to ground zero. Some suggest that it is an exercise in futility, and it is best to let more time pass before grappling with how God allowed the chosen people to be almost completely destroyed, with a loss of a third of the most active, energetic, vibrant, and dynamic part. What I therefore propose may not be acceptable to many, but it is my way of making sense of this unprecedented anti-God event, and for this I am indebted a bit to the teaching of Lurianic kabbalah, as described by the foremost expounder of kabbalistic thinking, the late Gershom Scholem.

Isaac Luria (known as the "Holy Ari," or the Lion), propounded the bold idea of how the world came into being. Basically, he portrayed the preexistent creator God, known as the *ein sof*, the Infinite God, as assuming several forms in the process of creation. This was preceded by a process that Luria termed *tsimtsum*, of self-contraction of God's presence in order to make room and allow creation to take place. In this empty space, elements of the Godhead were injected in the forms of vessels containing divine sparks. However, these vessels were for some reason not able to contain the sparks, and they shattered, sending the sparks flying in all directions in this primordial setting. This tragic event, so to speak, forced the hand of the Infinite God to the act of creation in order to restore the sparks, now mixed with the shards of the vessels (representing evil), to their original home within the Infinite Godhead. Luria's model is more intricate and arcane than presented here, and open to several interpretations by his many followers, including Hasidic rebbes. As for me, I beg to borrow from his contraction idea and expand it a bit so as to make some sense of the Holocaust. That is, I propose to view God's presence in our lives as a constant one, but of different degrees; it has ebbs and flows. It contains both emanations (*atzilut* in kabbalah language) as well as contractions, and this is an ongoing process. That, whenever there is much contraction, then evil has a greater sway—and the Holocaust was such an event, due to a severe contraction, a grievous *tsimtsum* of the divine flow. This left a greater void of the divine presence in the state of affairs of the world. The shards then took on more strength and more destructive capacity, and embedded in Nazism struck back at the sparks, at the teaching of brotherhood and compassion, enunciated in the biblical teachings and an integral part of the Jewish religion and people. Hence the Holocaust.

During the Holocaust, the divine sparks were almost in a total disarray, but then they became manifest and reasserted themselves, though in a reduced form but still very vibrant, in the acts of the Righteous Gentiles, of those non-Jews who risked their lives to save Jews from destruction–so that the biblical ethical teaching, the opposite counterpart of the Nazi social Darwinistic and racial thinking, upheld by the Jews, the principal carriers of the divine sparks, not be completely overwhelmed and obliterated. The defeat of Nazism corresponded to the stoppage of the contraction phase, and to the flow of a new divine manifestation, leading to the creation of the

State of Israel, as the principal carrier of Jewish survival and creativity. But the shards of wickedness have not been completely eliminated, as witnessed by daily events.

I am not sure whether my two explanations—of Nazism and of theodicy (God's justice)—will prove acceptable to the reader, since, by my own admission, I am not myself fully convinced of their infallible logic. At the same time, perplexed and puzzled as we still are by the Holocaust, we will remain so for a long time to come, and for the moment I feel at peace with these explications. I wish also to add that I have great admiration for my cousin, Rabbi Mordecai Schreiber who, coming from a secular background, and after having sketched a most gloomy picture of the Holocaust, is still able to come up with an uplifting message of hope and religious fortitude. For myself, I am a bit more hesitant and doubtful. While acknowledging the goodly deeds of the Righteous, the rescuers of Jews, close to seventy years after the Holocaust we are still witnessing the struggle between good and evil, between compassion and cruelty, that continues unabated, as evidenced by events in places like Cambodia, Rwanda, Darfur, and Syria. But this should not lead us to despair but rather, paradoxically, to a greater need for a continuous emphasis on the deeds of the Righteous of the Holocaust, of people like Raoul Wallenberg, Varian Fry, Jan Karski, and Chiune-Sempo Sugihara, as outlined in this book, who, in their separate ways, defied the Nazi teachings of race superiority and contempt and mistreatment of other ethnic groups, combined with the extermination of the Jews. In saving Jews, they tried in their individual and isolated ways to leave a legacy to future generations of civilized life based on certain ethical standards.

Such was expressed by the Dutch rescuer Johtje Vos to her mother, who one day came to visit her daughter and was stunned to find a Jewish child. The mother said: "You shouldn't do this, even though I agree with what you're doing, because your first responsibility is to your own children." To this Johtje Vos responded: "That's exactly why I'm doing it!" She added in her testimony, "I thought we were doing the right thing, giving our children the right model to follow." Or that through the help he received in Auschwitz from Lorenzo Perrone, an Italian civilian construction worker, Holocaust chronicler Primo Levi said, "I managed not to forget that I myself was a man"—this, in spite of Auschwitz and its bosses, the Nazis. For that reason alone, the uplifting message Mordecai Schreiber offers us is a necessary healing message to minds troubled by the enormity of the Holocaust.

Mordecai Paldiel
Fort Lee, New Jersey

# Preface

I would like to offer my deepest thanks to my cousin, Dr. Mordecai Paldiel, the former director of the Righteous among the Nations section at the Yad Vashem Holocaust Memorial Museum in Jerusalem. He checked every word of my manuscript for accuracy, making sure that my dealing with this most intricate subject was as close to the facts as possible. He also wrote a heartfelt foreword, which I greatly appreciate. My cousin and I represent the two absolute extremes of the Jewish world. He was born to a Hasidic family in Poland that miraculously managed to survive the Holocaust in Belgium, France, and Switzerland. I was born to a secular Zionist family in Palestine under the British Mandate and was raised as a secular Israeli in Haifa, a city of highly secular labor Zionist working-class Jews and moderately or nominally religious Muslim and Christian Arabs. As a child, I remember how we all lived in harmony and respected one another.

In 1949, when I was ten and the new State of Israel was only one year old, a bearded man wearing black Hasidic garb and his twelve-year-old son showed up at our apartment in Haifa. My mother explained to me that the boy's mother was her cousin, and that he and his father came to Israel from America, having survived the Holocaust in Europe, to receive a blessing from their Hasidic rabbi, the Belzer Rebbe. I instantly made friends with my new cousin, and we remain friends to this day. Over the years, however, there were times when we were in close touch, and times when we lost track of each other. This was due to the fact that we both have had very eventful lives. We lived in different parts of the world, and we pursued different careers. But looking back, we had one essential thing in common. We both found our way to graduate schools in the United States—I to the Hebrew Union College in Cincinnati, Ohio, where I was ordained as a rabbi; and my cousin to Temple University in Philadelphia, where he received his doctorate in Holocaust studies. By doing so we both traveled quite a distance from our early life—he from the closed world of the Hasidim in Brooklyn (who do not attend secular universities), and I from the highly secular world of the Jews of Haifa, who hardly ever set a foot inside a synagogue. It is safe to say that we both reinvented ourselves, as we both shared a passion for the Jewish people, or *klal yisrael*. By that I mean, not only one segment of the Jewish people, such as a Hasidic sect or secular Israelis, but for all Jews everywhere. Paldiel's career focused on discovering Righteous Gentiles who rescued Jews during the Shoah, and mine focused on bringing Jews back to their Jewish heritage, and later on biblical scholarship, where I have done research and written books about the Hebrew prophets.

While one could argue that neither one of us followed in our parents' footsteps, in reality we were both deeply rooted in the long history and the peculiar fate of our people, and we both felt the need to find meaning and purpose in the glorious albeit tragic saga of the Jews. As for myself, I remember as a child listening avidly to my parents' stories about their families in Europe. I never knew any of my grandparents, any of my aunts and uncles (except for one), or any other relatives whom my parents had left behind when they went to Palestine as pioneers at a very young age. Looking back, it did not feel peculiar to me not to have an extended family, because most children my age in Haifa in those days did not have one either. Ironically, it felt peculiar to meet someone my age who did have an extended family, because, in the final analysis, after the Holocaust we were an orphaned community. Instead of relying on an extended family, Jews in Haifa in the '40s and '50s made close friends with two or three other families that consisted of a father, a mother, and two or three young children, and this was our extended family.

In the years immediately before and after the establishment of the state, boatloads of Holocaust survivors began to arrive at the Haifa harbor. One distant cousin named Mordecai Abrabanel, who survived the camps, became a frequent visitor in our home. Like many other survivors who could not find a job, he peddled black-market food products. After the war food was scarce, and the only way to get some coffee or a piece of chocolate was through the black market. As a child I instinctively felt the difference between him and us. He was small and frail, and it was clear he had been through hell. As time went on, I kept running into other survivors, and I remember some of them had a number tattooed on their arm, and they were different from us who grew up under the blazing sun of the Promised Land. Unfortunately, our parents' generation did not know how to deal with them. They remained outsiders for a long time. That so many of them were exterminated with impunity in Nazi-occupied Europe was an embarrassment to our parents. We were the few who had to take on the many and prevail. They

## Preface

were the many who were killed en masse by relatively few. So as a child I had a skewed view of them, which I regret to this day.

In the late '50s my family went to Uruguay, where we had several relatives, to start a business. It was the first time I came face-to-face with anti-Semitism. For the most part, Uruguay was a progressive democracy where people enjoyed freedom and had many opportunities. But there was no lack of prejudice, particularly against Jews. In neighboring Argentina it was much worse, and we heard about top Nazis such as Eichmann and Mengele hiding there. Eventually my family returned to Israel, but in 1959 I enrolled in the Hebrew Union College in Cincinnati, and when I came back in the summer of 1960 to visit my family in Montevideo, Eichmann was captured in Argentina. Looking back, I remember it was a defining moment for me in regard to the grim reality of the Holocaust, as I believe it was for the rest of the world.

After I was ordained as a rabbi, I kept pursuing a side career as a writer. I often wrote and lectured about the Holocaust. When I took a pulpit in the New York area in 1970, I took a side job as an editor and translator for a Jewish publisher in New York City, which published quite a few memoirs of Holocaust survivors. I edited or translated or even ghostwrote many of those memoirs. Most of them sounded like carbon copies of all the others. Descriptions of the same atrocities were repeated over and over again until you could not tell them apart. But then again, this was the nature of the Holocaust. Yet once in a while a story stood out. Such a story was Sandra Brand's book *I Dared to Live*, in which a young blonde Jewish girl who easily passed for a Polish Catholic was hidden in Warsaw by a German policeman, who later paid with his life for his crime. Another was the story of Naftali Salsitz and his wife. He fought as a partisan in the forests of southeast Poland, and she was disguised as a German girl and worked for the Nazi high command in Krákow. Between them, they saved Krákow, the historical capital of Poland, from being blown up by the Nazis.

In the late '70s I moved my family to the Washington DC area where I started a translation company providing services for the U.S. government. My first government contract was with the U.S. Department of Justice Office of Special Investigations, which looked for former Nazis who found their way illegally into the United States. For the next six years I was involved in translating thousands of World War II documents. Those included Nazi documents such as concentration camp records, Gestapo interrogations, Wehrmacht military documents, survivors' testimonies, and more, from all the European languages. I was also sent to interpret at trials of former Nazis who had entered the United States with false documents. This was perhaps my most in-depth involvement in the Shoah, and some of those documents continue to haunt me to this day.

I have one confession to make: I have never visited Auschwitz. Nor, for that matter, have I visited my parents' old home in eastern Poland (now Ukraine). I have always been afraid that it would be more than I can bear. I am still working on getting up the courage to do it, and I believe someday I will. Perhaps now that I have written this book, I will finally find closure. I have written this book because the Holocaust has been haunting me all my life. I cannot understand why it happened to them and not to me. I look back and I wish I would have been there to share their suffering, and to be able to do something for them. So I finally decided that the least I could do is tell their story as best I could, to try to look at it from all sides, and to make sure that the world at long last has learned the lesson of their martyrdom, so that they would not have died in vain.

# Acknowledgments

First, to my mother and father, who left Europe in 1931 because they saw what was coming, and therefore I am here today, and because they gave birth to a state called Israel. Second, to my many British and Australian friends, whom I always remind that had it not been for their boys who stopped the German advance in Al Alamein in 1942 on its way to Palestine where I was born three years earlier, I would not be here today. Third, to my wife of fifty-three years, who always stood by my side, and to my wonderful children and grandchildren, who always make me proud.

To my cousin Mordecai Paldiel, former director of the Righteous Gentiles section of the Yad Vashem Holocaust Memorial Museum in Jerusalem, whose vast expertise as Holocaust scholar helped me get it right, and who wrote a heart-felt introduction.

To all the Holocaust survivors I have known over the years, many of whom I have helped write their memoirs, and whom I have always admired as heroes of the human spirit who have been to hell and came back.

To the wonderful Jews of Rhodes, Greece, and particularly to Carmen Cohen and Aron Hasson, who so graciously helped me with my quest for the identity of the boy with the star.

To my friends at the U.S. Holocaust Memorial Museum, particularly to Michael Berenbaum; to my friends at Yad Vashem; to my friends at the Hollywood, Flordia, Holocaust Museum, particularly Jim Kravit.

Last but not least, to my editor at Cascade Books, K. C. Hanson, and to the staff, whose warmth and friendship I cherish.

# Part 1

# Bottomless Evil

### THE NEED TO EXPLAIN

In the winter of 2012, while serving as a ship rabbi on a world cruise, I visited synagogues around the world. The most remote one was the synagogue of what has become known as the Shanghai Ghetto, now a memorial to a Jewish community of refugees from the Nazi horrors that lived there during World War II. The Shanghai Ghetto is located in an old and crowded part of this huge city of twenty-four million inhabitants, but the Chinese authorities have turned it into a dignified memorial for the Jewish refugees who once lived in their midst. They have restored an entire enclave, which one enters through a beautiful gate with commemorative plaques, leading to a small yet well-preserved synagogue. From there the path continues to former homes and courtyards—one of which has been converted into a small museum, which narrates the history of the ghetto. As my group visited the synagogue, once again I felt, as I have on several occasions over the years, the unfathomable presence of the Holocaust. I asked the group to join me in the reciting of the Kaddish, the Jewish prayer for the dead that reaffirms life. We all prayed, Jews and non-Jews.

During the Holocaust, Shanghai was about the only place in the world open to refugees from Nazi terror. Some twenty thousand Jews from Europe made the long journey to China and took residence in what is still known today as Ghetto Shanghai. The German regime contacted the Japanese authorities who occupied Shanghai at that time, and asked them to deal harshly with the Jews. The Japanese seemed to have their own agenda and did not pay much attention to the German request. The Jewish refugees were not disturbed, and after the war most of them found their way to America, to Israel, and elsewhere. Some of them pursued important careers and made major contributions to their adoptive countries.[1]

The story of the Shanghai Ghetto is one of the few happy-ending stories in that endless darkness known as the Holocaust. That darkness is still with us today and will continue to haunt us for generations to come. By "us" I don't mean only the Jews, I mean everyone. Here human evil had reached its apex. Here civilization lost its moral compass. Here is where questions begin and answers cannot be found. Thousands of books have tried and failed. People continue to ask why. They continue to read the books, see the photos and the films and the plays, visit the museums, listen to the lectures, but two questions remain unanswered: First, why did the Germans, with the help of many non-Germans, systematically murder millions of Jews all throughout Europe? Second, why did God allow it to happen?

I am not so presumptuous as to think I can answer such questions. Human evil is unfathomable, and the ways of God are not known to man. But these two questions cut deep into the heart of human existence and demand some explication. I think it is safe to say that human evil is bottomless, and I do believe in a merciful God. If there was any doubt before the Holocaust that human evil is bottomless, Hitlerism has put this question to rest once and for all. As for God's mercy, after Auschwitz, to use Richard Rubenstein's famous book's title, not only can it be argued that God is not merciful, but it can be argued that God does not exist altogether or has ceased to exist. I, for one, choose to believe that God does exist, and that God is merciful. I fully respect those who think otherwise, and I do realize that we have to make room for the entire human spectrum of belief and disbelief.

It seems to me that in order to fully understand the Holocaust it has to be considered in the context of the totality of human history, and even more specifically in the context of both Jewish and Christian history. Some have argued that the Holocaust stands apart from the rest of human history. When the celebrated Israeli Canadian architect Moshe Safdie designed the new Yad Vashem Holocaust Museum in Jerusalem, he cut a long wedge through a rocky hill on the museum grounds into which he designed the museum.[2] He explained that to him the Holocaust was a rupture of history,

---

1. Among the Jews who found their way to Shanghai on the eve of the Holocaust were some who became very accomplished people in the U.S., Israel, and elsewhere.

2. This was told to me by my cousin and longtime friend Dr. Mordecai Paldiel, the former director of the Righteous Gentiles Section at the Yad Vashem Holocaust Memorial Museum in Jerusalem.

as though an invisible knife had cut a wedge in time, altering human history forever. In explaining the Holocaust it will be necessary to show that no matter how incredible and incomprehensible the Holocaust may be, it is very much a part of human history, and yet it stands apart and defies all the rules of both individual and collective human behavior.

The Holocaust scholar and historian Lucy Dawidowicz has argued that Hitler conceived the idea of exterminating the Jewish people early on in his political career and had alluded to it in his political autobiography, *Mein Kampf*.[3] Thus, to follow her line of thinking, the Holocaust was not a by-product of World War II but the main goal of the Nazi ideology that started the war in the first place and sought to impose the Nazi race theory on a world cleansed of Jews. This is a very compelling argument because it is the only way to explain German behavior during the last year of the war (mid-1944 to mid-1945), when the Germans were losing the war, and instead of marshaling all their resources to fight the enemy at their gates, they squandered them until the very last minute on killing Jews. Hitler's last testimony before he shot himself in his bunker in Berlin blamed the Jews for starting the war, and concluded with the following sentence: "Above all I charge the leaders of the nation and those under them to scrupulous observance of the laws of race and to merciless opposition to the universal poisoner of all peoples, international Jewry."[4]

It is a given that Hitler's obsession with Jews was a form of mental disease, and that it played a huge part in the human tragedy known as the Holocaust. Hitler did not invent anti-Semitism, but he was able to put it into practice unlike anyone else in history. And yet, the Holocaust in all its enormity cannot be explained solely as the work of Hitler and his satraps. We do need to take a close look at this murderous gang, for the Holocaust would have not happened the way it did without them. But we cannot stop there, because there were others who, directly and indirectly, aided and abetted, and there were many factors, all of which converged through some satanic confluence and created the conditions for this unleashing of the most murderous event in all of history.

Some have learned the lessons of the Holocaust, but some have not. When NATO, representing the nations of Western Europe, intervened in the genocidal conflict in the Balkans and, with the help of U.S. President Bill

---

3. In *Mein Kampf*, Hitler writes, "If at the beginning of the War and during the War twelve or fifteen thousand of these Hebrew corrupters of the people had been held under poison gas, as happened to hundreds of thousands of our very best German workers in the field, the sacrifice of millions at the front would not have been in vain" (Hitler, *Mein Kampf*, 679).

4. Hitler, "Final Political Testament."

Clinton put an end to it by dispatching its peacekeeping force, it was obvious that the lessons of the Holocaust were well learned. But in places like the Congo, Rwanda, Cambodia, and, more recently, Syria, it was not learned. Nor was it learned by the Ayatollahs of Iran, who have been threatening Israel with annihilation; or by all the radical forces in the Muslim world that have been using murder as a political weapon, are depriving women of their human rights, and preventing the people of the Middle East from experiencing peaceful progress. Here much still needs to be done.

The Jews are a tiny fraction of the human race, but it has been their fate to be the conscience of the world. It has been a given throughout time that wherever Jews were persecuted, evil reigned and decline followed. Conversely, wherever Jews were allowed to lend their talents and energy for the common good, the host society flourished. Perhaps this is what the Nazis meant when they spoke about the "world Jewish conspiracy." Perhaps this has been the root cause of traditional Christian anti-Semitism, namely, the inability of the daughter religion to replace the mother religion as the moral compass of the world. Hitlerism, as we shall see, sought to replace both the Jewish God and the Christian God with a new religion, that of the "Aryan race."

Perhaps the most shocking realization when we revisit those years of darkness will be to find out that the Nazis were not uneducated savages. Many of them had advanced degrees; came from upright middle-class or upper-class families; had refined tastes; and appreciated good music, art, and literature. Once we exhaust all the reasons why they fell prey to history's greatest aberration, the question will still remain why they did what they did. Be that as it may, we will be left with a warning for all people and for all time that it can happen to anyone at any time.

# 1

# Not Just Another Genocide

The history of the human race is to a large extent a history of genocides. Yet the word *genocide* was not coined until 1944, when the Holocaust was at its peak.[1] The problem with words like *Holocaust* and *genocide* is that they are imprecise terms. *Holocaust* is an archaic term derived from Greek, which means "a sacrificial offering that is consumed *entirely* by flames." *Genocide* means the killing of an *entire* race or people. Both words denote complete destruction, yet they have been modified in our time to mean *partial* murder of a people, presumably with the *intent* of achieving total annihilation. While the capitalized term *Holocaust* has been universally accepted as applying only to the German war of extermination against the Jews, the term *genocide* took on an international legal meaning in the Genocide Convention of the United Nations of 1948, wherein the term refers to both intent and physical action, yet its precise meaning has been heatedly debated by scholars and by governments ever since. In recent years several events have been legally defined as genocides, including the Srebrenica Massacre during the conflict in the Balkans, in which thousands of Muslim Bosnians were systematically murdered, and the massacres of the Tutsi minority by the Hutu in Rwanda where some eight hundred thousand died.[2]

The twentieth century has topped all other centuries in the numbers of people killed by human action, not only on the battlefield but in

1. The term *genocide* was coined by Raphael Lemkin in 1944.

2. A note on statistics: All figures of genocides are approximate. There is no way of obtaining exact figures regarding events that were the result of regime or group brutality, much of which is often covered up to remove the evidence.

premeditated genocidal assaults on unarmed civilians. The exact number is unknown, but it is estimated in the hundreds of millions. Interestingly, one of the first known genocides of the century was committed in 1904 by German settlers in the African country of Namibia, where the Herero tribe, deprived of its grazing lands, was driven into the desert where many died of thirst and starvation. A century later, in 2004, the German government made an official apology.

Herero tribe survivors of the genocide in Namibia, 1904

In 1915 the Namibian genocide was eclipsed by the genocide perpetrated by the Turks in which about one and a half million Armenians perished. Despite the urging of many countries, Turkey is yet to apologize for this historical crime. The indifference of the world towards the fate of the Armenian people was not lost on Hitler. In August, 1939, as he was preparing to invade Poland, Hitler said:

> I have issued the command—and I'll have anybody who utters but one word of criticism executed by a firing squad—that our war aim does not consist in reaching certain lines, but in the physical destruction of the enemy. Accordingly, I have placed my death-head formations in readiness—for the present only in the East—with orders to them to send to death mercilessly and without compassion, men, women, and children of Polish derivation and language. Only thus shall we gain the living

space [*Lebensraum*] which we need. *Who, after all, speaks today of the annihilation of the Armenians?*[3]

While he was speaking of killing Poles, which he did, what he specifically had in mind was Polish Jewry. Hitler firmly believed that the world would be even less interested in a genocide committed against the Jews than the world had been in the genocide committed by the Turks against the Armenians. In his foreword to the *Encyclopedia of Genocide*, titled "Why Is It Important to Learn about the Holocaust and the Genocides of *All* People?" Archbishop Desmond Tutu of South Africa writes:

> The compelling reason why we should learn about the Holocaust, and the genocides committed against other peoples as well, is so that we might be filled with a revulsion at what took place and thus be inspired, indeed galvanized, to commit ourselves to ensure that such atrocities should never happen again. It is sadly true what a cynic had said, that we learn from history that we do *not* learn from history. And yet it is possible that if the world had been conscious of the genocide that was committed by the Ottoman Turks against the Armenians, the first genocide of the twentieth century, then perhaps humanity might have been more alert to the warning signs that were being given before Hitler's madness was unleashed on an unbelieving world.[4]

**A Jewish child dying in the streets of the Warsaw Ghetto, c. 1942**

Despite the United Nations' Genocide Convention of 1948, genocides continued throughout the second half of the twentieth century and into the

---

3. See http://en.wikipedia.org/wiki/Obersalzberg_Speech/.
4. Charny, *Encyclopedia of Genocide*, lvii.

twenty-first. Perhaps the most gruesome of those was the one perpetrated by the Khmer Rouge communist regime under Pot Pol in 1975 against the Cambodian people. Here mass murder was utilized in the pursuit of creating a utopian society. It was the regime's belief that Cambodia had to be converted into an agrarian society and do away with its "decadent" urban lifestyle and its traditional Buddhism. What resulted was a weird and macabre combining of the Stalin-era forced collectivization and the Nazi methods of mass murder. Some two million people died by execution, poisoning, hard labor, and starvation. Today, Cambodia is in the process of recovering from this long nightmare.

Africa, where the first twentieth-century genocide took place, has been the scene of a succession of genocides since the end of World War II, and there is still no end in sight. Countries like Nigeria, Congo, Rwanda, and Sudan stand out but are by no means the only ones. More recently, the Middle East has been the scene of violent conflicts, most notably in Syria, where the regime under Bashar al-Assad has been massacring its own people, a grim reminder of similar actions by Assad's father thirty years earlier that resulted in the Hama massacre in which some twenty thousand people were murdered. Rounding out this grim record is the ethnic cleansing in the Balkans in 1995 that pitted Serbs, Croats, and Bosnians against one another before the forces of NATO were able to put an end to the conflict.

The near extermination of the Jews of Europe during World War II by the Germans and their willing collaborators can certainly be classified as genocide, for it was an attempt to exterminate an entire people. But there was a fundamental difference between what we call the Holocaust and all the other genocides. Typically, genocide is the result of an escalation of a conflict between two or more groups of people that have conflicting interests and seek to resolve their conflict through violent means. The stronger group reaches the point of deciding that only by physically eliminating its adversary will it be able to achieve its goal, and proceeds to utilize all the means at its disposal to accomplish this elimination. This is not at all what the Holocaust was all about. When the Nazis came to power in Germany in 1933, they had scores to settle with the Allies who defeated them in World War I. They were defeated in that war by an alliance led by France and Great Britain, who were later joined by the United States as well. German Jews as well as Jews in the Austro-Hungarian Empire fought on the side of Germany, many with distinction. German Jews, at least half of whom were intermarried and assimilated, were true German patriots. Polish Jews, whom the Nazis thoroughly despised, considered Germany the epitome of European culture. Yet the Nazi leadership was able to convince the German people that the Jews—all Jews everywhere, even in places like Shanghai or

Timbuktu—were the mortal enemies of Germany, and, miracle of miracles, were secretly plotting across the world to do Germany in. I once lived in Guatemala, where there was a small community of German Jews. One of them once told me that his old uncle was whisked out of Germany on the eve of World War II and taken to London. He used to listen to the BBC news reports on the radio, and each time Hitler scored a victory he would cheer. When his family asked him why he was cheering, he explained that he had always been on the side of Germany.

National Socialism, or Nazism, following the delusional *Weltanschauung* or worldview of Adolf Hitler enunciated in his book *Mein Kampf*, came to articulate that the Jews controlled two opposing world forces that ostensibly threatened Germany—namely, Bolshevism, which came to power around that time in Russia, and Western capitalism, represented mainly by the United States. Never mind that Stalin, who took full control of the Soviet Union, systematically eliminated all his Jewish associates, most importantly Leon Trotsky.[5] And never mind that Roosevelt basically turned a blind eye to the plight of the Jews under Nazism and did little to help save them. The Nazis, who needed a visible and vulnerable victim to direct all their anger, frustration and hatred against, turned on that 1 percent of the Third Reich's population which they believed to be the "universal poisoner of all peoples," and later on all the Jews of Europe, and proceeded to carry out an ever-expanding campaign that culminated in the murder of two-thirds of that Jewry.

In other words, the Holocaust lacked all the common reasons of all other genocides, past and future, and was a misplaced unleashing of murderous hatred not only against those who were not the enemies of Germany, but also against those who were mostly either loyal German citizens or residents of other European countries and who looked up to Germany as a beacon of civilization. The Jews of Poland, for example, would have expected Poles to turn on them much sooner than Germans. In Poland most Jews lived under miserable conditions, while in Germany before Hitler many did very well. Polish Jews never trusted the Poles, while they did trust the Germans. This was one reason why it was possible for the Germans, once they began to occupy Eastern Europe, to round up Jews with little resistance or mistrust, and make them believe they were simply being "relocated," or taken to labor camps, when in reality they were being shipped to their death.

---

5. In the '30s, Stalin staged what has become known as "show trials" in which top leaders of Jewish origin in the Soviet Union, such as Kameniev, Zionviev, and so forth, were made to confess their "betrayal" of the revolution and were executed. Stalin effectively eliminated all of his Jewish comrades who had made the revolution possible.

So the Holocaust became an unprecedented event in human annals, and while it had its roots in traditional German and Christian anti-Semitism, its total impact by the time the war ended was beyond anything the world had ever known, and it is impossible to simply classify it as just another genocide.

It should perhaps be also pointed out that Nazi Germany, in looking to establish what Hitler called "the thousand-year Reich," was not merely interested in exterminating the Jews. That was only the first step in establishing German world domination. It was to be followed with mass destruction of other "inferior" races, such as Slavs and blacks, among others.[6]

It was also to be followed by the elimination of other political systems—communism, socialism, and even capitalism, and, most important, democracy. In addition, it was to be followed by the elimination of the clergy and the institutions of Christianity, Catholic and Protestant, both of which were somehow seen as Jewish inventions and as enemies of the German Aryan state. When we consider this master plan of the Nazi regime, it becomes clear that the Holocaust as the first round of this plan (and the only one the Nazis were able to carry out before they were defeated) was an event unlike any the human race has ever known.

---

6. See Shirer, *Rise and Fall of the Third Reich*, 937.

# 2

# How It All Started

Hitler suffered from pathological Judeophobia. He was deathly afraid of the Jews. He believed in an international Jewish conspiracy to take over the world and specifically to destroy Germany. In his autobiography, *Mein Kampf* (*My Struggle*), he discusses the genesis of his aversion to the Jews without being able to give any rational explanation for such virulent hatred. In fact, there is very little about his sprawling personal and ideological autobiography that is rational. It is a platitudinous diatribe against the so-called enemies of Germany, both external and internal, specifically against what he calls the "Judeo-Bolsheviks,"[1] who play the main role in this lurid drama. To his dying day, Hitler was driven by his relentless conviction that was emblazoned on giant banners during Nazi mass gatherings, *Die Juden sind unser Unglück*: "The Jews are our misfortune." His dying thought, before he shot himself in his bunker in Berlin, must have been, "Those rotten Jews have won after all."

Ironically, it was not the Jews who defeated Germany, not in World War I and certainly not in World War II. Hitler's military thinking was shaped by Germany's defeat in the First World War, which he blamed on the Jews. He refused to accept the fact that Germany did not stand a chance against the Allies, despite its great army and its great fighting spirit. Hitler subscribed to the theory that Germany was stabbed in the back by Jewish traitors. Those traitors somehow morphed into Judeo-Bolsheviks and, miracle of miracles,

---

1. Hitler repeatedly refers in his book to the so-called Judeo-Bolshevik enemy. Later his lackeys Goebbels and Himmler will adopt this term and use it indiscriminately.

also into Judeo-Americans who persuaded President Roosevelt to enter the war against Germany. Hitler was totally mistaken in his assessment of Jewish influence in the U.S. during the '30s, when anti-Semitism was widespread in the U.S., and when some top captains of American industry, such as Henry Ford, were avowed anti-Semites.[2] The leadership of American Jewry was afraid to speak up, and Roosevelt seemed to take the Jewish vote for granted.[3] None of this made any impression on Herr Hitler. To him, the Jews were the ultimate enemy of everything he believed in, which meant, above all, the supremacy of the German or Germanic people. He regarded Jews as base or even subhuman and grouped them with a whole host of ethnicities and nations, ranging from Slavs to Africans and Asians. Better yet, he called those others subhuman, while he argued that the Jews were vermin rather than human. Until and unless every last Jew in the world was eliminated, Germany could not regain its rightful place in the world as a triumphant, prosperous, and successful master race.

As I indicated before, Hitler's extreme anti-Semitism was not an end in itself, but rather a means to an end, namely, the subjugation and domination of other nations. Therefore, the question arises whether Hitler told what he believed to be the truth each time he spoke or wrote about the Jews (which was quite often) or whether he used anti-Semitism as a powerful tool to radicalize his own people and others in his struggle to elevate Germany to the status of a world power. For years I believed in the second possibility, namely, the scapegoat theory, a belief shared by many. But my renewed study of his writings and speeches and my redoubled effort to understand what appears to be Hitler's demented behavior convinced me that indeed Hitler was a true believer who believed in the most demonic aspects of anti-Semitism. As I will try to prove in this book, he even elevated his belief to the level of a mystical, quasi-religious creed, in which the Judeo-Christian theodicy, which posits the existence of a good God in the face of evil, takes on a satanic, twisted reality, which in effect glorifies evil. In other words, at some point in his life, probably quite early on, Hitler must have come to the conclusion that the only way to achieve his goals was through decisive, brutal means that stopped at nothing. If Hitler had to sacrifice his own mother for the greater glory of Germany, so be it. He would not think twice. Indeed, it did not take much for him, once he was in power, to eliminate not only political adversaries but also those closest to him, if he had the slightest suspicion that they were not unconditionally loyal to him. In this he closely resembled another contemporary brutal dictator, namely, Joseph Stalin of

---

2. Baldwin, *Henry Ford and the Jews*; Woeste, *Henry Ford's War on Jews*.
3. Morse, *While Six Million Died*; Hecht, *Child of the Century*.

the USSR, and it appears that the two quite often not only vied with each other but also imitated each other.

To understand the extent of Hitler's fear of and hatred towards the Jews, we have to consider how he let those feelings overtake his better judgment so that, in the end, they brought about his downfall.

The great paradox of this extreme phenomenon known as Nazi Germany is that a highly rational people, who gave the world some of the greatest philosophers of all time—Leibnitz, Hegel, Kant, Schopenhauer, Nietzsche, only to name a few—managed, under the leadership of a fanatic and delusional demagogue, to take leave of their senses and of their better judgment, and to subject themselves to a state policy that was short on rationality and long on atavistic behavior, and which carried within itself the seeds of its own destruction. As we shall see, an entire nation had lost touch with reality and had followed a philosophy (if that is the right word) that flew in the face of all the laws and rules of civilized society. By putting the state above all else, and especially above all other people (*Deutschland über alles*), German leaders were able to justify every act, no matter how heinous.

In other words, Hitler succeeded in getting the German people to accept his fear and hatred of the Jews as basic tenets of what was good for Germany. If only the Jews were to disappear, the argument went, Germany could rise again and regain its rightful place in the family of nations, namely, as a *Herrenrasse*, or Master Race. It is this irrational belief that needs to be studied, for such study will enable us to penetrate the mind of an otherwise mediocre person who was able in a short time to commit the greatest crime in all of human history.

## THE PATHOLOGY OF ANTI-SEMITISM

Anti-Semitism did not start with Hitler, nor has it ended with his demise. However, under his reign it became an official state policy and resulted in what Jews call the Shoah, or the Catastrophe: perhaps the greatest catastrophe in Jewish history. Its implications are not limited to the Jewish people. They have a far-reaching significance for all humankind. As of this writing there are regimes and groups around the world—the regimes in Iran and Syria, the terrorist group Al Qaeda, only to mention a few—who engage in Nazi-like behavior, giving free reign to murder and mayhem. And there are those, including some major countries, that condone the behavior of those enemies of humanity. Yet for the past several decades the crimes of Nazism have been ever-present in the consciousness of the world, a grim reminder of how far human evil can reach.

Much has been written about the causes of anti-Semitism. Political, religious, sociological, economical, psychological, and other kinds of explanations abound. But it seems to me that it all boils down to one simple explanation. The Jews were always a small people, yet their impact on the human race has been enormous. After all, they gave the world the most influential book ever written, namely, the Bible. They also gave the world the one God most of the human race believes in. To this day, the Jews continue to contribute to the progress and welfare of humanity far beyond their small numbers. The ratio of economically successful Jews far exceeds that of many other groups. Inevitably, such a high profile elicits envy, and when conditions are right leads to animosity that can result in extreme violence.[4]

The two best examples of this anti-Semitic cycle are Spain in 1492 and Germany in 1938. The similarities between the two are astounding. Never before or after in the history of Europe did Jewry achieve more than Spanish Jewry achieved prior to the expulsion of the Jews from Spain in 1492, or German Jewry prior to Kristallnacht (Night of the Broken Glass): the night of November 9, 1938—when the windows of Jewish homes, stores, and synagogues were shattered; when Jews throughout Germany were attacked; when Jewish stores were looted and synagogues desecrated or destroyed, signaling the beginning of the Shoah.

Like the Jews in the Golden Age in Spain several centuries earlier, Germanic Jewry in the twentieth century reached the apex of human achievement in every field of human endeavor. Names like Albert Einstein, Sigmund Freud, Franz Kafka, Gustav Mahler, Franz Werfel, Walter Benjamin, and Martin Buber stand out. While they formed less than 1 percent of the general population of the German-speaking countries, they contributed to German culture relative to their numbers immeasurably more than the rest of the population. None of this prevented the average German from harboring anywhere from mild to extreme anti-Semitic feelings. When Albert Einstein formulated his theory of relativity, he was reported to have said, "If my theory of relativity is proven successful, Germany will claim me as a German and France will declare that I am a citizen of the world. Should my theory prove untrue, France will say that I am a German and Germany will declare that I am a Jew."[5]

Germany, not unlike most of Europe, never accepted the Jews as equals, no matter how much they contributed to German life and prestige, and no matter how loyal and devoted they were to their motherland. It has

---

4. One could argue that the contributions of Jews in Germanic lands to world culture rivaled any group in history.

5. Comment made during an address at the Sorbonne in Paris. See McGarty, *Categorization in Social Psychology*, 117.

been said that German Jews were more German than the Germans themselves. But obviously the feeling was not mutual. In fact, even the Jews of Eastern Europe loved German culture and regarded Germany as the standard-bearer of civilization. This did not prevent the German people (and to some extent even German Jews!) from looking down on them as *Ostjuden*, Eastern Jews, an inferior kind of a Jew, and when the Germans invaded Eastern Europe the main thrust of their overall campaign was the brutalization and extermination of several million East European Jews.

Hitler's lurid fascination with Jews, which, according to his book, began in his youth, seems to have been fueled by two characteristics of his personality. The first was his tendency to look at the world in global, universal terms, almost like a latter-day Napoleon. The second was his penchant for seeing the world in black and white, without any shades of gray. As a young German soldier emerging from the defeat of Germany in World War I, in which he was wounded and temporarily blinded by gas used on the battlefield, Hitler spent many hours pondering the root cause of his country's humiliating defeat and the terrible aftermath of the war, during which time Germany was brought to its knees by the Allies, was made to pay staggering reparations, and experienced an astronomical inflation and widespread starvation. Hitler witnessed the rise of communism in Russia, the success of the Communist party in Germany, and the rise of the United States as a world power. Hitler's *Weltanschauung*, or worldview (one of his favorite words)[6] needed a common global denominator to explain all the great misfortunes that had just befallen his country. Incapable of looking inwardly and accepting any responsibility on behalf of Germany for its military adventures, and equally incapable of any kind of an objective analysis of the various forces at work in his time, he arrived at what physicists might call a "unified field theory" which provided one easy answer to the myriad problems of Germany and the world. That answer was the "world Jewish conspiracy."

It was not an original idea. It appeared in a book titled *The Protocols of the Elders of Zion*, first published in Russia in 1903 and translated into multiple languages. (Henry Ford funded a printing of five hundred thousand copies, which were distributed throughout the United States in the 1920s.) For Hitler, this theory became the cornerstone of his political thinking and, as we shall soon see, it enabled him to rally around him like-minded people who within a few short years were able to turn a small radical party, which was initially outlawed, into a mass movement able to take control of the country, eliminate all the other parties, and whip the German masses into

---

6. It appears in his book numerous times.

a frenzy of patriotic fervor that erupted in a relentless drive to overtake Europe and create a new world order of superior and inferior races. Instead all this ended up bringing about the loss of fifty million human lives and the utter rout of Germany.

One, it appears, can safely speak of the "pathology of anti-Semitism." Anti-Semitism can be looked upon as a form of mental disease. Like other mental diseases, it affects the behavior of its subject, for whom it has deleterious consequences. Jewish history proves this over and over again. Those who have turned on the Jews throughout time have met an inglorious end, not so much because of what the Jews could do to retaliate, but because such action has always been erratic and self-damaging rather than rational and well thought out. In a sense, the treatment of the Jews has been the measure of the conscience of the world, or its moral compass. The rationality and morality of the nations was and can still be measured today by the way they treat the Jews. It has almost been axiomatic throughout history that enlightened regimes have treated the Jews with respect and have enabled them to contribute to the welfare and success of their country of residence. Oppressive regimes, on the other hand, have nearly always treated the Jews badly, and their decline or demise always went hand in hand with the degree to which they mistreated Jews.

In Germany between 1933 and 1945 anti-Semitism broke all the records of human history before or since. The idea of physically exterminating the Jews, or having them give up their faith and their heritage dates back to the ancient Pharaohs of Egypt and to many other subsequent political or ecclesiastic tyrants. Hitler's Germany, however, almost made it a reality. It was as if centuries of European anti-Semitism finally came to a head, and all throughout Europe Hitler and his hordes, with the help of many other nationals and with the tacit approval of entire populations, was able to mow down the Jews with impunity. The question remains, has the world at long last learned the lesson of the disastrous consequences of the disease called anti-Semitism as well as all other forms of racism, or will the ghastly phenomenon of Nazism and racism repeat itself again in the future?

## THE "LEGITIMACY" OF ANTI-SEMITISM IN PRE-WORLD WAR II EUROPE

As the Israeli historian of the Holocaust, Yehuda Bauer, has point out, after the Holocaust no one is any longer an anti-Semite. In other words, anti-Semitism is no longer respectable and has gone underground. Not so before the Holocaust. In post–World War I Europe, anti-Semitism was quite respectable. Anti-Semitism, rather than decline after World War I as Europe was getting rid of its monarchies and replacing them with nationalism and emerging democracies, enjoyed a rebirth. Even in France, running for office on an anti-Semitic ticket was perfectly legitimate. In Eastern Europe, anti-Semitism was virulent. And in Germany it certainly did not lag far behind. One may wonder if Hitler could have made anti-Semitism the cornerstone of his ideology if the rest of Europe had been less anti-Semitic. But he certainly did not have to worry about it. For centuries, blaming the Jews for the ills of the world was fashionable almost everywhere. Those who were born after World War II may find this difficult to understand. But a good parallel today is the criticism that is constantly heaped on the State of Israel by people and countries whose own record is far from stellar. The attitude of the world toward the Jewish people remains very complex, as the world often applies a double standard when dealing with Jews. Much has changed for the better since pre-Holocaust times, but we should keep in mind that when Hitler, after World War I, began to organize what would eventually become the National Socialist party (*Nazi* for short), a virulently anti-Semitic party, he found fertile ground. Germany was ready to blame the Jews for all its problems, and turned a blind eye when the persecution and finally the extermination of the Jews became a state policy enunciated in the Nuremberg Laws in 1935.

# 3

# Germany and Europe after World War I

The Hitler phenomenon did not happen in a vacuum. In fact, one may wonder what Hitler might have done if he were born at a different time, say, a time when Germany was doing relatively well. A charismatic yet cantankerous and delusional personality, would he have gone into politics, business, entertainment, or something else? He tried his hand at being a painter but did not do well. He tells us in his book he was attracted to architecture but did not pursue the necessary studies. Clearly, he was obsessed with power. He had little or no sense of humor, so it is doubtful he would have succeeded in show business. He had little ability to compete with political opponents, so it is equally doubtful he would have gotten anywhere in politics in normal times. He might have become a tyrannical CEO of a major corporation, but it is doubtful he had an interest in profit and loss. Most likely, he would have become a cult leader à la Jim Jones or David Koresh and would have led his obedient disciples to some apocalyptic showdown after failing to take on the powers that be.

Hitler was a typical and clearly defined product of his place and time. His entire career was shaped by his personal experience in World War I, and particularly by Germany's capitulation in November 1918. Almost to the end of his life he vowed that November 1918 would never be repeated. Germany, he argued, should rather cease to exist than repeat the surrender of

1918. This seemed to be his idée fixe, indeed, his obsession. But he certainly did not stop there. He wanted to go much, much further.

In a sense, the time of Hitler was somewhat similar to the time of Napoleon, namely, to the aftermath of the French Revolution, some 120 years earlier. The French Revolution was the turning point in the political history of Europe, in that it brought the monarchy in that country to a violent end and showed the rest of the world how to shift the center of power from a ruling dynastic monarchy to the common people. Napoleon was a common person, and so was Hitler. Napoleon made himself an emperor, and Hitler made himself the absolute ruler of his country. The road from the Bastille leads to such European capitals as Berlin, Vienna, and Moscow in the aftermath of World War I, when long-ruling powerful monarchs lost their thrones, and new regimes, which at first appeared to reflect the will of the people, came into being. New movements and ideologies, all of which in their own way purported to represent the will of the people, came into prominence, namely, nationalism, socialism, communism, and fascism. While they all claimed to speak in the name of the people, none of them was all-inclusive, and all of them in order to succeed resorted to the use of force to impose their will. Europe as a whole in 1918 was still a long way away from being defined by democratic regimes where power is determined by ballots rather than bullets. The movements created by the common man to represent the people soon found themselves in a conflict that before long would become lethal, whereby the nationalistic movements (running the gamut from moderate democrats to far-right fascists) came into direct conflict with the transnational communists, most powerfully represented by the Bolsheviks, who in 1917 took over the former Russian Empire.

While a well-intentioned contemporary American president named Woodrow Wilson promoted the idea that Europe after World War I was heading for peace and democracy, the truth, alas, was quite different. Postwar Europe was a tangle of restive and frustrated nations, nations-in-the-making, and political ideologies that were simmering under the surface and waiting to explode. It was only a question of time before they would reach the boiling point and all hell would break lose. Europe in 1918 was a volcano about to erupt, and there were many players waiting in the shadows for the moment when they could climb onto the stage of history and wreak havoc. There was much unfinished business in Europe when the Great War ended, many accounts to settle, and the idea of living in peace and harmony was a mere illusion. Something tragic had to happen, and it did.

Part 1: Bottomless Evil

## PRE-HITLER GERMANY

Nowhere was this drama more sinister than in Germany. In his book *Hitler's Willing Executioners*, Daniel Goldhagen makes a compelling and well-documented case that the common man in Germany had lost his moral compass during and after Hitler's rise to power. Goldhagen gives the lie to the myth that most of the German people did not know about the Holocaust or did not participate in one way or another in the persecution of the Jewish people. He relentlessly exposes the pervasiveness of the common German's complicity in the ghastly enterprise that resulted in the violent death of millions. What is remarkable about his book is that it became a runaway bestseller in both Germany and Austria, and quite possibly greatly contributed to an awakening among Germanic people, examples of which I have personally experienced on several occasions in recent years. *Hitler's Willing Executioners* also ignited a firestorm of criticism among Holocaust scholars around the world, who have taken Goldhagen to task over several aspects of his scholarship and its resulting conclusions. A comparative study of those criticisms shows that they are inconsistent, and to a large extent reflect jealousy on the part of the critics because of the author's popular success.

In my search to penetrate the mind of Adolf Hitler and of the German people under his reign, I took a look at the causes of World War I, the event that shaped Hitler's life and thought. One book that helped me gain a clear perspective on the subject has been Barbara Tuchman's magisterial work, *The Guns of August*. For me, the author brought two important things into focus. Both deserve some attention.

The first is the death throes of Europe's monarchic system—the Russian czar, the German kaiser, the Austro-Hungarian emperor, and a host of others. The second is Germany's dream of empire, which was dashed against the rocks of harsh reality during the Great War. Both events had a decisive influence on Hitler and on the German people, and explain a great deal about the twin catastrophes known as World War II and the Holocaust.

Let us begin with the second: Germany's dream of empire.

On the eve of World War I, Europe was an imperial and a colonial continent, ruling much of the world. The leading countries of Europe had colonies around the world which played a key role in their economic well-being. The most powerful and far-reaching colonial power at that time was Great Britain, whose naval power was unmatched. Britain was hard at work striving to maintain a balance of power in continental Europe, achieved through a series of treaties. The Treaty of London, to which Prussia committed itself in 1871, guaranteed the neutrality of the small country of Belgium, which separates Germany from France—two countries that had been at war with each other for generations. Belgium's neutrality at the time was a cornerstone for nonbelligerency in Europe. In retrospect, it becomes quite clear that Germany was not comfortable with the rules of the political and diplomatic game in Europe, which seemed to reflect the dominance of other European powers rather than its own. The vying for power in Europe on the eve of the Great War was spiraling out of control. The Russian Empire was rebuilding its armed forces. The Austro-Hungarian Empire was threatening Bosnia. The Italian Empire was looking to expand its colonial reach in Africa. And the German Empire was discussing war plans to preempt the Russians and the French before its own position in Europe became too weakened. Germany, quite clearly, wanted a bigger role in the world. Its military leaders felt that their country, which had an impressive military tradition, was shortchanged by history. Germany could do better and needed to assert itself to achieve its goals.

The Great War, which would later become known as World War I—a war which claimed the lives of many of Europe's best and brightest and put an end to the late nineteenth-century dream of a world at peace—has been endlessly analyzed by historians, who have taken many differing stands as to its causes. One of the bones of contention among those historians and scholars is to what extent Germany was responsible for starting the war. The spark that ignited the European gunpowder keg was the assassination of the Austrian Crown Prince Ferdinand by a Bosnian agitator. But the resulting conflict could have simply ended with Austria taking action against Bosnia, rather than with a world war. Germany wasted no time in allying itself with its sister country of Austria, and in turn all of Europe began to take sides, plunging the entire world into a global war.

Barbara Tuchman in her book *The Guns of August* puts a great emphasis on Germany's role in starting the war and raising it to new levels of brutality, especially against civilian population. The key event she brings into focus is what became known as the "rape of Belgium." Germany decided to ignore the Treaty of London and outflank the French forces by invading France through neutral Belgium. This in itself was enough of a breach of an international treaty, but it did not stop there. The Germans did not expect the Belgians to put up a resistance. Germany was operating on a tight timetable. It knew from the beginning it had to win quickly, or else face defeat. This was due to the fact that the odds were stacked against it. It was facing the Russian giant in the east, and in the west it did not see fulfilled its wish of keeping Britain out of the conflict. Germany did not have the manpower or the material resources to face such combined forces. This, ironically, will become its main problem in striving to win World War II as well. Clearly, Hitler did not learn the lesson of the first war.

As the German forces were approaching Belgium, the Belgians blew up railroad tracks and engaged in other activities designed to slow down the German advance. The German field commanders were furious. They had their marching orders, which did not include bad behavior on the part of puny Belgium. As a result, the German forces resorted to savage behavior against the locals. They would walk into local homes near the site of an act of sabotage, ransack the place, take out some of the men, including the local mayor, and execute them as an object lesson for other Belgians. These acts, which became known around the world as the "rape of Belgium" turned world opinion against Germany, and convinced the United States to enter the war against the "Huns" to save civilization.

In the early twentieth century, Germany, so to speak, believed in its own Manifest Destiny. Tuchman cites Thomas Mann, the great German writer of the century, as speaking of "the establishment of the German idea in history, the enthronement of *Kultur*, the fulfillment of Germany's historical mission."[1]

German academic standards were, indeed, the most advanced in the world. Germany was in the forefront of nearly every area of human endeavor. The president of my rabbinical school, the Hebrew Union College in Cincinnati, Ohio, Dr. Nelson Glueck, a pioneer in the field of biblical archeology, did his doctoral studies in Germany in the 1920s, as did many Jewish scholars from around the world who were attracted to Germany as the center of the *Wissenschaft des Judentum* (science of Judaism). My mother told me that Jews in her town in eastern Poland memorized the poems of Goethe and Schiller. Young Zionists avidly studied the philosophical writings of Nietzsche and Karl Marx. And a German-speaking Austrian Jew named Dr. Theodor Herzl became the founder of political Zionism and the father of modern Israel. And then of course there were Albert Einstein and Sigmund Freud, and the list goes on and on.

And yet, as many can attest, there was also a dark side to Germanic civilization. It seems to me that the idea of a national character invites generalizations. Not all Frenchmen are romantic. Not all Italians are artistic. Not all the Dutch are frugal. Yet we do attribute national characteristics to all nationalities. The Germans are known for their virtues of orderliness, cleanliness, precision, and self-discipline. But at the same time those virtues often seem to be carried to an extreme and become vices. The behavior of the German military in Belgium at the outbreak of World War I was a clear example of German virtues gone awry and resulting in a disaster. "The

---

1. Tuchman, *Guns of August*, 369–70. In his book *The Green Hills of Africa*, Ernest Hemingway makes the point that Thomas Mann was the greatest novelist of his time, and that in the U.S. there was no novelist who equaled him (19).

## Germany and Europe after World War I

trains must run on time," seemed to be the conventional German wisdom, "or else you will be shot." It is quite possible that in Belgium in August of 1914 the seeds for World War II and the Holocaust were sown. The lesson Hitler and his ilk learned from the Belgian experience was not that savaging a small nation was a sure way to alienate world opinion, which they deeply despised, but that the officers of the "Old Reich" were not brutal enough. They had failed to whip the Belgians into submission, something the Nazis practiced with great vigor before they were finally brought down to their knees by the Allies.

As I mentioned before, Hitler was a product of Germany's defeat in World War I. As a failed artist and a young man who was lost in his prewar world, Hitler saw the Great War as a dream come true. Here was an opportunity to find instant success, to become a soldier and attain glory on the battlefield. The thought of war and destruction was music to his ears. This was the greatest adventure of all. Germany's Manifest Destiny was about to be fulfilled. He, a nobody, could become a somebody. All he had to do was join the army, and join he did. Years later it would become clear that Hitler was a gambler by nature, perhaps the greatest gambler who ever lived. He was not afraid to put his life on the line, and later on he would not be afraid to put the life of his entire country on the line. Whatever Hitler was, he certainly knew how to think big. He had little patience for details.

Hitler was wounded in the Great War and was awarded the Iron Cross for bravery. Before the war ended, he became temporarily blinded by gas on the battlefield. And then came November 1918 and Germany's surrender. The Austro-Hungarian Empire ceased to exist. His native Austria was separated from Hungary and stripped of its empire. The German Empire was gone, replaced by the Weimar Republic. A new treaty, known as the Treaty of Versailles, was imposed on Germany. The country was mutilated, with portions of it given to its neighbors. Heavy reparations were imposed on Germany, which was blamed for starting the war, and therefore had to compensate the victors.

Democracy, so to speak, was now forced upon Germany, but Germany, unlike England or France or the United States, did not have a democratic tradition. Political parties proliferated, but the republic proved to be weak, ill managed, and dispirited. The economy, burdened by the war reparations and by an economic crisis, was rapidly deteriorating. Unemployment kept growing, and starvation became common. Many were attracted to the doctrine of communism, which had now taken over the former Russian Empire. Others turned for answers to various forms of extreme nationalism. But the future of Germany remained grim at best. The country that was to lead Europe as the beacon of civilization had become a basket case.

Germans began to ask themselves what went wrong. After all, their soldiers had shown great valor on the battlefield. The country boasted some of the best minds of Europe. What had happened to that glorious Manifest Destiny?

Many Germans, it appears, could not bring themselves to take responsibility for their country's military misadventures. The answer had to be found elsewhere. Something had gone terribly wrong, and it was not the fault of the German people. But what was it?

And so the idea began to emerge: Germany was stabbed in the back by internal enemies. Who were those enemies? Slowly but inexorably the finger began to point at a small minority among the German people that constituted less than one percent of the population. For centuries, that minority was looked upon as pseudo-German. It was rejected by both of Germany's dominant churches—the Catholic Church and the various Lutheran churches. Both had always looked upon the Jews as a cursed people who had committed deicide and therefore were condemned to wander the face of the earth and never find peace. They were never accepted as truly German or given full rights. At best, they were tolerated and accommodated. At worst, they were burned at the stake. Clearly, even though many Jews fought for Germany and for Austria in the Great War and distinguished themselves on the battlefield, the presumption among many Germans was that they really hated Germany and wished its downfall. They were the ones who supported Germany's enemies—most notably Bolshevik Russia and capitalistic England and the United States—and made it impossible for Germany to win the war.

And so, what was perhaps the most logical nation in the world was now on its way to taking leave of all logical thinking and was finding an answer to all its woes in a theory worthy of the darkest ages of history.

And this is where a young war veteran, a man without credentials of any kind, stepped onto the stage of history. Like a parasite finding a carcass, the future savior of Germany found the ideal feeding ground to nurture his grandiose yet nefarious dreams.

# 4

# Satan's Prophet
## The Rise of Hitler

Nazi hierarchy: Hitler on left, Goebbels in the middle.

I am not the one who is bestowing the title of prophet on Hitler. The Führer was the first one who applied this title to himself. On January 30, 1939, the sixth anniversary of his rise to power, Hitler told the Reichstag:

> I have often been a prophet in my life and was generally laughed at. During my struggle for power, the Jews primarily received

with laughter my prophecies that I would someday assume the leadership of the state and thereby of the entire nation and then, among many other things, achieve a solution of the Jewish problem. I suppose that meanwhile the laughter of Jewry in Germany that resounded then is probably already choking in their throats [loud applause follows].

Today I want to be a prophet again. If international finance Jewry within Europe and abroad should succeed once more in plunging the peoples into a world war, then the consequence will be not the Bolshevization of the world and hence a victory of Jewry, but on the contrary, the destruction of the Jewish race in Europe.[1]

Nor am I the first to refer to Hitler as the emissary of the devil. This title has been bestowed upon him innumerable times before, even by some of the most respectable scholars who have dealt with this subject in painstakingly dispassionate terms, and by former close Hitler associates. Nor, for that matter, did Hitler, who was not a churchgoer, shy away from employing theological terminology in his political speeches, words like *providence*, *good* and *evil*, and even *God*. In my referring to Hitler as Satan's prophet, one may wonder whether I believe in the existence of a supernatural being known as the devil. Without engaging in a theological discussion, suffice it to say that for our purposes the devil or Satan is invoked here only metaphorically, not as an article of faith. Since Hitler kept referring to himself as a prophet, which by definition is someone who is believed to be the emissary of God, it appears necessary to emphasize that Hitler was the emissary of some satanic force, and he serves as tangible proof that a single human being has the ability to inflict enormous harm on humanity.

Where does such an evil force emanate from?

Hannah Arendt in her book on the Eichmann trial titled *Eichmann in Jerusalem: A Report on the Banality of Evil*, portrays Adolf Eichmann, one of Hitler's key lieutenants in carrying out the "Final Solution of the Jewish Problem," as a gray bureaucrat, a banal person who was given the power to organize the shipping of millions of human beings to their death. Evil, in the final analysis, is indeed banal, pointless, hollow. Hitler was an empty vessel, a charlatan, a false prophet by the admission of some of his closest associates who had originally fallen under his spell and survived to tell the tale in their memoirs—men like Albert Speer, his chief architect; or Otto Dietrich, his press chief. But at the same time that he was an empty vessel, Hitler was endowed with some unusual gifts that enabled him to emerge from total

---

1. Hitler's speech to the Reichstag on January 30, 1939, "On the Jewish Question."

obscurity, with a nonexistent record as a politician, to become the absolute ruler of eighty million people. Perhaps his most useful gift was his power of oratory. Once he entered the political arena after the First World War, he discovered he had the ability to work himself up to a high emotional pitch in front of massive audiences and to hypnotize his listeners. In addition, he followed a clear and consistent course in his speeches, always dwelling on the same few key points, which he repeated endlessly until they began to sound like the gospel truth. Hard as it may be to believe, he did make sense to millions of Germans, especially in the early years, and once he was able to turn the German economy around, he became even more credible, amassing a political capital that increased immeasurably when he began to score his first territorial victories. Moreover, Hitler was endowed with a photographic memory that enabled him to keep track of his growing number of associates and to take unilateral action without having to consult anyone or resort to notes or records.

Hitler was baptized in the Catholic Church and showed an interest in Lutheranism as an adult. But his words and deeds make it clear that he was only proud of the dark side of Catholicism and of Martin Luther in his later years, when Luther became a rabid anti-Semite. Everything he said and did points to the fact that he despised the moral and humanitarian teachings of both the Old and the New Testaments. He regarded Christianity as weak and corrupted by the teachings of Judaism, and he refused to believe that the Christian Savior was born to Jewish parents. To him this was one more falsification of history, concocted by the world Jewish conspiracy. Hitler spoke of the true Jesus, who of course was an Aryan, born to the northern tribe of the Amorites. That blond, blue-eyed Nordic Jesus fitted into Hitler's Wagnerian belief system, which enshrined the heroic ancestors of the Germanic people and the pagan Teutonic gods of war and glory, whom Hitler sought to resuscitate as the future gods of the thousand-year Third Reich he was about to establish. In other words, Hitler's views provide history's prime example of the complete distortion of the moral teachings of both Judaism and Christianity, which posit the sanctity of human life and the equality of all human beings as children of the one God. Once he rejected those teachings, everything became fair game. Human life—whether that of the Jews of Europe or of his own soldiers fighting losing battles and dying unnecessarily by the hundreds of thousands in places like Stalingrad—became expendable. A Soviet writer named Ilya Ehrenburg said during the war that "a good German is a dead German." Ironically, Hitler, more than anyone else in those years, sided with Ehrenburg.

It took the German people twelve long years of endless brutality to learn that Hitler, rather than being their savior, was their executioner. By then it was too late. Germany lay in ruins. Europe, from Moscow to Madrid, was devastated. The so-called civilized world would never be the same again.

The reason it took so long for people to see the obvious had a lot to do with three additional aspects of Hitler's political talent, namely, his great skills as a propagandist, his ability to dissimulate his true intentions and actions, and the deep secrecy that typified his years in power.

As a propagandist, Hitler understood that people—masses of people—often choose to believe what they want to believe, especially in times of a great crisis. He also knew that if you repeat something often enough in a very loud voice and with great conviction and fanfare, it begins to sound like the truth. In fact, as early as 1925 in his book *Mein Kampf* Hitler coins the term "the big lie," which of course he imputed to the Jews. It was actually he and his sidekick, Propaganda Minister Joseph Goebbels, who were history's greatest practitioners of the Big Lie (so much so that they caused writers like George Orwell and scholars like George Steiner to conclude that in the post-Hitler world language was bankrupt). Hitler writes:

> All this was inspired by the principle—which is quite true within itself—that in the big lie there is always a certain force of credibility; because the broad masses of a nation are always more easily corrupted in the deeper strata of their emotional nature than consciously or voluntarily; and thus in the primitive simplicity of their minds they more readily fall victims to the big lie than the small lie, since they themselves often tell small lies in little matters but would be ashamed to resort to large-scale falsehoods. It would never come into their heads to fabricate colossal untruths, and they would not believe that others could have the impudence to distort the truth so infamously. Even though the facts which prove this to be so may be brought clearly to their minds, they will still doubt and waver and will continue to think that there may be some other explanation. For the grossly impudent lie always leaves traces behind it, even after it has been nailed down, a fact which is known to all expert liars in this world and to all who conspire together in the art of lying.[2]

As dissimulators, Hitler and his associates, particularly the ones who engaged in the persecution and elimination of the actual and the imagined "enemies of the Reich," became experts in covering up their real intentions, so much so that they actually invented a jargon known as *Nazi Deutsch*, or Nazi-speak. Thus, for example, when Heinrich Himmler, the head of the SS, composed a manual on how to build a concentration camp (which I was

---

2. Hitler, *Mein Kampf*, 231.

once asked to translate for the U.S. Department of Justice), he did not use the term "concentration camp" (*Konzentrationlager*) but rather "protective camp" (*Schutzlager*), a camp in which Jews and other undesirables could be protected, as stated in the introduction, "from the justified rage of the public."

In his recent book *Hitlerland*, the veteran American journalist Andrew Nagorski focuses on the failure of American journalists, politicians, and public figures during the '30s to grasp the enormous danger to world safety and peace embodied in the new Nazi regime. The following paragraph about Charles Lindbergh, who visited Germany after Hitler's rise to power, speaks for itself:

> Also from Denmark, Charles wrote to Truman: "While I still have many reservations, I have come away with a feeling of great admiration for the German people." As for Hitler, Lindbergh wrote in a letter to the banker Harry Davison, "He is undoubtedly a great man. And I believe he has done much for the German people." While conceding that Hitler and the German people exhibited fanaticism, he added: "It is less than I expected . . ." And many of Hitler's accomplishments would have been impossible "without some fanaticism."[3]

All those who have written about Hitler's life agree that from the day he became chancellor in 1933 to the day he died in 1945, Hitler became an unknown entity to his own people and even to his closest associates. The Nazi propaganda machine, headed by Goebbels, created a public image of Hitler that had little to do with reality. He was portrayed as the kind and caring leader of the nation who was above reproach and could do no wrong. Not only did he love children, but he was also a lover of nature and animals. As Speer makes clear in his memoir, *Inside the Third Reich*, nothing could be further from the truth. Speer writes:

> Hitler's decision to settle on Obersalzberg seemed to point to a love of nature. But I was mistaken about that. He did frequently admire a beautiful view, but as a rule he was more affected by the awesomeness of the abysses than by the harmony of a landscape. It may be that he felt more than he allowed himself to express. I noticed that he took little interest in flowers and considered them entirely as decorations. Sometime around 1934, when a delegation of Berlin women's organizations was planning to

---

3. Nagorski, *Hitlerland*, 206. Lindberg's support of Nazi Germany and his isolationism have been the subjects of many articles and books, most recently Philip Roth's *The Plot against America*.

welcome Hitler at Anhalter Station and hand him flowers, the head of the organization called Hanke, then the Propaganda Minister's secretary, to ask what Hitler's favorite flower was. Hanke said to me: "I've telephoned around, asked the adjutants, but there's no answer. He hasn't any."[4]

From the day Hitler became sole master of Germany, the German propaganda machine made sure his image was everywhere, like Big Brother always watching his people. But in reality his people had little or no contact with him and did not know him as a real human being at all. Better yet, even his closest associates, the likes of a Goebbels or a Göring or a Himmler, were usually kept at arm's length, only meeting him for state business and always addressing him as the commander in chief. (*Mein Führer* was a common salutation.) His girlfriend, Eva Braun, was unknown to the public until the very end, when he finally married her immediately before the two of them committed suicide. Speer offers the following explanation as to why Hitler always kept himself so isolated:

> There was actually something insubstantial about him. But this was perhaps a permanent quality he had. In retrospect I sometimes ask myself whether this intangibility, this insubstantiality, had not characterized him from early youth up to the moment of his suicide. It sometimes seems to me that his seizures of violence could come upon him all the more strongly because there were no human emotions to him to oppose them. He simply could not let anyone approach his inner being because that core was lifeless, empty.[5]

Once again, one cannot help but marvel how an empty vessel like Adolf Hitler could have been built up by his propaganda machine to appear like a caring human being and one of the greatest leaders of all time.

---

4. Speer, *Inside the Third Reich*, 47.
5. Ibid., 471–72.

# 5

# The World according to Hitler

Hitler's approach to knowledge was eclectic and narrow-minded to an extreme. When he went to war in 1914, he claimed he had taken along a copy of Schopenhauer's philosophical writings, but there is no indication that he was well-versed in the teachings of this particular or any other German philosopher. He adopted ideas from the likes of Friedrich Nietzsche and Charles Darwin, and even from the Bible and from Martin Luther. But he was not the follower of any of them. He was always consistent in being inconsistent. He would pick and choose whatever validated his narrow worldview, and by doing so would always demean the particular author whose idea he would borrow. According the Speer, his chief architect, Hitler had no taste in either art or architecture. He had a distorted notion of classical Greek architecture, which he admired, and he had ordered Speer to build massive Greek-style buildings, stadiums, victory arches, and monuments, mainly in Berlin, which were intended to grace and perpetuate the thousand-year Reich. Speer's father was a prominent architect before Hitler's rise to power. Speer writes about his father's reaction when he was invited to view some of his son's designs ordered by Hitler:

> My father too came to see the work of his now famous son. He only shrugged his shoulders at the array of models: "You've all gone completely crazy." The evening of his visit we went to the theater and saw a comedy in which Heinz Rühmann was appearing. By chance Hitler was at the same performance. During the intermission he sent one of his adjutants to ask whether the

old gentleman sitting beside me was my father, then he asked us both to his box. When my father—still erect and self-controlled in spite of his seventy-five years—was introduced to Hitler, he was overcome by a violent quivering such as I had never seen him exhibit before, nor ever did again. He turned pale, did not respond to Hitler's lavish praise of his son, and then took his leave in silence. Later, my father never mentioned this meeting, and I too avoided asking him about the fit of nerves that the sight of Hitler had produced in him.[1]

Ironically, the man who fancied himself a latter-day Napoleon and was out to conquer the world had hardly traveled and did not know the world. An unworldly megalomaniac, he passed judgment on races and nations without having the slightest idea of what he was talking about. One of the main reasons he lost the war was his excessive faith in the greatness of the German soldier and his belief that Slavs, Africans, and Asians were inferior people who did not know how to fight, Americans had no will to fight, and Jews were devoid of any military skills. In the end, Russian, American, and British generals gave German generals a run for their money; many Africans and Asians fought bravely on the side of the Allies; and as for Jews having no military skills, the verdict of history is quite different.

From Nietzsche, Hitler borrowed two key ideas. The first was the idea of the *Übermensch* or Overman, more commonly known in English as the Superman, which Hitler took to mean the super-race, namely, the German people. He never paid attention to—or may have never been aware of—Nietzsche's severe criticism of German nationalism and of German anti-Semitism. Nor, for that matter, was Hitler aware, as far as we know, of the philosopher's prediction that in the twentieth century Germany was going to cause great harm to the world. While there are varying opinions on what Nietzsche actually meant by *Übermensch*, an idea he develops in his ecstatically visionary book *Thus Spoke Zarathustra*, we do know that Nietzsche was not out to glorify the German people but rather to find an alternative to Christian civilization, which he believed had lost its validity. In its place he sought to introduce not a divine but a human authority, embodied in a highly accomplished human being who was able to transcend those around him and their value system, which was based on the worn-out teachings of Christianity, and to achieve fulfillment as a creative force in this life rather than in the Christian promise of an afterlife. Who exactly this particular individual is remains unclear. Whether or not this obfuscation was deliberate, it allowed Hitler to put his own spin on this idea, and since he felt contempt

---

1. Speer, *Inside the Third Reich*, 133.

for the basic values of his own religion, he seized upon the idea of the Superman and twisted it to represent the super-race, while claiming Nietzsche as a precursor of Nazism, something Nietzsche would have found appalling.

The second idea Hitler seems to have borrowed from Nietzsche was his view of life as a perpetual struggle. Hitler's main knowledge of Nietzsche's writings came from Nietzsche's surviving sister, Elisabeth. Elisabeth was a devout Nazi and a friend of the Führer. She tampered with her brother's writings to suit her extreme views and misinterpreted the idea of struggle to mean that life was meant to be a perpetual *military* struggle, and that the critical issues of life could only be decided on the battlefield.

From Darwin, Hitler borrowed the idea of the survival of the fittest, which was the result of Darwin's observations of behavior patterns in the animal kingdom. Here again Hitler chose to ignore the humanitarian side of Darwin, who, among other things, was a staunch opponent of slavery during the American Civil War. Ignoring all the laws and beliefs of civilized society, Hitler became convinced that life is guided by the principle of "might is right." In other words, "the strong shall inherit the earth." In his pursuit of a strong and abiding Germany, Hitler, with the aid of German physicians and scientists who bought into his superman philosophy, launched a program of disposing of the physically and mentally weak members of German society, and of breeding strong and mentally fit babies by selective mating of young German girls with members of the SS. What becomes obvious here is that in the world according to Hitler, human beings were little more than biological entities whose individuality and whose intrinsic worth meant little, since they existed primarily for the greater glory of the state, which for Hitler replaced God. The will of the state, interpreted of course by the infallible Führer, superseded that of any individual German.

And herein resided the crowning idea of Hitler's worldview: the state does not exist for the sake of human beings; human beings exist for the sake of the state. Never mind that human beings make up the state. The whole is greater than the sum of its parts. Better yet, human beings are expendable. The supreme leader of the state has the right to do anything he deems right to any member of the state since he is the supreme arbiter and knows better than anyone else what the best interest of the state is.

How did one of the most advanced nations in the world allow itself to give up all individual freedom and let the will of one person control all matters large and small? One of the best answers I have ever seen was given by the psychologist Erich Fromm in his book *Escape from Freedom*. Fromm shows how people in distress—whether as a small group or as an entire nation—unable to take charge of their own affairs, are willing to forgo their freedom and put their fate in the hands of a strong personality without asking too many questions. After their defeat in World War I and their failure at democracy in the form of the Weimar Republic, Germans were yearning for a strong leader and traded their freedom for a ruler with absolute powers whom they regarded to be their savior. Clearly, this can happen to any people at any time when conditions are right.

Hitler felt great contempt for all figures of authority in the Nazi state. Those included, among others, the clergy, the intellectuals, the judges, and even the top military commanders. He and his lieutenants often clashed with the German clergy, whom they considered to be a nuisance and a stumbling block in their drive towards world domination. Only those members of the clergy who fawned before them and praised them to high heavens were acceptable, and unfortunately there were more than a few of those. But as we shall see, there were also brave souls among them who spoke out and paid dearly for doing so.

The only intellectuals looked upon with favor by the Hitler gang were pseudo-intellectuals whose main intellectual contribution was Nazi propaganda and pseudo-ideas. Germany's real intellectuals and its creative artists—writers and scientists, the likes of a Thomas Mann or an Albert Einstein—had to leave the country. There were some unusual exceptions, such as the philosopher Martin Heidegger or the composer Richard Strauss, who were willing to work within the Nazi system, and whose collaboration remains controversial to this day. But the general attitude promoted by Hitler during his reign was one of anti-intellectualism carried out by a relentless campaign to force German culture into the narrow bed of the Nazi racist ideology.

Hitler always showed deep aversion for the German legal system. In his memoir, *The Hitler I Knew*, his press chief, Otto Dietrich, writes:

> Hitler incessantly attacked the nation's judges for being "remote from life," without links to their race, sticklers to the dead letter of the law," "petrified bureaucrats," and the last pillars of reaction. In his private conversation violent abuse of magistrates was one of his constant themes. He made no bones about his hatred of them. Undoubtedly one of the reasons for this feeling was the sense that judicial independence constituted concealed resistance to his absolutism.[2]

Last but not least, from the day he took power in 1933 to the day he lost the war in 1945, Hitler was always attacking his generals. A critical component of the Hitler myth was the idea drummed into the German people that Hitler was one of history's greatest military geniuses, on par

2. Dietrich, *Hitler I Knew*, 101.

with Napoleon. In 1961 I visited the Pentagon in Washington DC, a guest of my cousin, who served at the time as the comptroller of the United States Air Force. My cousin told me he had lunch the other day at the cafeteria in the Pentagon and he overheard two West German generals at the next table who were guests of the U.S. Air Force talk about Hitler. One told the other that he believed Hitler surpassed Napoleon as a military genius. This was during the height of the Cold War, and the German general added that if the Americans had appreciated Hitler's gifts as a military strategist they would have allied themselves with him and together would have put an end to communism then and there.

From the time of the 1918 defeat, Hitler distrusted and disliked the top brass of the Wehrmacht for two reasons. First, Germany lost the war. Second, the generals in the main came from the old Prussian aristocracy and were regarded by Hitler, the pseudopopulist, as elitists who were more loyal to their class than to the state. Only those who followed him blindly and never questioned his decisions were considered acceptable. The others were always mistrusted. As a general rule, Hitler always lay down the law in all major military decisions, and no matter how removed those decisions were from reality, the generals had to obey unquestioningly. As Germany's fortunes of war began to decline in late 1941, the clash between the Führer and his generals became more and more severe. It mattered little if a particular battle or campaign were lost despite the brilliant performance of a particular general. Since losing a battle was not an option (even though sometimes it is necessary to retreat in order to advance), generals, including some of the best, were summarily replaced or demoted or worse. It is no wonder that von Stauffenberg and his colleagues tried to assassinate Hitler. What is surprising is that it took so long for such an attempt to take place.

The only figures of authority in the Hitlerian galaxy that had freedom of action were his close lieutenants, who acted as his tentacles, protecting their master and carrying out his murderous policies. As I noted, this did not mean that he clutched them to his bosom as close friends. Essentially, as the supreme leader, he had no friends. But the likes of a Goebbels, a Heydrich, a Himmler or a Göring, as we shall see, vied among themselves to outdo one another in implementing their master's policies and often exceeded his wishes and expectations in order to outdo one another and advance their personal careers. (They all saw themselves as the next Führer.) Needless to say, they were always extremely careful not to challenge his authority and lavished constant praise on him, real or feigned.

In light of all this, one does not need a rich imagination to envision what the world would have been like had Hitler won the war. True, Stalinism and communism as a whole would have disappeared. But so would democracy, human freedom, and human rights. The world would have been ruled by the likes of a Mussolini, a Franco, a Hirohito, and others like them. Entire populations would have been exterminated with impunity. The human race would have been reengineered. Civilization as we know it would have ceased to exist.

# 6

# The Complicity of the World
## A Tale of Two Conferences

The enormity of the destruction of the Jews of Europe, known as the Holocaust, cannot be understood without considering two conferences that took place within three years of each other: the Évian Conference in July 1938, and the Wannsee Conference in January 1942. For me, revisiting those two events is an extremely painful experience, and I am not sure which one is more painful. The first was convened in France by democratic nations and their allies, ostensibly with good intentions of finding a solution to the problem of Jewish refugees fleeing Nazi Germany and Austria about a year before the outbreak of World War II. Instead of finding a viable solution, the Évian Conference made it clear, after several days of deliberations, that the so-called enlightened world did not care about the fate of the Jews, and, in effect, gave Hitler a free pass to proceed with genocide. The second conference was held in Berlin by top Nazi leaders after Germany had taken control of the lives of several million Jews in Eastern Europe and was looking for the best way to wipe them off the face of the earth. This conference, which was bureaucratic in nature and only lasted ninety minutes, spelled out the "Final Solution" to the "Jewish Question." There seems to be a correlation between the two conferences, which caused the world at that time to be divided into two parts: those who killed the Jews and those who stood by and watched without lifting a finger.

The Évian Conference was convened at the initiative of President Franklin D. Roosevelt, and was attended by representatives of thirty-two countries, including the United States, Great Britain, the countries of Latin America, the democracies of Western and Northern Europe, and the member countries of the British Empire. By that time Germany had passed its Nuremberg Laws, which deprived the Jews of Nazi Germany of their citizenship rights and turned many of them into stateless refugees who had nowhere to go. The Évian Conference was an opportunity for those countries to take a stand against the racist and supremacist policies of Hitler's Germany, but they failed to do so. The conference was also an opportunity for countries like Australia and Brazil to welcome German and Austrian Jews, who could have contributed greatly to the welfare and progress of those countries. Forty years later, Walter Mondale would sum up the Évian conference as follows:

"At stake at Évian were both human lives and the decency and self-respect of the civilized world. If each nation at Évian had agreed on that day to take in seventeen thousand Jews at once, every Jew in the Reich could have been saved. As one American observer wrote, 'It is heartbreaking to think of the . . . desperate human beings . . . waiting in suspense for what happens at Évian. But the question they underline is not simply humanitarian . . . it is a test of civilization.'"[1]

We will never know how many future Nobel Prize winners could have been saved. We only know that the world was greatly diminished by the inaction of the Évian conference.

How are we to explain such blatant failure to act?

A careful study of the main players of the conference, particularly the heads of state and their representatives at the conference, reveals what may come as a shock to many today. The Jews did not have a single true friend among those thirty-two countries' leaders—not at the White House, not at 10 Downing Street, and not at any of the other seats of power. Worse yet, anti-Semitism seems to have played a major role in the decision-making process among those world leaders. This applied to the leaders of the United Kingdom, Canada, Australia, and other nations. Roosevelt, who was believed at the time to be a friend of the Jews, and who had several Jews in his cabinet, remained consistent before and during the entire war in not extending a helping hand to the Jews of Europe. We should keep in mind that the only topic of discussion at the Évian Conference was the Jews of Germany and Austria. The millions of Jews in Eastern Europe, for whom the writing was already on the wall regarding genocide, did not even figure in the discussion. They did not seem to matter at all.

One may wonder, why would the countries of the British Empire be so opposed to letting those people in? After all, countries like Canada and

---

1. Mondale, "Geneva and Evian."

# The Complicity of the World

Australia were sparsely populated, and could have used the talents of what was at that time the most advanced Jewry in the world. Both of those countries' heads of state gave a clear answer. They did not like the idea of increasing their Jewish population. Australia in particular, until recent years, has had very restrictive immigration laws. Canada claimed that it needed farmers, not merchants. A. A. Heaps, a Canadian member of Parliament who had advised his fellow Jews to keep silent for fear of an anti-Jewish backlash and to put their trust in its leaders, was shocked at the Canadian government's reaction to Évian. He wrote a passionate, bitter, and accusing letter to his friend, Prime Minister Mackenzie King, as he felt betrayed by the promise that a reasonable number of refugees would be allowed to come to Canada, but this had proved "a cruel hoax." He made a last desperate appeal to King, pointing out the iniquitous behavior of his government, hoping that it might shame the prime minister to take action. Heaps wrote:

> The existing regulations are probably the most stringent to be found anywhere in the whole world. If refugees have no money they are barred because they are poor, and if they have fairly substantial sums, they are often refused admittance on the most flimsy pretext. All I say of existing regulations is that they are inhuman and anti-Christian . . . Practically every nation in the world is allowing a limited number to enter their countries . . . The lack of action by the Canadian government is leaving an unfortunate impression . . . I regret to state that the sentiment is gaining ground that anti-Semitic influences are responsible for the government's refusal to allow refugees to come to Canada.[2]

Heaps never received a reply to his letter. One should marvel at his courage in writing such an appeal. Jewish leaders in the United States and around the world at that time were afraid to speak up. If they did, they were either censured or, as in Heaps's case, ignored. The British government under Prime Minister Neville Chamberlin set the tone for the rest of the empire. It refused to take a strong stand on the issue of German Jewry and, a year later, in 1939, issued a White Paper for Palestine, which greatly curtailed Jewish immigration to what was to become (to quote the British Balfour Declaration of 1917) the "national home for the Jewish people."[3]

---

2. The McAdam Report, No. 377, 04/11/03, 21.

3. "Balfour Declaration. A letter from the United Kingdom's Foreign Secretary Arthur James Balfour to Baron Rothschild, dated November 2, 1917, supporting the establishment of a Jewish home for the Jewish people in Palestine" (*Wikipedia*, "Balfour Declaration").

The only tangible result of the conference was the formation of an Intergovernmental Committee to look into solutions to the problem. It proved to be an empty gesture, since nothing came of it. And yet both the United States and the United Kingdom touted it as a great achievement. Lord Winterton in his Report to the British Cabinet said that it had been possible at Évian to "reach a conclusion which was not only unanimous, but which was more satisfactory than seemed likely at the outset." The *London Times* stated on July 16, 1938,

> Évian has done its work admirably . . . It has devised machinery which, if not blocked by the countries of origin should transfer the haphazard flight of destitute Jews into the orderly exodus of not wholly impoverished emigrants . . . The representatives of one country after another . . . held out the prospect that his Government would relax its immigration laws to the outmost possible extent . . . 200,000 can be settled.

One may wonder whether the editors of the *Times* were being naïve or cynical.

Myron Taylor, President Roosevelt's emissary to the conference, wrote in his conclusions to his Report of the meeting of the Intergovernmental Committee on Political Refugees at Évian:

> As I look over the situation, I am satisfied that we accomplished the purpose for which the Intergovernmental Meeting at Évian—which we consistently regarded as an initial session—was called. We have obtained approval of machinery which should prove effective, if skillfully used, to alleviate the condition of political refugees.[4]

One gets the impression of collusion between the United States and the United Kingdom, as well as the other countries, all of whom were looking to assuage their conscience and to appear to be on the side of justice and fairness, as if they cared about the fate of the hapless victims of Nazi persecution. The truth was different. Hardly ever in the history of the world was there a moment like that day in July 1938, when the Jews of the world found themselves all alone in the world, without hope, as if their fate was sealed. The road to Auschwitz was opened on that day.

"Nobody wants them," claimed the German Nazi newspaper *Völkischer Beobachter* after the Évian Conference.[5] Gloating, Hitler commented: "It is a shameful spectacle to see how the whole democratic world is oozing

---

4. The McAdam Report, No. 376, 04/07/03, 21.
5. *Völkischer Beobachter*, July 1938.

## The Complicity of the World

sympathy for the poor tormented Jewish people, but remains hard hearted and obdurate when it comes to helping them."[6]

The conference was a bitter disappointment to Jewish leaders, who were only allowed to attend as observers. One of them was Golda Meyerson, later Golda Meir, who wrote in her memoirs:

> Sitting there in that magnificent hall and listening to the delegates of thirty-two countries rise, each in turn, to explain how much they would have liked to take in substantial numbers of refugees and how unfortunate it was that they were not able to do so, was a terrible experience. I don't think that anyone who didn't live through it can understand what I felt at Évian—a mixture of sorrow, rage, frustration and horror.[7]

Dr. Chaim Weizmann, the man who secured the Balfour Declaration from the British government and later became the first president of the State of Israel, pointed out that the world was now divided between countries who killed the Jews and those who would not let them in.[8]

In Palestine, a few months later, David Ben-Gurion, the founder of the State of Israel, would say in a speech in reaction to the British White Paper, the Arab riots, and the outbreak of World War II: "We will fight the White Paper as if there is no war, and fight the war as if there is no White Paper."[9] It had become crystal clear to the future founder of Israel that the only hope left for the Jews was to take their fate into their own hands and fight for their survival.

Perhaps the greatest irony of the Évian Conference is that while the Nazis at that time claimed that the Jews were running the world, the conference made it clear that the Jews in the world of 1938 were politically powerless. Hitler, who originally speculated that the world did not care when the Turks massacred the Armenians before World War I, must have now realized that the world would not get too upset when he started to exterminate the Jews. What we have here is the complicity of the world in the Holocaust. Hitler and his Nazi hordes may have been the executioners, but

---

6. Hitler, "On the Jewish Question."

7. Meir, *My Life*, 158. The total helplessness felt by such Jewish leaders as Chaim Weizmann and Golda Meir is well attested to. It is against this background that David Ben-Gurion made it clear that he would continue the struggle for the establishment of a Jewish state in Palestine against all odds.

8. Dr. Chaim Weizmann in a speech on 25 November 1936, testifying before the Peel Commission for Palestine.

9. See Ben-Ami, *Scars of War, Wounds of Peace*, 27.

those countries that could and should have done something are not blameless. We shall return to this point later on.[10]

Unlike the delegates to the Évian Conference, the men who met in January 1942 in a beautiful suburb of Berlin at the beautiful villa at 56–58 Am Großen Wannsee, stolen by the Nazis from its Jewish owners, were not interested in pretending to be just and fair. As their leader, Hitler, stated in one of his speeches, "The world calls us barbarians, and indeed we are." The meeting was organized by one of Hitler's top henchmen, Reinhard Heydrich, the only member of the Führer's coterie who physically fitted the image of the Nordic superman (the rest, including Hitler, looked like a group of circus clowns). Ironically, he was purported to have Jewish blood running through his veins. Heydrich is considered by historians to have been the most evil figure in the Nazi elite. Still in his thirties at the time, he was chief of the Reich's main security office, which included the Gestapo. Therefore, he reported to Himmler, who was the head of the SS, the Nazis' paramilitary organization that committed the majority of the war crimes during the Nazi era. Fortunately for the world, Heydrich was assassinated the following year by a British-trained team of Czech soldiers who had their own accounts to settle with him. Intelligence falsely linked the assassins to the Czech villages of Lidice and Lezaky. Lidice was razed to the ground; all adult males were executed, and all but a handful of its women and children were deported and killed in Nazi concentration camps. Hitler proposed to further retaliate by killing several thousand additional Czechs, but was dissuaded by his advisors who were afraid of destabilizing that entire country.

Heydrich had received an order from Hitler's second in command, Hermann Göring, to convene a meeting of Nazi state functionaries for the purpose of formulating the "Final Solution to the Jewish Question." In reality, by January of 1942 the Germans were in full swing of exterminating the Jews in Eastern Europe. But in order to kill millions more they had to come up with a master plan that took into account the intricate and costly logistics of rounding up entire populations, transporting them to discreet locations where they could be forced to do hard labor, tortured, killed, and disposed of without disrupting the daily life of other people in the area, and without attracting too much world attention. Historians have been pondering the

10. In 1939, 937 passengers left Hamburg, Germany, for Havana, Cuba, on the MS *St. Louis*. Despite holding visas, Cuba denied the 922 Jewish passengers entrance, and then the U.S. and Canada did the same. The ship's captain, Gustav Schröder, refused to return the ship to Germany until all the passengers were given safe haven outside Germany. Eventually, the Jewish passengers were accepted into Belgium, France, the Netherlands, and the U.K. This story was recounted in the book (written by Gordon Thomas and Max Morgan-Witts) and movie *The Voyage of the Damned* (directed by Stuart Rosenberg).

## The Complicity of the World

real purpose and significance of this historic conference and have offered various interpretations. Some have argued that the top Nazis wanted to spread the responsibility for this satanic plan among lesser functionaries of the regime. Heydrich invited Adolf Eichmann, whom he had charged with the task of facilitating the mass transportation and managing the logistics of mass deportation of Jews to ghettos and extermination camps in German-occupied Eastern Europe, to act as the recording secretary of the meeting. During his trial in Jerusalem after the war, Eichmann would testify that he was charged with providing a list of all the Jewish populations of Europe, and was told to sanitize the minutes by not using words like *extermination* but rather *evacuation* or *resettlement*. Eichmann further explained that after the meeting, which only lasted ninety minutes, the attendees had a glass of cognac and spoke openly about the total extermination of the Jews.

Heinrich Heydrich

The Wannsee Conference was originally scheduled for December 1941. However, on December 5 the Soviet Army began a counteroffensive outside Moscow, and the prospect of a rapid conquest of the Soviet Union did not materialize. On December 7, the Japanese attacked the United States at Pearl Harbor, causing the U.S. to declare war on Japan the next day. To fulfill its obligations under its Tripartite Pact with Italy and Japan, the Reich government began on December 11 preparing to issue a declaration of war against the United States.

With the Nazi hierarchy busy with those major events, Heydrich had to postpone his meeting to January 20, 1942. One can only marvel why those top Nazi leaders were focusing their attention at a time like this on the systematic murder of helpless men, women, and children who had nothing to do with the war the Germans themselves had started when it became clear that, first, the Germans were facing a devastating war with the Russian giant who vastly outnumbered them in personnel and matèriel, and when it became clear that, second, the Germans were facing a new giant, namely, the United States. All this put the Germans in an untenable position and made their chances of winning the war practically nil.

According to Lucy Dawidowicz in her book *The War against the Jews*, Hitler's primary purpose in launching World War II was to wage war not against his neighbors but against the Jews. In other words, exterminating the Jewish people was his primary objective, which took precedence over everything else. Seen in this light, the Wannsee Conference may make sense. One perhaps could go a step further and argue that the military defeats the Germans began to suffer in late 1941 on the Russian front redoubled their determination to complete the task of making Europe *Judenrein* ("cleansed of Jews"). This argument was advanced by Princeton University historian Arno Mayer, as mentioned in Richard Breitman's book *The Architect of Genocide: Himmler and the Final Solution*.

Hitler and his minions were victims of the demonology they themselves had invented. While they were fighting Soviet military forces, they had convinced themselves that the real and most insidious enemy within the Soviet Union were the Jewish people—men, women, and children—who invented Bolshevism in the first place. They were the incarnation of the devil, and if that devil could be destroyed the Germans somehow would emerge triumphant. Here again it is quite impossible to grasp how educated people in the middle of the twentieth century could have degenerated to the point of thinking like the most backward zealots of the darkest Middle Ages, the ones who burned people at the stake because they were "possessed by the devil." Moreover, while Hitler continued to insist almost until the end of the war in 1945 that Germany was going to win the war, by the beginning of 1942 Germany chances of winning were becoming dimmer and dimmer. Only in one area could the Master Race show its ostensible superiority, namely, in its ability to murder Jews with impunity. Beyond that, one can only speculate. History's greatest crime remains a mystery, and may never be solved. There was certainly no logic in the Nazis' relentless pursuit of their genocidal goals in late 1941 and in the beginning of 1942. Thus, Évian and Wannsee are two acts in the same tragic drama of two conferences in which the so-called good guys failed to act, and the murderers acted to the full extent of their ability.

# 7

# Those Who Did the Dirty Work

We have no written records of Hitler personally ordering the Wannsee Conference. We can only deduce that Göring would not have ordered Heydrich to convene such a conference without the Führer's blessing. This was typical of the way Hitler operated. He was not a hands-on chief executive. As Führer, he cultivated the image of someone removed from the ordinary business of government. Unlike Himmler, he never visited a concentration camp. He kept his distance from the atrocities committed on his behalf and with his blessing. What Hitler had going for himself was the ability to find like-minded people whom he would groom as his disciples, who were always ready to do his bidding. He would weed out the ones who were not totally and unconditionally devoted to him, and promote the true disciples, whom he always kept guessing as to his next move, while playing them off one against another. In this way he was literally able to clone himself and let his underlings do all the dirty work while he focused on what he liked to do best, which was to play the role of prophet and savior, and to give fiery speeches.

Hitler's henchmen—men like Himmler and Eichmann and many of the other top Nazis—were consummate bureaucrats, sticklers for details, and hard workers, while Hitler was basically lazy, disorganized, and completely impulsive. As a result, he surrounded himself with evil geniuses who became the embodiment of his will, and who worked tirelessly not only on carrying out his wishes but on exceeding them. When it came to killing Jews, they all vied with one another for the dubious distinction of being the greatest Jew hater and destroyer, the one who could do more than the rest to further the cause of ridding the world of what they considered its worst enemy. If Hitler was Satan's prophet, they were the angels of death who worked tirelessly on turning their master's satanic prophecies into reality.

These utterly depraved members of the human race, history's greatest criminals, deserve some of our attention. Without them, Hitler—according to many historians—would not have been able to carry out his nefarious plans. For our purposes, we will single out four of them, namely, Heinrich Himmler, Joseph Goebbels, Adolf Eichmann, and Josef Mengele. The mention of their names sends a shiver down one's spine. They each played a decisive role in promoting and implementing the "Final Solution," and they all went to great lengths to make it as vicious and satanic as possible. If their true intention was to become history's greatest villains, they certainly succeeded. To be sure, there were others, like Göring, for example, who could be included in this evil council. But when it comes to the Holocaust, these four played a decisive role in the preparation and implementation of the Final Solution and in taking it to unprecedented levels of ferocity and cold-blooded sadism.

What truly defies understanding is the fact that they were not uneducated lowlifes. On the contrary, many in the Nazi hierarchy came from respectable middle-class or even upper-class families. More than a few had PhDs. Many were raised in God-fearing Catholic or Lutheran homes. They were all familiar with the Ten Commandments, particularly with the one that states, "You shall not commit murder." Many had loving wives and children and were good family men. They loved to listen to classical music, and they read classical literature. Many loved their dogs or their more exotic pets (in the case of Göring). They treated them with kindness and were shocked when anyone mistreated an animal. For all good purposes, these were very genuine human beings. And yet they were all infected by the same virus, namely, the virus of racism in its most extreme manifestation. This virus must have entered their brain and destroyed that part of it known as human conscience. They were able to operate the way they did because their value system shifted from respect for human life to the belief in the "survival of the fittest." As George Orwell put in aptly in his book *1984*, good became evil, war became peace, and so on.

Had Hitler won the war in Europe, and had the Nazi vision been fulfilled, Germany would have done away with the institutions of Christianity, replacing Jesus with the Führer, and his henchmen would have become the apostles of the new faith. Instead of worshiping God, the Germans and those living under their yoke would have been worshiping the new "gods" of Nazism. This would not have been the first time this had happened in human history. The Nazi gods had their precedents in the ancient Pharaohs, in the kings of ancient Assyria (who, arguably, were history's first Nazis), in demented Roman Caesars like Caligula and Nero, and (more recently) in Stalin, who was deified in the Soviet Union as the "Sun of the Nations."

Let us take a look at some of the top perpetrators of the Final Solution, and let us try to understand what made them tick. By gaining some insights into those masters of evil, we will better understand their lord and master, Adolf Hitler, and why the greatest act of murder in all of human history took place at the heart of so-called civilized Europe in the middle of the twentieth century.

## HEINRICH HIMMLER

**Himmler (right) inspecting Auschwitz**

Himmler (1900–1945) may deserve the title of history's greatest murderer. As head of Hitler's police state, he started his career overseeing the killing of German and Jewish "enemies of the Reich" to help his patron and idol become the absolute ruler of Germany. The main venue for those activities was the Dachau concentration camp near Munich, where Himmler's SS personnel honed their skills as torturers and murderers. After the war broke out, Himmler applied the Dachau model to Nazi-occupied Poland, where he established similar camps, and masterminded the activities that turned that country into a graveyard for millions—Jews and non-Jews. Most notorious were the camps at Auschwitz, Himmler's premier project, where about 1.5 million people, mostly Jews, were either gassed and burned upon arrival or systematically dehumanized by being starved, tortured, worked to death, or subjected to medical experiments by the likes of a Josef Mengele. While his boss never visited places like Auschwitz, Himmler was a frequent visitor.

Mythology or science fiction would have portrayed Himmler as a larger-than-life monster, and yet he hardly looked the part. Awkward looking, unattractive, shy, and reserved, he possessed none of his boss's theatrics and charisma, yet he complemented Hitler as if they were two sides of the same coin. Himmler came from a perfectly normal, God-fearing Catholic family. His father was a schoolteacher, strict with his children (as many German fathers in those days were) but also a caring father who took interest in his children's well-being and education. His mother was devoted to her three sons, who were quite close. Heinrich's two brothers (he was the middle son) were perfectly normal young Germans. In 2007, Himmler's grandniece, Katrin Himmler, published a book titled *The Himmler Brothers: A German Family History*. One learns from this book that during the Nazi era the Himmler clan was very proud of having a top Nazi leader in their midst, which accorded them a high status in German society. It turns out that both of Himmler's brothers joined the SS—the elite Nazi organization responsible for most of the regime's war crimes. In the final analysis, the Himmler brothers were fairly ordinary Germans who at some other time would have been upstanding citizens. It seems that the times they lived in and their opportunity to attain power far beyond their normal social status and personal skills drove them to become the monsters they ended up being. Their story is a chilling reminder that almost anyone is capable of committing monstrous crimes.

While growing up, Heinrich Himmler lived in the shadow of his older brother. He was neither good-looking nor an overachiever. He was awkward with the girls and remained a virgin late into his twenties. When World War I broke out, Himmler was only fourteen, too young to enlist. His older brother saw action and was awarded the Iron Cross. Heinrich dreamed of military glory but never achieved it. As head of the SS he donned the uniform of this quasi-military organization and tried hard to cut a figure of a brave soldier. But like the paths of many of the top Nazi leaders, his career had little to do with bravery on the battlefield or distinguished military service. Rather, his was the career of a party hack; he was a member of violent political gangs and was a delusional right-wing, *völkisch* racist, whose rise to power was the result of political machinations, deception, and assassinations.

In his early twenties, Himmler lost his Catholic faith, which he considered the faith of the weak who stood in the way of Germany recovering its old glory and its true identity. The ideology of the new National Socialist Party, or Nazi Party, became his new religion. He joined the Nazi Party and embraced its belief in the superiority of the Aryan race, its fear of the dangers facing Germany on all sides, and its faith in the noble ancestry of the

Germanic people, whose ranks had been diluted by inferior races like Slavs, Jews, and others: Himmler saw it as his life's mission to root out and destroy those enemies at all costs.

It is not clear at what point in his young life Himmler embraced the notion that human life was expendable and bought into Hitler's policy of political assassination and, later on, into mass murder of innocent civilians demonized by the Nazi regime. Like other top Nazis who turned their backs on their parents' values and the teachings of their religious traditions, Himmler came under the spell of the all-knowing Führer who preached murder as a legitimate means to attain political goals. Furthermore, he also came under the spell of the great mission of the Germanic people to rid the world of inferior races and particularly of the most evil form of human life, namely, the Jews, so that Germany could become the master race it was meant to be.

To better understand Himmler, we should consider the nature of the organization he was put in charge of by Hitler, which, under his command, became the elite Nazi killing machine, namely, the *Schutzstaffel* (Defense Corps) or SS. During the Nazi Party's formative years, the SS was a small organization charged with protecting the Nazi leaders, mainly during their public appearances, which often resulted in violent disturbances. It was an adjunct to the SA, or *Sturmabteilung* (Assault Division), also known as the Brownshirts, which functioned as the original paramilitary wing of the Nazi Party. The SA consisted of unruly thugs who terrorized the members of other political parties and initiated the persecution of German Jewry once the Nazis came to power. The SA was headed by a former German army officer named Ernst Röhm, who was Himmler's superior when Himmler first joined the Nazi Party in 1923. During the following ten years, a power struggle began to brew between Röhm and Hitler's close associates, a group that included Himmler. When the Nazis came to power in 1933, Röhm sought a larger role for his SA organization, which he believed should become the new German army.

Hitler saw Röhm as a threat to himself as the sole leader of the new Germany, and in 1934 decided to eliminate him along with other prominent Nazi and anti-Nazi leaders, including many SA leaders. This event of ruthless political assassinations became known as the Night of the Long Knives. It helped consolidate Hitler's position as the absolute ruler of Germany, and it gave Himmler the opportunity to show his unconditional loyalty to the Führer. After the Night of the Long Knives, Hitler and his close associates realized that they could achieve their political goals through acts of murder that they justified as actions necessary for the protection of the German people from both internal and external enemies.

While the SA continued to exist until the fall of Nazi Germany, it was now emasculated and stripped of its political power. This was Himmler's golden opportunity to turn the small SS into a state within a state, a terror organization without which a dictatorship cannot exist, since a dictatorship's very existence depends on repression and intimidation. Unlike the SA, which threatened Hitler's claim to total power, the SS was his loyal and unquestioning servant, which above all enabled him to come close to making his "prophecy" about the defeat of world Jewry a reality. Himmler acted as Hitler's alter ego. Unlike the temperamental Röhm, Himmler was cool and calculating, self-effacing, and utterly obedient to the Führer. In his biography of Himmler, Richard Breitman writes:

> Himmler consulted Hitler about major and minor matters—from the basic laws for the SS to appointments and promotions. He became, in the identical words of two quite knowledgeable contemporaries, Hitler's "voluntary tool." Those who saw him with the Führer described him as almost hanging on Hitler's every word. Himmler's personal staff office manager, who saw him virtually every day, described his attitude towards Hitler as reverence and love. Rudolf Höss, commandant of Auschwitz, described Himmler as probably the truest, most unselfish follower of Adolf Hitler.[1]

One may wonder whether Himmler's total zeal in exterminating Jews was a function of deep-seated, insane hatred towards them, or the result of his unconditional loyalty to his leader. Breitman describes an encounter in Minsk between Himmler and a group of Russian partisans about to be executed. Himmler notices among them a blond, blue-eyed youth. The following exchange takes place:

> Are you a Jew?
>
> Yes.
>
> Are both your parents Jews?
>
> Yes.
>
> Do you have any ancestors who were not Jews?
>
> No.
>
> Then I can't help you.[2]

---

1. Breitman, *Architect of Genocide*, 23.
2. Ibid., 195.

## Those Who Did the Dirty Work

Clearly, Himmler must have thought that this particular youth had Aryan features, and perhaps could be spared by him. When the condemned person answered him as a proud Jew, he did not fly into a rage, and he did not abuse him. He made a simple, factual statement, "Then I can't help you." Himmler, it appears, was always under orders, and would not deviate from fully executing the tasks entrusted to him.

It is precisely in the way he went about reorganizing the SS that his personality and beliefs come into sharp focus. From the very beginning, he reorganized the SS as much more than a policing and paramilitary body. His long-term purpose was to make the SS the racial-ideological elite of the German state. In other words, it was to become the epitome of German racial superiority, the embodiment of the true essence of an invincible people destined to rule the earth. The SS under Himmler became the fulfillment of the Nazi ideal. To become an SS officer, one had to be able to prove pure Aryan ancestry dating back to the eighteenth century; one had to be a totally dedicated member of the Nazi Party; one had to swear total loyalty to the Führer; and one had to be willing to die for fatherland.

Himmler, in a sense, saw himself as the spiritual leader of the SS, who was accountable only to the prophet of the fatherland. As Reichsführer-SS, or commander in chief of the SS, Himmler became personally involved in the lives of his officers. He would lecture his officers about their great historical mission, and he turned them into a quasi-mystical order reminiscent of medieval knights, claiming that he was re-creating ancient orders and rites of Teutonic tribes. By doing so he bypassed centuries of Christian civilization and Christian morality, and legitimized the breaking of the basic rules of civilized society. During the war in the east Himmler redefined the mission of the SS as a war to the death against the "Judeo-Bolshevistic" enemy out to destroy Germany. The SS were put in charge of the concentration camps, and formed the special units that murdered Jewish and other civilian populations all throughout Eastern Europe. By that time Waffen-SS (Armed SS) units were fighting alongside Wehrmacht (Armed Forces) units, and as Germany began to lose the war, those SS units took control of the front to ensure total loyalty to the Führer.

But this was not all. Himmler became personally involved in the intimate lives of his SS men. He insisted on personally approving potential brides for his subordinates. Those brides had to be racially pure, ideologically reliable, and capable of bearing children. The presumption was that the SS was giving rise to the pure Germanic race destined to rule much of Europe and perhaps the world. Himmler was thus playing midwife to this transformation of his master race. Later on, Himmler, whose own marriage (according to his grandniece in her aforementioned memoir) was not a happy one, took on a mistress. He argued that monogamy was an insidious and unnatural invention of the Church, and he fathered children outside his own marriage. It appears that Hitler did not disagree with him on this score. After all, the survival of the Nazi state was the highest moral good.

The picture that emerges from everything we know about Heinrich Himmler and his role as the "architect of the Holocaust" is one of a complex and enigmatic personality. Under different circumstances, he might have turned out to be a successful German businessman or head of a corporation. He would have found harmless outlets for his Teutonic fantasies. But history called upon him to serve as the one who complemented a demonic personality named Adolf Hitler, thus becoming a demonic personality himself. From his early days as a National Socialist agitator, Himmler went through all the stages that culminated in history's greatest crime. Once he sold his soul to the devil, there was no going back. Like a character in a Greek tragedy, he courted doom for himself and for his people. At the end of the war, when it finally became clear to him that he had followed the wrong god, Himmler tried to contact Jewish leaders and later the Western Allied forces and sue for peace. But it was too late. As he turned himself over to the British forces, he realized he would be prosecuted and executed as a war criminal, and he committed suicide. Many members of the SS went into hiding, changed their identities, and found refuge in other countries. More than a few were prosecuted. The myth of the Germanic master race was officially rejected by postwar Germany.

Hitler used to say that the only person who was more loyal to him than Himmler was Goebbels. As we shall see, Joseph Goebbels played a crucial role in making the Holocaust possible. But Himmler was the executioner, the one who personally supervised all the dirty work, who from the very beginning planned and ran the concentration camps and the death camps, the mass deportations and the mass murders. A good German from a good German family had turned himself into one of history's greatest criminals, the man who drove a wedge known as Auschwitz into human history, after which nothing could be the same again. People like Himmler force us to reexamine the entire human condition, to question our faith in God and our faith in man's capacity for good. The scale of human suffering that places like Auschwitz inflicted on the human race is beyond human understanding.

A few years ago I visited the U.S. Holocaust Museum in Washington DC. I went through the exhibits, many of which were familiar to me, and I came upon a white plaster scale model of the death camp at Auschwitz, showing the process of the selections, the showers, the gas chambers, and the crematoria. I suddenly felt I was one of the victims, and the sheer horror of it made me gasp. I was only halfway through the museum, but I couldn't go any farther. After Auschwitz, to paraphrase Dylan Thomas's poem "A Refusal to Mourn the Death, by Fire, of a Child in London," there is no more.³

## JOSEPH GOEBBELS

Joseph Goebbels

If Jews are history's most maligned people, then Joseph Goebbels (1897–1945) may deserve the title of history's greatest maligner of Jews. During his years of service to the Führer, he perfected the art of fabricating lies against Jews and disseminating them at mass rallies, in the print media, in films, and over the radio to millions of Germans. He was certainly the master of what Hitler called in his book *Mein Kampf* the "Big Lie." Goebbels continued to lie to the German people almost to the bitter end. When Germany lay in ruins, he continued to insist that the war was not lost, since Germany was about to launch some devastating secret weapons and turn an imminent defeat into a decisive victory. As Nazi Germany's minister of propaganda, he played a critical role in enabling and sustaining the murderous program known as the Holocaust.

With the possible exception of Himmler, Hitler had no follower more loyal or more willing to go to any lengths to do his master's bidding than Goebbels. Goebbels became attached to Hitler at the hip, so to speak. When the failed prophet of German national socialism decided to commit suicide, Goebbels did not hesitate to follow suit. He had his six young children

---

3. See Thomas, *Collected Poems*, 112.

poisoned, whereupon he and his wife killed themselves. Apparently, it was clear to him that once Hitler was dead, the only option left for him was suicide. He did not have a separate existence from Hitler.

In other words, while Himmler was the master of secrecy—keeping a low profile, working behind the Führer, always taking great pains to cover up the nefarious work he was doing—Goebbels was the man up front, the one in the limelight, vying with his own master in delivering fiery, hate-filled speeches, acting as the regime's cheerleader, and not missing an opportunity to voice his opinion on all matters large and small. As a result, we can read Goebbels like an open book and analyze him as though he were lying before us on the analyst's couch and spilling out his guts. We can turn to YouTube and listen to his speeches (or rather, rants) and be impressed with his demagoguery and his ability to make the most blatant lies sound like a higher truth.[4] We can read his extensive diaries and find out about his love affair with lying to large masses of people and creating his own twisted world in which anything of merit is evil and anything evil has merit. As we read these diaries, what also becomes clear is that the service Goebbels rendered Hitler as propaganda minister was invaluable, since the entire house of cards known as Nazi Germany was built on and sustained by a constant flow of words and images that excluded any rational thinking.

Like Hitler and Himmler, Goebbels was born a Catholic and gradually lost his Catholic faith. Like Hitler, he turned to the arts but failed as a literary writer. Like Himmler, he dreamed of military glory but attained none. Unlike those two, he was a bright and diligent student and received a doctorate in literature from Heidelberg. His two most influential teachers, Friedrich Gundolf and Max Freiherr von Waldberg, his doctoral supervisor, were Jews. His intelligence and political astuteness were generally acknowledged even by his enemies. Sir Neville Henderson, the British ambassador to Germany during the Nazis' rise to power wrote of him:

> The 'little doctor' was probably the most intelligent, from a purely brain point of view, of all the Nazi leaders. He never speechified; he always saw and stuck to the point; he was an able debater and, in private conversation, astonishingly fair-minded and reasonable. Personally, whenever I had the chance, I found pleasure in talking to him. In appearance and in character he was a typical little Irish agitator . . . When, however, he was on a public platform or had a pen in his hand no gall was too bitter and no lie too blatant for him.[5]

4. See http://www.youtube.com/watch?v=PHA-A0BUfDo/.
5. Quoted by Manvell and Fraenkel in *Doctor Goebbels, His Life and Death*, 149.

Goebbels had a deformed right leg and walked with a limp. He was short and thin and had a large head. He was rejected for military service in World War I, which he bitterly resented. He later would misrepresent himself on occasions as a war veteran and his disability as a war wound. Goebbels was also embittered by the frustration of his literary career; his novel did not find a publisher until 1929, and his plays were never staged. He found an outlet for his desire to write in keeping a diary from 1923 to the end of his life. Another outlet for his poor self-image was his womanizing, especially seducing young actresses who had come under his patronage as the custodian of German Nazi culture, including the movie industry.

In one case, Hitler had to intervene and order him to break up a steamy romance he had initiated with a Czech actress, which was about to wreck his marriage.

Before he joined the Nazi Party at age twenty-seven, Goebbels worked as a journalist, but he finally found his true vocation as a Nazi agitator. Although his political views did not at first fully coincide with Hitler's, once the future Führer realized he could mold the insecure intellectual into a true disciple, a love affair was born that would burn bright till the end. Goebbels capitulated completely, offering Hitler his total loyalty—a pledge that was clearly sincere, and that he adhered to until the end of his life. "I love him . . . He has thought through everything," Goebbels wrote. "Such a sparkling mind can be my leader. I bow to the greater one, the political genius." Later he wrote: "Adolf Hitler, I love you because you are both great and simple at the same time. What one calls a genius."[6]

The impression one gets from the romance between these two satanic characters is that they both must have sensed that by joining forces they could achieve something greater than each could achieved separately. In fact, we may find a clue here to how this infernal machine called Nazism was able to commit evil on such a large scale. While the dirty work was done by more than a few, the ones at the top—the likes of a Goebbels and a Himmler and the others closest to the chief—were evil geniuses consumed with their own personal anger and hatred, which, given the circumstances of post–World War I Germany, afforded a singular opportunity to gain a broad appeal among the German masses who themselves were frustrated and disillusioned and, most of all, scared of the future, and needed a radical solution, which could only be provided by unscrupulous charlatans.

Hitler rewarded Goebbels's loyalty by making him *Gauleiter*, or Nazi Party leader of Berlin. The German capital was also its cultural center, and provided a good learning ground for the future chief propagandist of the

---

6. Goebbels, *Goebbels Diaries* (in German), November 1938 entry.

Nazis. Here Goebbels came face to face with a strong Jewish community, which he began to harass. He was able to satisfy his thirst for violence by ordering party thugs to engage in street fighting. He began to hone his skills as a pamphleteer and an agitator, and learned that effective propaganda has no scruples. And here is where he found out he could speak in front of crowds and bend them to his will. In *The Face of the Third Reich*, Joachim Fest wrote:

> He drove his listeners into ecstasy, making them stand up, sing songs, raise their arms, repeat oaths—and he did it, not through the passionate inspiration of the moment, but as the result of sober psychological calculation.[7]

In 1933, when the Nazis finally came to power, Goebbels became Reich Minister of Public Enlightenment and Propaganda. This effectively put him in control of all aspects of German cultural and intellectual life, particularly the press, radio and the visual and performing arts. Now the "little doctor," the frustrated writer, the armchair warrior, and the deformed agitator who could not find legitimate glory, became the cultural czar of one of the most cultural countries in the world, empowered to control the lives and careers of the real creative minds, and of stunting all forms of cultural creativity, particularly by those who until now brought much glory to Germany but happened to be Jewish or simply to be in disagreement with the new "enlightened" regime.

As could be expected, one of the first manifestations of Goebbels genius as the cultural czar of the new Germany was something straight out of the darkest Middle Ages, namely, the public burning of books written by "enemies" of the regime. Goebbels organized groups of students in several universities throughout Germany and ordered them to round up books by classical and contemporary writers (German and non-German), pile them up in public places, burn them, and dance around the fire to celebrate the purging of Germany of all decadent books. In a speech to students at a book burning in Berlin Goebbels said:

> The era of extreme Jewish intellectualism is now at an end. The breakthrough of the German revolution has again cleared the way on the German path . . . The future German man will not just be a man of books, but a man of character. It is to this end that we want to educate you. As a young person, to already have the courage to face the pitiless glare, to overcome the fear of death, and to regain respect for death—this is the task of this

---

7. Fest, *Face of the Third Reich*, 92.

young generation. And thus you do well in this midnight hour to commit to the flames the evil spirit of the past. This is a strong, great and symbolic deed—a deed which should document the following for the world to know—here the intellectual foundation of the November Republic is sinking to the ground, but from this wreckage the phoenix of a new spirit will triumphantly rise.[8]

Among the books student leaders burned that night were those of well-known socialists such as Bertolt Brecht and August Bebel; those of the founder of the concept of communism, Karl Marx; those of critical "bourgeois" writers like the Austrian playwright Arthur Schnitzler; and those that spread "corrupting foreign influences," such as works by American authors Ernest Hemingway, Jack London, and Helen Keller. Also burned were works by the English writer H. G. Wells and works by notable Jewish authors such as Franz Werfel, Max Brod, and Stefan Zweig. Especially notable among those works burned were the writings of beloved nineteenth-century German Jewish poet Heinrich Heine, who wrote in his 1820–1821 play *Almansor* the famous admonition "Dort, wo man Bücher verbrennt, verbrennt man am Ende auch Menschen": "Where they burn books, they will in the end also burn people."

Germany's greatest writer, Thomas Mann, fled to Switzerland, and when the war broke out, he went to the United States. Mann said, "Where I go there goes German culture." Stefan Zweig escaped to Brazil where he committed suicide. Zweig was one of Germany's most popular writers and an avowed pacifist. He happened to be a Jew, as were a large number of Germany's best-known writers. Erich Maria Remarque, a non-Jew, who wrote the famous pacifist novel about World War I, *All Quiet on the Western Front*, had to leave Germany. In short, the best and the brightest were put in jail, killed, exiled, or had to escape. For twelve years a dark night descended upon Germany, and the master of ceremonies of that gruesome witch hunt was Herr Doktor Joseph Goebbels.

In November 1938, Goebbels finally got the opportunity he had been waiting for to go all out against the Jews, when a seventeen-year-old Jewish youth, Herschel Grynszpan, shot a German diplomat named Ernst vom Rath in Paris, in revenge for the deportation of his family from Germany to Poland and the persecution of German Jews in general. On November 9, the evening vom Rath died of his wounds, Goebbels was at the Bürgerbräu Keller in Munich with Hitler, celebrating the anniversary of the 1923 Beer

---

8. April 8, 1933. See The History Place, *The Triumph of Hitler*, "The Burning of Books."

Hall Putsch with a large crowd of veteran Nazis. Goebbels told Hitler that "spontaneous" anti-Jewish violence had already broken out in German cities, although in fact this was not true: this was a clear case of Goebbels manipulating Hitler for his own ends. When Hitler said he approved of what was happening, Goebbels took this as authorization to organize a massive, nationwide pogrom against the Jews. He wrote in his diary:

> [Hitler] decides: demonstrations should be allowed to continue. The police should be withdrawn. For once the Jews should get the feel of popular anger . . . I immediately gave the necessary instructions to the police and the Party. Then I briefly spoke in that vein to the Party leadership. Stormy applause. All are instantly at the phones. Now people will act.[9]

The result of Goebbels's incitement was *Kristallnacht*, the "Night of Broken Glass," during which the SA and Nazi Party members went on a rampage of anti-Jewish violence and destruction, killing at least ninety people, destroying almost all synagogues and hundreds of Jewish businesses and homes, and forcing some thirty thousand Jews off to concentration camps, where some died before the remainder were released after several months of brutal treatment. The longer-term effect was to drive eighty thousand Jews to emigrate; most left behind all their property in their desperation to escape. Foreign opinion reacted with horror, bringing to a sudden end the climate of appeasement of Nazi Germany in the Western democracies. Goebbels's pogrom thus moved Germany significantly closer to war, at a time when rearmament was still far from complete. Göring and some other Nazi leaders were furious at Goebbels's actions, about which they had not been consulted. Goebbels, however, was delighted. "As was to be expected, the entire nation is in uproar," he wrote. "This is one dead man who is costing the Jews dear. Our darling Jews will think twice in future before gunning down German diplomats."[10]

Once the war started, Goebbels's role in the Nazi hierarchy was diminished, since the emphasis now was on the war effort and not on domestic propaganda. Himmler and Göring became more prominent than the minister of propaganda. So as not to lose ground, Goebbels became even more vituperative in his verbal attacks on the Jews and in his demand to pursue their total annihilation. On February 14, 1942, he wrote in his diary:

> The Fuehrer once more expressed his determination to clean up the Jews in Europe pitilessly. There must be no squeamish

---

9. See Gilbert, *Kristallnacht*, 29.
10. Ibid.

sentimentalism about it. The Jews have deserved the catastrophe that has now overtaken them. Their destruction will go hand in hand with the destruction of our enemies. We must hasten this process with cold ruthlessness. We shall thereby render an inestimable service to a humanity tormented for thousands of years by the Jews. This uncompromising anti-Semitic attitude must prevail among our people despite all objectors.[11]

One may wonder what is meant here by rendering "an inestimable service to a humanity tormented for thousands of years by the Jews." Does Goebbels refer to Jews as moneylenders who robbed their Gentile clients? Does he mean to say that the Jews have secretly ruled the world to their own benefit? Or perhaps he is insinuating that the Jews gave the world the Christian Redeemer, who made unfair demands on humanity and particularly on the German people, who were now yearning for a new faith?

Be this as it may, this sanctimonious sentence affords an interesting insight into the Nazi mentality. According to the Nazis, the Jews are not the victims of history but the victimizers. A month later, on March 27, 1942, as the extermination of the Jews of Poland went into high gear, Goebbels wrote in his diary:

> Beginning with Lublin, the Jews under the General Government [the Nazi occupation of Poland] are now being evacuated [actually exterminated] eastward. The procedure is very barbaric and is not to be described here more definitely. Not much will remain of the Jews. About 60 percent of them will have to be liquidated. Only about 40 percent can be used for forced labor. The former Gauleiter of Vienna [Odile Globocnik, the butcher of Polish Jewry], who is to carry out this measure, is doing it with considerable circumspection and in a way that does not attract too much attention . . . One must not be sentimental in these matters. If we did not fight the Jews, they would destroy us. It's a life-and-death struggle between the Aryan race and the Jewish bacillus. No other government and no other regime would have the strength for such a global solution as this.

The total lack of humanity of Hitler and his sidekick, Goebbels, comes best into play when the war is being lost in the spring of 1945. Now the victims of Goebbels's lies are no longer the Jews but the German people themselves. As Berlin lies in ruins, Goebbels is selling the Germans his megalomaniac idea of a "total war." At this point both he and his boss have become suicidal. They must sense that their end is near, and they are

11. The Nizkor Project, "Joseph Goebbels' Diaries: Excerpts, 1942–43; Part 2 of 2."

determined to take the German people down with them. Hitler declares that if the Germans lose the war, they do not deserve to live. Now the Gauleiter of Berlin is calling upon all people—men, women, children, and the elderly—to become soldiers. If every last German becomes a soldier, a miracle will happen: Germany will win after all. Ironically, there are more than a few who buy into this macabre scheme. We see Goebbels in old photos pinning medals on the chests of children in uniform about to put their lives on the line as the Soviet tanks roll into Berlin from the east, and as the Western Allies move in from the west. The man whose entire life was one long delusion remained delusional to the very end. There could be no other outcome to the Goebbels story. When he spoke to the German students in Berlin at the burning of the books, he encouraged them to face death. It is a pity that the death wish of some delusional opportunists resulted in the actual death of so many millions.

## JOSEF MENGELE

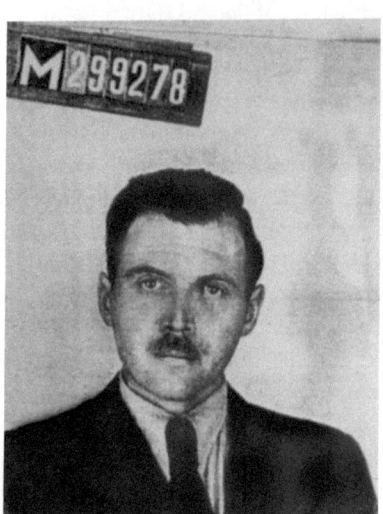

**False ID photo of Mengele hiding in Argentina**

Known as "the angel of death," Josef Mengele (1911–1979), the Auschwitz physician in charge of medical experiments on human subjects, personified the bottomless brutality of Nazism in its most extreme manifestation. Unlike Himmler or Goebbels, Mengele was not part of Hitler's entourage. Nor was he one of the architects of the Holocaust. He was assigned to Auschwitz in 1943, when the mass murder machine was already going full steam, and by engaging in his medical or pseudomedical work, which gave him unrestricted power over countless human lives, he achieved the dubious distinction of becoming one of history's most brutal criminals. His career is an object lesson in what happens when a society demonizes other societies, and when human life becomes expendable.

Mengele was the eldest of three sons born to an affluent Catholic family in Günzburg, Bavaria. His father, Karl, was a founder of Karl Mengele & Sons, a company producing farm machinery for milling, sawing, and baling, which prospered under the Nazis. The young Mengele was expected to go into the family business, but, like Himmler and Goebbels, he dreamed of leaving his mark on the world, and as the Nazis came to power in 1933, he came under their spell and became a fervent adherent of the Nazi ideology, to which he remained loyal till the day he died in 1979, long after the Nazi hierarchy was gone.

In 1935, Mengele earned a PhD in anthropology from the University of Munich. Two years later, he became an assistant to Dr. Otmar Freiherr von Verschuer at the Institute for Hereditary Biology and Racial Hygiene [!] in Frankfurt. Verschuer was a leading scientist mostly known for his research in genetics, with a particular interest in twins. Mengele became a close disciple of the celebrated scientist, who, after the war, was never tried for war crimes despite many indications, not only that had he been fully cognizant of Mengele's work at Auschwitz, but also that he had even encouraged and collaborated with Mengele in some of his most gruesome research. This miscarriage of justice can perhaps be explained by the thin line that separated legitimate medical research during the Nazi era from pseudoscientific studies based on the Nazi belief in biologically superior and inferior races. Such studies became common in Nazi Germany under the encouragement of the regime. The new applied science of eugenics, which advocates the use of practices aimed at improving the genetic composition of the population, became popular during the early decades of the twentieth century, and was seized upon by the Nazi regime to pursue its goal of purifying the Aryan race and improving its stock. It seemed to be very important for the Nazi leadership to find a scientific basis for its extreme racism, which would enable the regime to justify the quest for racial dominance, and at the same time would provide a new ethos that would enable the world's "superior races" to rule the world unhindered. Moreover, everything the Nazis did was done under great time constraints because, in reality, somewhere in the dark recesses of their twisted minds they knew that what they were doing was extremely blatant and risky. To begin with, they were taking on several powerful countries that, in the aggregate, had far greater resources than they did; to defeat the combined power of the British Empire, the United States, the Soviet Union, and all their many allies, they had to be victorious on a very tight timetable (as had been the case in World War I). As a result, German scientists like Verschuer and Mengele were taking shortcuts in their research and breaking all the rules of medical ethics. Once they became convinced that Jews, Slavs, and others were subhuman, everything became permissible. Nature, the Nazi argument seemed to run, created inferior races to serve the needs of the superior ones, which included experimenting on the living flesh of the "subhumans" in order to help improve the stock of the "superhumans."

Before the war broke out, Mengele received his medical degree (his second doctorate) and became a member of the SS. He was recruited for military service and later volunteered for medical service in the Waffen-SS, the combat arm of the SS. He distinguished himself on the battlefield in the Ukraine, serving with a panzer unit, where he rescued two soldiers from a burning tank, for which he received the Iron Cross. Mengele was wounded during this campaign, and since he was medically unfit for combat, he was posted to the Race and Resettlement Office in Berlin, the organization responsible for "safeguarding the racial 'purity' of the SS" within Nazi Germany. Mengele resumed an association with his mentor, Verschuer, who was at the Kaiser Wilhelm Institute for Anthropology, Human Genetics, and Eugenics in Berlin; and it is believed that his mentor was responsible for posting Mengele to Auschwitz where, according to Verschuer, there was a golden opportunity to do experiments on a wide variety of ethnic groups, including a free supply of twins.

In May 1943, a thirty-two-year-old doctor with little medical experience and a passion for eugenics was assigned to the concentration camps at Auschwitz-Bierkenau. He was given two equally grisly tasks. The first task was to wave the new arrivals either to the left or to the right, namely, either to be sent directly to the gas chambers and to the crematoria, or to become slave laborers in the camp and die within a short time of starvation, exhaustion, disease, or execution. The second task was to run the medical-experiments section for the benefit of the master race. Even though he was not the chief doctor of the camp complex, his enthusiasm, total absorption in his work, and relentless viciousness in discharging his duties made many surviving inmates believe that he was the camps' ultimate medical authority. The name Mengele became synonymous with torture and death. To thousands of hapless human beings he became the incarnation of the angel of death, the name by which he was known to many.

Twins at Auschwitz

During his twenty-one-month tour of duty at Auschwitz, from May 1943 to the final stage of the war in early 1945, Auschwitz was a death factory the likes of which the world had never seen. In one single day in 1944, nine thousand Jews were gassed in a twenty-four hour period in the five facilities of gas chambers and crematoria. All the while, Mengele was busy in his laboratory dissecting human beings, mainly twins in the early stages of childhood, with or without anesthesia, injecting chemicals, subjecting his victims to extreme cold and extreme heat, and sending the results to his mentor in Berlin. Jewish and non-Jewish inmate physicians who were pressed into service by him have provided a great deal of blood-chilling testimony about his brutality and nonchalance during the operations, when he would often whistle tunes from operas and from German classical music. Quite clearly, he derived great pleasure from his demonic work, and most probably was hoping for a scientific breakthrough that would, in his words, "put my name in the encyclopedia."[12]

In their book *Mengele: The Complete Story*, Gerald Posner and John Ware quote from the West German indictment against Mengele:

---

12. See *Hitchhiker's Guide to the Galaxy: Earth Edition*. "Josef Mengele—The Angel of Death."

The research into twins occupied a large part of the pseudo-experiments of the accused according to the Court's preliminary investigation. This was especially interesting to the Nazi regime, in particular with regard to a desired increase in the birth rate through medically manipulated increase in the number of the births of twins.[13]

No one benefited from Dr. Mengele's research, but the resulting suffering and loss of life, mostly of Jewish life, has little parallel in human history. As in Himmler's case, so for Mengele: while the rest of his family engaged in normal occupations such as teaching or producing farm equipment, Himmler (who as the head of the SS was Mengele's supreme commander) and Mengele and others like them, driven by an insatiable thirst for power and acclaim, were willing to forgo all the rules of human decency and spurn the teachings of their Catholic faith in pursuit of an alternate view of human history that posited brute power à la Genghis Kahn and Attila the Hun as a viable and acceptable modus operandi for twentieth-century Germany.

When the war ended, members of the Nazi hierarchy either ended their lives, were put on trial by the Allies at Nuremberg, or were pursued and captured one by one. The process of pursuing Nazi war criminals—mainly by the governments of Israel, West Germany, and the United States, and by private Nazi hunters such as Simon Wiesenthal and Serge and Beate Klarsfeld—continued for a long time. I myself worked for six years as a translator in the 1980s with the U.S. Justice Department Office of Special Investigations, which mainly pursued former Nazis and Nazi collaborators who had entered the U.S. illegally. The two main cases I was involved with were those of John Demjanjuk (who was suspected of being Ivan the Terrible, the butcher of Treblinka) and Klaus Barbie, the butcher of Lyon, France, who headed the Gestapo in that city during the Nazi occupation, and who was responsible for the death of Jean Moulin, leader of the French Resistance. Barbie hid for many years in Bolivia, and was one of many former top Nazis who found refuge in South America. Another top Nazi who managed to live in South America under an assumed name was Adolf Eichmann, who was captured by the Israeli Mossad in 1960, brought to Israel, put on trial, and executed. But no one rivaled Josef Mengele in evading capture and so dying a natural death in 1979, at the age of sixty-eight, while practically the whole world was looking for him. The story of Mengele's evasion of justice defies human understanding, and as a result has given rise to countless unfounded reports and to the popular novel and movie *The Boys from Brazil*. According to these reports, Mengele was moving around South America with armed

---

13. Posner and Ware, *Mengele*, 31.

guards and watchdogs and was engaged in hair-raising medical experiments. According to these reports, those who tried to capture Mengele either were gunned down or died mysteriously in the wilds of South America. Nothing could be further from the truth. In 1960, when the Mossad was in the process of kidnapping Eichmann in Buenos Aires, its operatives were only a step away from also capturing Mengele, who was also living in the Argentinian capital under an assumed name and even under his own name. At the last moment, they decided not to risk the Eichmann operation and deferred the capturing of Mengele to a later date. At that point everything started going wrong. Aware of the great danger he was in, Mengele moved first to Paraguay and later to Brazil, not far from Sao Paulo, where he lived as a farmhand on a small farm owned by a Hungarian couple sympathetic to the Nazi cause. He did receive support from his relatives in Germany, and he had many connections in South America with former Nazis. For years, West Germany was looking for him, and tried to elicit the help of the Argentine government as well as Paraguay's dictator, Alfredo Stroessner, but did not seem to be getting anywhere. The Mossad had to cut back on this operation because of financial problems. The U.S. did not seem too interested, and private investigators like Wiesenthal repeatedly failed to get good leads. In the meantime, the butcher of Auschwitz, who had the power of life and death over countless people, was living the miserable existence of a hunted man afraid of his own shadow, and withered away. At one point he was visited by his son, whom he only met once after the war. The son grew up haunted by the fact of having such a notorious criminal for a father. He was eager to find out what his father was all about, and especially how he would explain what he did at Auschwitz. He spent hours questioning his father, but in the end he gave up the likelihood that his father would ever own up to what he had done. Mengele remained unrepentant to the very end, arguing that he did not invent Auschwitz, that he was forced to do what he did in the name of science, and that he had never harmed anyone. On the contrary, he helped people who were marked for death to survive.

Probing the mind of a Josef Mengele helps us gain insight into the Nazi mentality in general. Many of the things he did and said parallel the utterances of Himmler, Goebbels, and other top Nazis, including Hitler himself. They all argued that they were doing the world a favor by getting rid of the Jews. They did not understand (a) that the whole world did not hate the Jews—not even all Germans did; (b) that the Jews played a special role in world history, important far beyond their small numbers, and that the world needed the Jews as both a spiritual and an economic catalyst; (c) that the Jews were not out to do Germany in, and German Jews in particular were very loyal to Germany; and (d) that the long record of Jewish history shows that those who rose against the Jews were never successful, and by turning on the Jews the Nazis were sowing the seeds of their own destruction.

Mengele hated the new regime that followed Nazism in Germany. He saw the government of West Germany as a traitor to its people and to the cause of Germany as a master race. He and other ex-Nazis like him in South America and elsewhere continued to dream of a return to power. Unlike Albert Speer or Otto Dietrich who, as we have seen, realized after the war that Hitler had betrayed them and their country, Dr. Mengele, like Dr. Goebbels, continued to believe to the very end that Hitler was right, that Germany (once again, as had happened after World War I) was stabbed in the back because a misguided and shortsighted world hates Germany and loves the Jews.

Mengele might have escaped and survived in South America, but he did not live happily ever after.

## ADOLF EICHMANN

**Eichmann in his days of "glory"**

Adolf Eichmann (1906–1962) was not a flashy personality like Goebbels or Mengele. Like Himmler, he was a superb organizer who for the most part kept a low profile and did his work away from the limelight. He was born into a God-fearing German Lutheran family, and raised by his grandmother on Bible stories. Throughout his youth and even during his entire career as a key Nazi figure he had many dealings with Jews, and while he was an avowed National Socialist who believed that the Jews were Germany's most dangerous enemy, he was always able to be discerning in his views on individual Jews whom he regarded as an exception to the rule. It could be argued that he was deeply anti-Semitic from the very beginning, but certainly the Eichmann at the beginning of his career is not the same as the one in the last stages of the war, when he was sending hundreds of thousands of Hungarian Jews to their deaths.

The world might have never heard of Adolf Eichmann except for two things: as a young man he joined the Nazi Party and the SS, and he was assigned to the Jewish Section of the SD, the Security Service of the SS. Eichmann came to this position with meager credentials: he had been a high school dropout, a mechanic who did not finish his training, and a clerk at several companies. It was in the SD, however, that he began to make a name for himself. In 1937 he was sent to Palestine, which was under the British Mandate, to examine the possibility of massive Jewish immigration from Germany to Palestine. During the early years of the Nazi regime a great deal of time and effort was expended by the Nazi leadership on plans to evacuate the Jews from Germany, and later from those parts of Europe occupied by the Reich, and to have them resettled in places that did not threaten Germany's strategic interests, such as South America, Africa, or Palestine. Most prominent among these plans was the Madagascar Plan, which promoted the idea of sending millions of Jews from Europe to the African island of Madagascar, which was under French rule. Eichmann's trip to Palestine did not produce any results, since the British did not allow him to stay in the country and would not negotiate with him. Three years later Eichmann became involved in the Madagascar Plan, which gained momentum after Germany defeated France in May 1940. Hitler, drunk with victory (old footage shows him dancing in his train car after he crossed the border into France), expected to defeat England soon thereafter, take over the British navy, and control the sea routes to Africa. Plans were being drawn up for using confiscated Jewish funds to finance the operation. Madagascar was to become a vast reservation for European Jewry under the control of the SS, where they would be kept as hostages to prevent American Jewry from causing problems, and it was expected that living under the harsh conditions of the island the Jewish population would quickly wither away. By that time, Germany had occupied Poland, and Jews from Germany and elsewhere were being sent from Germany and other places to the General Government in Poland. The construction of the Warsaw Ghetto was stopped, since it was no longer necessary for absorbing more Jews. Soon, however, it became clear that Britain was not about to fall, and the British navy was not about to come under German control. Without much fanfare, the Madagascar Plan was shelved, the construction of the Warsaw Ghetto was resumed, and the German word for "resettlement" became a euphemism for mass murder.

In autumn 1941, Reinhard Heydrich disclosed to Eichmann that all the Jews in German-controlled Europe were to be eliminated. In January 1942, Heydrich ordered Eichmann to attend the Wannsee Conference, where Germany was to spell out its official policy of genocide, as a recording secretary. Eichmann was given the position of Transportation Administrator of the "Final Solution to the Jewish Question," which put him in charge of all the trains that would carry Jews to the death camps in the territory of occupied Poland. It was at this point that Adolf Eichmann became a willing accessory to genocide. From now on he would distinguish himself as a highly efficient administrator who under adverse wartime conditions managed to send millions to their deaths. His good work earned him regular promotions through the ranks of the SS and several decorations.

In 1944, as they were losing the war in Russia, the Germans occupied the buffer state of Hungary, where they took control of the last major Jewish population in Europe, which numbered close to eight hundred thousand. Eichmann was transferred to Budapest, where he took control of evacuating Hungarian Jews to Auschwitz. The Germans were now facing a dilemma. They had no desire to slow down the Final Solution, but they also saw an opportunity to trade Hungarian Jews for equipment they needed for the war effort, such as trucks. Eichmann became the negotiator, making contacts with a local Jew named Joel Brand, who before the arrival of the German occupiers did rescue work in Hungary, helping Jews in Nazi-occupied countries to escape to the relative safety of Hungary. Eichmann proposed to release one million Jews for ten thousand trucks and other goods, but the deal did not come to fruition. Eichmann resumed his work as chief of transportation and managed to ship off four hundred thirty thousand Hungarian Jews, most of whom ended up in the gas chambers at Auschwitz. As the war was coming to an end in 1945, his commander, Himmler, issued an order to halt the deportations. Eichmann ignored the order and continued his work until the Russians started pushing the German forces out of Hungary.

Before the Russians could get their hands on him, Eichmann escaped to Austria and was captured by the U.S. army (which failed to identify him since he was travelling with false papers). He managed to hide for several years until he was able to leave for Argentina in 1950, where he also brought his wife and two sons (a third son was born in Argentina). Eichmann lived in Buenos Aires for ten years under the name of Ricardo Klement, doing odd jobs. All during the '50s Eichmann was on lists kept by organizations and individuals in the U.S. and Europe who were looking for Nazi war criminals. One of the players was the Israeli Mossad, the intelligence arm of the Israeli government. The Mossad chief, Isser Harel, was tipped off by Simon Wiesenthal, the renowned Jewish Nazi hunter, that Eichmann was living in Buenos Aires. This was the start of a major operation that involved Mossad operatives and others, who located Eichmann in 1960 and managed to kidnap him and bring him to a safe house in Buenos Aires, drug him and transport him to a waiting Israeli airplane and fly him out of the country to stand trial in Israel.

The Eichmann trial took place in Jerusalem in April 1961 and lasted for fourteen weeks. It caused an international sensation. Israel allowed the world media to report the trial live, and it was broadcast around the world. One hundred prosecution witnesses took the stand, ninety of them concentration camp survivors. Their testimonies were heartrending. "There were two Adolfs," one witness said. "Adolf Hitler and Adolf Eichmann, both of them equally feared."[14] The trial brought the enormity of the Holocaust to the attention of the world by putting a human face on it. Eichmann's was not a very impressive human face. His was the face of a petty bureaucrat, such as might be found almost anywhere; without his SS uniform and his SS officer's hat with the death head and the other insignia, he looked rather pathetic. His appearance prompted Hannah Arendt, the Jewish American political theorist of German origin, an expert on totalitarianism, who attended the trial and wrote a book titled *Eichmann in Jerusalem*, to coin the term "the banality of evil." According to her account, Eichmann had abdicated his will to make moral choices, and thus his autonomy. Eichmann claimed he was just following orders, and that he was therefore respecting the duties of a "bureaucrat." Arendt thus argued that he had essentially forsaken the conditions of morality, autonomy, and the ability to question orders. In South America, and particularly in Argentina, the Eichmann kidnapping and trial resulted in a wave of anti-Semitic attacks. In *Mengele: The Complete Story*, Posner and Ware write:

> The Eichmann kidnapping unleashed a wave of anti-Semitism that spread like a brushfire across South America. In the face of the UN furor [Argentina protested to the UN about the kidnapping and the breach to its sovereignty], there was little Israel could do. Meanwhile, Jewish cemeteries were desecrated, Hebrew schools were set on fire, several Jewish restaurants were machine-gunned, and synagogues were bombed. In Colombia, Nazis held a memorial service for those war criminals executed

---

14. I heard this on TV watching the Eichmann trial back in the day. I haven't seen it in print anywhere.

at Nuremberg. Fascist youth groups held rallies in almost every South American capital. The home in the Israeli ambassador in Montevideo was bombed. A young Jewish woman, Gabriela Sirota, believed to be the daughter of the owner of the safe house where Eichmann had been held by the Israelis, was kidnapped, sexually abused, and tortured, a swastika burned into her breast.[15]

It goes on and on. I am bringing this up because I was on a visit to South America at that time. My sister was living in Montevideo, and I went to her wedding. When I got to Montevideo, I was given a Colt .45 revolver and told I had to do guard duty to protect Jewish businesses threatened by neo-Nazis. I also recall being told in secret that some Mossad operatives had found the two members of the neo-Nazi Tacuara movement who had kidnapped Gabriela Sirota, and had ambushed them, had tied them up, and had taken them to the River Plate, which runs between Argentina and Uruguay, had tied heavy rocks to their legs and had dropped them in the river. I also recall that when I landed in Ezeiza International Airport in Buenos Aires on my way to the wedding in Montevideo, the local customs officials refused to let me continue to Montevideo because my U.S. passport mentioned that I was born in Israel. Thanks to my American wife, who started crying, they changed their minds and let me travel to the local Aeroparque escorted by the airline officials, where my wife and I boarded the Alitalia plane and took the half-hour flight across the River Plate (or Rio de la Plata) to the Uruguayan capital.

---

15. Posner and Ware, *Mengele*, 147.

# 8

# The Evolution of the Holocaust

The Holocaust did not happen all at once. It was not a spontaneous outburst of anger that led to violence, as happens with most genocides. The Holocaust happened in stages, and it spread from Germany to Austria to Poland to Eastern Europe, and to the rest of Europe. Its last two major "accomplishments" as the war was almost over were the murder of some half a million Hungarian Jews, and the Death Marches as the concentration camps were evacuated at the end of the war, in which some three hundred thousand evacuees died. While Hitler came upon the idea of ridding Germany and Europe of Jews early on in his political career, mass physical extermination did not happen all at once. Once the Nazis came to power in 1933, they only had control over the Jews of Germany. They proceeded immediately to issue decrees designed to disenfranchise its Jewish citizens and prompt them to leave the country. These decrees culminated in the Nuremberg Laws of 1935, which put Jews outside German society and deprived them of German citizenship. When Germany annexed Austria in 1938, those laws were applied to Austria as well. A concerted effort was made in the Greater Reich to force the Jews out: this effort took the forms of harassment, incarceration, and torture. The Nazis, with their elaborate police-state system, introduced a reign of terror not only against Jews but also against anyone whom they perceived as an enemy of the state. Those included political dissidents, homosexuals, Jehovah's Witnesses, Gypsies, Freemasons, and others. Whoever they disapproved of was subject to mistreatment and could be disposed of without trial. Moreover, in their pursuit of a superior Aryan race, they launched a ruthless campaign of eliminating their own mental patients, disabled persons, and others who they felt diluted the pureblooded race. This led to a euthanasia program that claimed thousands of lives and gave the Nazis an opportunity to experiment with the use of deadly gas on humans as a means of mass extermination, which they would later use in the gas chambers of the death camps to kill millions. The net result of all of those actions was a devaluation of human life and the legitimizing of the principle of disposing of human life for the so-called interest of the state. In this kind of a political environment the mass murder of Jews was only a matter of time.

As I mentioned before, during the '30s the Nazis seized upon an idea that had been circulating among European anti-Semites since before the turn of the century, namely, the relocating of the Jews of Europe to the East African island of Madagascar. The presumption was that the Jews would not be able to last long in that inhospitable environment and would gradually disappear. I also mentioned earlier that when Germany defeated France in 1940, it took possession of the French colony of Madagascar. It hoped to defeat Great Britain in short order and take possession of the British navy. British ships were to be used by the Germans to transport masses of Jews from Europe to Madagascar under the supervision of the SS. When Britain refused to capitulate and subsequently took control of Madagascar, the Madagascar plan disappeared. Instead, the Germans, who had halted the construction of the Warsaw Ghetto, proceeded with the work. The construction of the Warsaw Ghetto was part of a master plan to relocate the Jews from the Reich and from the Nazi-occupied parts of Europe to enclaves in Poland, which included ghettos and concentration camps. With its three million Jews, Poland was home to one-third of European Jewry. When Germany invaded Poland on September 1, 1939, ushering World War II, the USSR invaded from the east, and the two divided Poland between themselves. It was not the first time in modern history Poland was divided among its powerful neighbors. The Nazis, who worshiped power, had deep disdain for the Poles, whom they considered a backward people or, worse yet, subhumans. Their first order of business for Germany after defeating Poland was to remove Polish populations from western Poland and make room for ethnic Germans (*Volksdeutsche*) to take their place. German nationalistic ideology dating back to the nineteenth century believed in the concept of *Drang nach Osten*, the "push eastward," which meant expanding the German Reich to the east, which included the Ukraine and parts of Russia; this push gave the Germans *Lebensraum* or "living space," as well as possession of the breadbasket or wheat fields of the Ukraine, and possibly also the Russian oilfields.

In all of this strategic planning, the millions of Jews living in Poland and in the surrounding countries were clearly a nuisance to be gotten rid of, which meant that the Nazis had no intention of keeping the Jews in Poland alive for any length of time. The ghettos and the camps were only a temporary measure, and the Nazi leadership made it clear that there was an urgent need to further resolve the "Jewish Question."

On June 22, 1941, Germany invaded the Soviet Union and reached the outskirts of Moscow. Jews were being massacred throughout Eastern Europe, from Latvia to the Ukraine, by the Germans and their willing collaborators, of which there were many. The Nazi leadership kept talking about relocating the Jews from Poland and other places to remote locations in Asian Russia and letting them die of cold and starvation. But by late 1941, as the fortunes of war were turning against Germany when the Russians refused to capitulate in Moscow, it became clear that, like the Madagascar Plan, this plan too was not feasible. What was left was the plan for a systematic mass extermination of the Jews, mainly in the death camps in Poland: Chelmno, Majdanek, Belzec, Sobibor, Treblinka, and, most notoriously, Auschwitz.

## THE POLISH CONUNDRUM

Like an onion, the Holocaust was made up of many layers. The more you peel it, the more layers you find. One of the more complicated and vexing layers is the enormity of the extermination of the Jews in Poland. Poland has been and still is a land of paradox. Its history is both glorious and tragic. I once served as an interpreter at the trial of a former SS concentration camp guard in Chicago. An elderly Polish gentleman was flown in for the trial from Poland to serve as a witness. He and I had lunch, and he said to me: "We Poles lost six million people during World War II." I thought he was referring to the six million Jews. He went on to explain: "Three million Poles and three million Polish Jews." I had never before heard it put in those terms. But it was true. The Poles suffered terribly under the Nazi occupiers. I once saw a telegram addressed to Hitler by the German general who took Poland. It said, "Mein Führer, we have Poland. What should we do with it?"

Jews lived in Poland in significant numbers for a thousand years. Poland, an agrarian country, needed a merchant class to serve the needs of the king and the nobles, and the Jews were well suited for that purpose. In the late eighteenth century the fortunes of Poland and its Jews began to decline, as Poland was partitioned among its powerful neighbors—the Russians, the Austro-Hungarians, and the Prussians. Anti-Semitism became a growing problem through the nineteenth century and increased in the twentieth between the world wars. While Poles lived side by side with Jews, the two did not socialize, they hardly ever stepped inside each other's houses of worship, and with rare exceptions they did not intermarry (at a time when over 50 percent of German Jewry was intermarried). In fact, the common language of Polish Jewry before World War II was Yiddish rather than Polish. It was a German dialect mixed with Hebrew, and it gave rise to a rich literature which produced world-famous authors like Scholem Aleichem, Scholem Asch, and Nobel Prize winner Isaac Bashevis Singer.[1]

Polish Jews were in fact a people apart, who did not assimilate into the majority culture. On the eve of the war the great majority of Poland's Jews was poor and had very limited prospects. The Jewish masses coped with this grim reality in a variety of ways. Many joined the various Zionist organizations whose ultimate goal was to leave Poland and settle in the land of Palestine. Many more belonged to ultrareligious groups, most notably the various Hasidic sects, which separated themselves not only from their Polish neighbors but also from their fellow Jews, and lived with the hope of otherworldly messianic redemption. And a large number belonged to socialist organizations such as the Bund,[2] which sought to establish a new, equitable social order in which Yiddish-speaking Jews would have full rights in a new classless Europe.

This was the picture of Jewish life in Poland when the Germans arrived with their own agenda as to what was to become of Poland.

In other words, the Jews were far from united among themselves, as the Nazi ideologues chose to portray them, and were not living in harmony with their Polish neighbors, which suited the Germans just fine. Now, Poles and Jews were facing a common enemy, but both of them in their hour of greatest need did not know how to make a common cause against a common enemy. Nowhere was this more in evidence than in the failure of the Polish and the Jewish resistance organizations to work together in their struggle against the German occupier. While Jewish and Polish partisans could have inflicted much greater blows on the German occupier had they worked together, they operated separately, and quite often the Polish partisans turned on their Jewish counterparts to the common detriment of both.

---

1. The Yiddish language is experiencing a revival in our time.

2. The Jewish Labor Bund was a socialist Jewish organization that started in Eastern Europe in the late nineteenth century and continued in New York and in other parts of the world. It embraced the Yiddish language as the language of the Jewish people, and rejected Zionism and the revival of the Hebrew language. The rise of the State of Israel as the world center of Jewish life rendered the Bund irrelevant.

The only one who benefited from this divisiveness was of course the common oppressor.

On the other hand, thousands of Poles sheltered Jews, risking their own lives, and there were fewer Poles who collaborated with the Germans (less than 1 percent) than Latvians, Lithuanians, Ukrainians, or even French or Dutch. A Polish priest once told me that he could have saved many Jewish children by hiding them in Catholic institutions, but he had no contact with the local Jewish community and did not know how to initiate one. So here again the great divide among Jews and Gentiles worked against the Jews.

Ironically, another thing that worked against the Jews was the close family ties that were common among Polish Jews in those years. Many young Jewish men and women could have either escaped east to Russia or hidden in the woods of Poland, but they were reluctant to leave their parents and their extended family in time of war, and as a result entire families perished. Historically, strong family ties were one of the strongest factors of the survival of the Jewish people. But during the Holocaust in Eastern Europe it was the opposite. I heard this from more than one Holocaust survivor.

That many Jews did not speak Polish well and had Semitic features prevented them from blending into the general population. The Holocaust survivor Sandra Brand, author of the heartrending memoir *I Dared to Live*, survived in Nazi-occupied Warsaw because she was blond and blue-eyed, spoke fluent Polish, and could easily pass for a Pole. Better yet, she was sheltered by a German policeman, who was later caught by the Nazis and executed. (He was designated a "Righteous Gentile" by Yad Vashem in later years.) But she was the exception rather than the rule.[3]

Thus, Polish Jews became easy prey for the Nazi beast. But another casualty of the nightmarish five years of German occupation of Poland has been the conscience of the Polish people. To this day Poles are struggling with the near-total annihilation of their three million Jewish residents, in which they, for the most part, played either a passive role or worse. I keep getting mixed messages from Poland all the time. Two years ago in Venice I attended a European cultural exhibition. The theme of the Polish pavilion was, the return of the Jews to Poland. At the entrance to the pavilion I saw a poster that urged Jews to come back to live in Poland. It sounded quite far-fetched. Conversely, I keep hearing that anti-Semitism to this day is alive and well in Poland. The impression I get from these mixed messages is that the Poles to this day are confused about their feelings toward the Jews and Judaism. Having lived first under communism and then under Nazi

---

3. As a publisher of Jewish books, I had the honor of reissuing her remarkable book.

occupation, and then again under communism, and having regained their freedom only in recent years, Poles—we should not be surprised—are still struggling with their national identity and particularly with their attitudes towards Jews. No doubt, in Poland the Holocaust and the war years were a double tragedy, but it was made worse because they were also two separate tragedies played at the same time against Poles and Jews with the Jews being by far the ultimate victims.

## AUSCHWITZ

When the Nazis first came to power in Germany in 1933, they built large prisons in the form of camps with barracks to keep "undesirables," of which there were many, locked up. The most notorious was Dachau, outside of Munich. The mastermind, Heinrich Himmler, head of the SS, called them "Protective Camps" (*Schutzlager*), designed ostensibly to protect the inmates from the angry crowds. In actuality, they were used to abuse, torture, and kill the victims of the regime. After Germany occupied Poland, the Dachau model was replicated in the form of concentration camps and labor camps—mostly in Poland—and finally as death camps used for the sole purpose of mass killing. One of those, namely Auschwitz, stands out as a monument to man's bottomless evil. I am tempted to use the term "bottomless bestiality," but having perused literally thousands of World War II documents, including countless survivors' testimonies, I have run too many times into the term *bestiality*, and it finally occurred to me that we humans are so depraved that we consider animals capable of ultimate evil, when in reality man is the only animal that plans, in cold blood, the torture and suffering and mass killing of its own kind, and therefore *humanity* has far worse connotations than *bestiality*.

Auschwitz was more than just another death camp. It was the main venue for the implementation of the "Final Solution." Not only Polish Jews, but also Jews from all over Europe, including its most remote corners, were brutalized and ultimately perished at Auschwitz. Indeed, Auschwitz has become a metaphor for ultimate evil. Even the Nazis themselves, particularly Himmler, who oversaw its operations, felt compelled to keep those operations under a shroud of secrecy. As the Red Army was approaching the camp at the end of the war, the camp personnel went to great lengths to obliterate the evidence of what had taken place behind its electrified barbed-wire fences.

Auschwitz-Birkenau was a vast complex of camps, barracks, gas chambers, and crematoria, housing thousands of people while exterminating thousands on a daily basis upon their arrival by freight trains from many points of assembly around Europe. In addition, it was home to some major German war industries—particularly the industrial giant I. G. Farben, which was engaged in producing rubber and converting coal into oil for the German war effort. The transports of Jews and others provided slave labor for this industry (which for years after the war was made to pay reparations to its surviving victims). Another notorious section of Auschwitz was the medical-experiments center, which was discussed earlier in the section about Josef Mengele. If ever human life was rendered totally violable, it was certainly here. Primo Levi, who spent a year at Auschwitz, said the following concerning his camp experience:

> The German camps constitute something unique in the history of humanity, bloody as it is. To the ancient aim of eliminating or terrifying political adversaries, they set a modern and monstrous goal, that of erasing entire peoples and cultures from the world. Starting roughly in 1941, they became gigantic death machines. Gas chambers and crematories were deliberately planned to destroy lives and human bodies on a scale of millions. The appalling record belongs to Auschwitz, with 24,000 dead in a single day, in August 1944.[4]

Similarly, in his book *Treblinka*, Jean-François Steiner narrates an episode in which a guard at that camp shoots down a bird. Looking on, the narrator is paralyzed with fear. It becomes clear to him that even a bird cannot leave that place alive.[5]

Living conditions at Auschwitz for most of the inmates were deliberately appalling. The intent was clear: you did not come here to live; you came here to die. More prisoners died of exhaustion, despair, disease, mistreatment, and starvation than in the gas chambers. In the women's barracks in Birkenau there was one toilet for several hundred women. The barracks and the clothes did not protect the inmates from the severe winter cold. Medical attention for the most part was nonexistent. The smell of burning bodies and human feces was in the air at all times. Everything was designed to demoralize and to make one wish he or she were dead.

The historian Arno J. Mayer, in his book *Why Did the Heavens Not Darken?*, points out that Auschwitz has to be understood in the broader context of the Germans' inability to defeat the Russians, which made them turn all their fury on the captive Jews. He writes:

---

4. Levi, "Primo Levi's Heartbreaking, Heroic Answers."
5. Steiner, *Treblinka*, 408.

Any attempt to explicate Auschwitz requires facing up to the diabolic fusion between, on the one hand, the ideological and institutional press for extermination and, on the other hand, the contingent exigencies of an intractable and failing total war. Auschwitz was a microcosm not only of the systematic license of the Nazi regime's destructive impulses but also of its rising entropy. No doubt, Auschwitz was conceived and run by the SS, which eventually turned it into a hell on earth. But this hell was located in a space conquered by the regular army; it was capitalized and exploited by big industry; and was used for sinister medical experiments by licensed physicians . . . Auschwitz was the quintessential total institution, with no exit: of the over 400,000 registered and *countless unregistered prisoners*, only several score ever escaped without being recaptured and killed.[6]

Because of the absence of full records, we will never know exactly how many Jews perished at Auschwitz. The number fluctuates between one and two million. In his underground diary, which was actually found after the war under the human ashes in Auschwitz and published in Hebrew under the title *In the Heart of Hell*, Zalman Gradowsky pleads with us to seek revenge against his tormentors. Gradowsky was one of the leaders at the end of the war of the only revolt at Auschwitz, in which he and most of his comrades died. Is it possible to find a suitable punishment for a crime of the magnitude of Auschwitz? This is clearly a rhetorical question. What happened at Auschwitz transcends the human dichotomy of crime and punishment. It puts in question the validity and purpose of human existence. It makes any person with an ounce of human decency ashamed to be a member of the human race. It forces us to reexamine everything we have ever believed in, and to look for healing and a way out of the endless darkness it has cast upon our existence.

## THE COMPLICITY OF THE WEHRMACHT

In his book *Germany's War and the Holocaust: Disputed Histories*, Israeli historian Omer Bartov, an authority on the Wehrmacht during World War II, argues that it is untrue that the army was an apolitical force dedicated solely to military operations. After the war, a sharp distinction was drawn for years between the Wehrmacht and the various police and paramilitary forces, such as the SS, the Waffen-SS, the Einsatzgruppen, and so on, who had been charged with committing the war crimes with rare exceptions.

---

6. Mayer, *Why Did the Heavens Not Darken?* 354–55 (italics added).

Bartov accuses the Wehrmacht of being an accomplice in the process of the mass murder of civilians, particularly Jews, starting with the war in Poland and becoming more prominent with the invasion of Russia.

Another military historian, Stephen Fritz, in his recent book, *Ostkrieg: Hitler's War of Extermination in the East*, confirms Bartov's views. Of particular interest is the way he describes the complicity between General von Reichenau, Sixth Army commander in the Ukraine and a rabid anti-Semite, and SS Colonel Paul Blobel.[7]

After Kiev fell to the Germans, the close cooperation between the Wehrmacht and the SS under those two leaders led to a decision to massacre a large number of Kiev Jews. The result was what is considered to be the largest single massacre of Jews of the entire Holocaust. On September 29–30, 1941, over thirty-three thousand Jews were killed in a single operation on the outskirts of Kiev in the ravine of Babi Yar. It was a mass execution by firing a bullet to the back of the neck of each victim and piling the bodies, layer upon layer.

In her book *Into That Darkness: From Mercy Killing to Mass Murder*, Gitta Sereny, an award-winning Austrian-born investigative reporter, relates a conversation about Blobel she once had with one-time chief of the Church Information Branch at the Reich Security Office, Albert Hartl:

> Hartl had told me of a summer evening—that same hot summer in 1942—in Kiev when he was invited to dine with the local Higher SS Police Chief and Brigadeführer, Max Thomas. A fellow guest, SS Colonel Paul Blobel, had driven him to the general's weekend dacha. 'At one moment—it was just getting dark,' said Hartl, 'we were driving past a long ravine. I noticed strange movements of the earth. Clumps of earth rose into the air as if by their own propulsion—and there was smoke; it was like a low-toned volcano; as if there was burning lava just beneath the earth. Blobel laughed, made a gesture with his arm pointing back along the road and ahead, all along the ravine—the ravine of Babi Yar—and said, 'Here lie my thirty-thousand Jews.[8]

Blobel was tried at Nuremberg after the war, found guilty of the murder of some fifty thousand Jews during the course of the war, and executed, while Reichenau died a year after the Babi Yar Massacre. The two exemplify the close cooperation between the Wehrmacht and the SS when it came to killing Jews. Ironically, in the conduct of the war itself the two organizations were often in disagreement, especially after 1941, when the tide turned

7. Fritz, *Ostkrieg*, 102.
8. Sereny, *Into That Darkness*, 97.

against Germany, and Nazi ideology became further and further removed from military reality.

## EUROPEAN COMPLICITY

The Germans did not do it alone. They greatly benefited from the complicity of the regimes in countries they occupied where the local regime was left in place (such as France or Hungary), from the collaboration of local people whom they drafted into their various police forces' ranks, from the passivity of the local populations, and from the silence of the local church authorities (more on this later). When I visited relatives in Paris in 1956, my cousin's husband, who had fought in the French resistance, told me that during the war the Nazis succeeded in brainwashing the local population by spreading virulent anti-Semitic propaganda. One example I recall him mentioning was the placing of large posters throughout Paris with drawings designed to identify Jews by juxtaposing images of an "Aryan nose" and a "Jewish nose," of "Aryan eyes" and "Jewish eyes," and so on. It did not take much to awaken French anti-Semitism, which never suffered from a lack of devout followers.

The French defeat in 1940 resulted in the division of the country into Nazi-occupied France in the north, which included Paris, and the Vichy regime "free zone" in the south, headed by the aging Marshal Pétain. A national hero of World War I, Pétain officially declared a policy of collaboration with the Nazi regime.

On February 16, 2009, the British newspaper the *Guardian* published the following news release:

> France's highest court put an end to decades of legal timidity and moral taboo yesterday when it issued a ruling recognizing the state's responsibility in the deportation of tens of thousands of Jews during the second world war.
>
> Citing "mistakes" made by the collaborationist Vichy regime, the council of state said the government's share of blame was clear in acts which had not been forced on it by the occupiers and which "allowed or facilitated the deportation from France of victims of anti-Semitism."
>
> The ruling, which will be recorded in the official state legislative journal, marks the first time any French judicial body has acknowledged in such stark terms the government's role in Nazi-era atrocities.
>
> Calling for a "formal admission of the state's responsibility and of the prejudice collectively suffered," the court said it had concluded that acts such as the arrest, internment and

# The Evolution of the Holocaust

dispatching of Jews to transit camps were clear indicators of the government's guilt. "As they led to the deportation of people considered Jewish by the Vichy regime, the acts and activities of the state . . . became its responsibility," it added.[9]

Pétain, who was sentenced to death after the war (his sentence was commuted to life imprisonment), believed that Germany was going to win the war, and that he was acting in the best interest of France. He became, in effect, an ally of Hitler, which facilitated the deportation and killing of some seventy-eight thousand out of the three hundred thirty-three thousand Jews in France at the time (which included French Jews as well as Jews from Germany and other parts of Europe). On his own initiative, Pétain issued on October 2, 1940, a "Statute of the Jews," reminiscent of the Nuremberg Laws.

In his book *Nazi Germany and the Jews: 1933–1945*, the Israeli Holocaust historian Saul Friedländer, who was hidden in France during the German occupation in a Catholic monastery, writes:

> No Catholic prelate protested the "Statute of the Jews." Some bishops even openly supported the anti-Jewish measures. In fact, on August 31, 1940, after being informed of the forthcoming statute, the assembly of cardinals and archbishops meeting in Lyon discussed the "Jewish Question." Emile Guerry, Adjunct archbishop of Cambrai, summed up the assembly's official stand: "In political terms, the problem is caused by *a community [the Jews] that has resisted all assimilation* . . . The State has the right and the duty to remain actively vigilant in order to make sure that the persistence of this unity [of the Jews] does not cause any harm to the common good of the nation."[10]

The sentence "the community that has resisted all assimilation" speaks volumes not only about the state of mind of the Catholic Church during those dark years, which reminds us of the church during the Dark Ages, but also what I would call French xenophobia. Having had relatives in France since before the war, who came from Poland in search of more freedom and tolerance, and having visited France several times as a lover of French culture, I have experienced that the French are not particularly adept at accepting other cultures, belief systems, and customs on equal terms. Over the years, my French relatives had to assimilate into French culture and play down their Jewishness to be fully accepted in French society. Moreover, during the war they (as did Friedländer's family) had to turn their children over

---

9. Davies, "France Responsible."
10. Friedländer, *Nazi Germany and the Jews*, 194–95 (italics added).

to French Catholic families or to Catholic institutions to be sheltered from the Nazis and from the French regime, and in many cases those children were not returned after the war to their parents (many of whom perished) or to Jewish relatives but were raised as Catholics. Nevertheless, a large number of French people of all walks of life and French Catholic priests did help save Jews, and did show extraordinary courage and compassion. Those righteous people remind us of the great French writer Émile Zola, who was not afraid fifty years earlier to denounce the regime during the Dreyfus Affair, when the mob outside the courtroom in Paris where Dreyfus was being tried for treason he did not commit was shouting, "Mort aux Juifs" ("Death to the Jews.").[11]

In countries like Lithuania and Latvia, and in the Ukraine, where the local population believed that the Germans would help them establish their own independent states, many nationalistic Lithuanians, Latvians, and Ukrainians sought to show their gratitude to their "liberators" by outdoing them in brutalizing and murdering the accursed Jews. These misguided populations did not need too much encouragement to take an active role in massacring Jews. When we look at wartime photos from those countries, we see mass murder in the streets of cities like Kovno and Lvov, in which men with their sleeves rolled up are hacking to death defenseless Jews, using sticks and knives and farm tools, as armed guards—German and local—stand by and enjoy the show. Like the Jews in Poland, the Jews of those countries were also nearly wiped out. Major Jewish communities with a long history of scholarship and piety disappeared. The people of those countries, with whom the Jews lived side by side for generations, joined the foreign invader in significant numbers and became their neighbors' executioners.

Similarly, the fact that two-thirds of the Jews of the Netherlands, some one hundred thousand souls, also perished in the Holocaust, does not speak well for the Dutch people. Contrary to popular belief, the highly civilized and humane Dutch, who are mainly known to the world as the people who sheltered Anne Frank, did not, for the most part, save their Jews but rather facilitated their deportation to the death camps. The Dutch bureaucracy and police did most of the work of rounding up the Jews and putting them on the trains that departed for concentration camps in Holland and from there to Auschwitz and other death camps. Adolf Eichmann, who was in charge of transportation to the camps, was quoted as saying that "The transports [from Holland] run so smoothly that it is a pleasure to see."[12]

11. The Dreyfus Affair was a defining event in the European history of anti-Semitism. It made many Jews realize that under the best of circumstances, Europe did not accept the Jews as citizens with full rights.
12. Gerstenfeld, "Wartime and Postwar Dutch Attitudes."

# The Evolution of the Holocaust

Under the Nazi occupation, the Germans outlawed all Dutch political parties but allowed the Dutch National Socialist party, which mimicked Nazism, to operate. Holland provided more volunteers for the Nazi Waffen-SS than any country in Europe. To this day, the story of Dutch complicity in the Holocaust is still unfolding. According to some reports, some twelve billion dollars robbed from Dutch Jews by the Dutch banks in collaboration with the Nazi occupier are still unaccounted for.[13] While Germany has been paying reparations to Holocaust survivors for years, and still does, the Dutch seem to get a free pass from the world. Either the Dutch or the rest of the world seems to have a selective historical memory.

Other European countries where The Nazis' work was facilitated by local cooperation were Slovakia, Romania, and Croatia. Slovakia joined the Nazis in their war effort and deported two-thirds of its ninety thousand Jews to the death camps in Poland. Romania, which had a pro-Nazi regime during the war, spared the Germans the need to transport Jews to their death by doing most of the killing in house. Of its six hundred thousand Jews before the war, only half survived. Romania had a long history of anti-Semitism, and looked upon its Jews as subversive foreigners.[14] Matters got worse on the eve of World War II with the rise to power of the Iron Guards under Ion Antonescu, a rabid anti-Semite. The dictator launched a series of massacres that rivaled Nazi atrocities. In Croatia the situation was similar to Romania. Here too a pro-German fascist regime was in control, and by the end of 1941 about two-thirds of Croatia's thirty-two thousand Jews were put in local concentration camps where they were murdered by the Croatian authorities.

The last major collaboration between the government of a European country and the German occupier occurred in 1944 in Hungary. Of Hungary's eight hundred thousand Jews, five hundred fifty thousand Jews were murdered by the Nazis, mainly in Auschwitz. Hungary also had a pro-German regime when the war broke out, but at first Hungarian Jews fared better than those of Slovakia, Romania, and Croatia. Hungarian Jews played an important role in the Hungarian economy as bankers and financiers. They were also prominent in science and the arts. But as the war was coming to an end, Germany occupied Hungary and took charge of dispatching it Jewish population to the death camps. Adolf Eichmann, who was put in charge of this operation, was surprised to see how much cooperation he was getting from the Hungarian police. Winston Churchill commented that the

---

13. Ibid.
14. On Romanian anti-Semitism, see Sudetic, "World War II," 40–42.

deportation of the Hungarian Jews was the worst crime in human history.[15] It was a wanton murder of some half million human beings without any rhyme or reason. Even Eichmann realized that as Germany was losing the war, the effort put into sending these Jews to their death was counterproductive. He met with Jewish contacts like Joel Brand and tried to strike a deal of exchanging thousands of Hungarian Jews in return for trucks and other equipment for the Wehrmacht. Nothing came of it, and finally, towards the end, Himmler called off the transports.[16] In 1994, the fiftieth anniversary of the Holocaust in Hungary, the Hungarian government officially apologized for Hungary's complicity in the Holocaust.[17]

Clearly, the Holocaust was a joint venture initiated by the Germans but at the same time given ample support by more than a few European nations, including some of those considered to be in the forefront of human rights. No official apology by the present-day governments of those countries can atone for or erase the shame of their cowardly collaboration. In a way, their guilt is greater than the guilt of Germany, because Germany continues to carry the mark of Cain, while the others continue to play the role of victims who ostensibly were forced to do what they did.

## EXCEPTIONS TO EUROPEAN COMPLICITY

There were some exceptions to European complicity in the Holocaust, but they only accounted for relatively small numbers of Jews rescued from the long reach of the Nazi henchman.

Perhaps the most astounding exception is the case of Italy under Mussolini. Even though the Italian dictator was Hitler's main ally, Italy was not an enthusiastic accomplice to the Nazi madness of seeking to exterminate European Jewry. Of Italy's forty-five thousand Jews, nearly thirty-eight thousand survived the Holocaust. I was six months old when World War II broke out, and my mother later told me that she had taken me many times to the bomb shelter in our apartment house in Haifa, then Palestine's main seaport, as Italian aircraft were approaching the shore seeking to bomb the British oil refineries in Haifa Bay. Apparently, the Italian pilots never bothered to deliver their payload, but instead dropped the bombs in the Mediterranean Sea and flew back to their bases. Unlike the Germans, the Italians were neither enthusiastic empire-builders nor avowed racists. Hitler's war was not their war, and the Jews were not their enemies. Before the

---

15. Gilbert, "Churchill and the Holocaust."
16. Cesarani, *Becoming Eichmann*, 185.
17. International Holocaust Remembrance Alliance, "Hungary."

war ended, Italian partisans captured Mussolini and his mistress, executed them, and hanged them by their feet in Milan.

Another remarkable exception to the rule of complicity is the story of Danish Jewry. From the beginning of the Nazi occupation, the Danes refused to turn in their Jews. They argued that they did not have a "Jewish problem." Germany at the time depended on Denmark for food supplies and chose not to make an issue of the Danish refusal. But in 1943 the German occupier put the screws to the Danish government, making a series of demands the Danes could not accept. The Danish government resigned, and the Germans put their own administration in place. Hitler took advantage of the opportunity and ordered the "evacuation" of the Danish Jews. What followed is probably one of the most amazing rescue stories in human history. The Danes got word of the secret order and launched a countrywide effort to inform the country's eight thousand Jews that they were at risk. At the same time, the Swedish government was contacted (Sweden was a free country and it is a short sail from the Danish shore) and was asked to accept the Jewish Danish refugees. The Swedish government vacillated at first, but eventually agreed to let the Danish Jews into Sweden. What followed was a secret Danish operation that loaded almost all the Danish Jews on small boats and ferried them to safety in Sweden.

The Danish example demonstrates that rescue operations were possible even under the nose of the Nazis, but that the will of the Danes was a rare thing in a compromised Europe.

Another remarkable story is the rescue of the Jews in Albania. What makes this story particularly significant is that Albania is mostly a Muslim country. When the war started there were only two hundred Jews living in Albania, but by war's end their numbers grew to two thousand, which included refugees who were able to enter the country during the war. When the Germans occupied Albania they looked for Jews, but the Albanians hid every last Jew and ignored the orders of the occupier. This story was not known for many years because Albania came under a communist dictatorship after the war and was virtually isolated from the rest of Europe. A retired Jewish businessman from New York by the name of Norman Gershman, who became an accomplished portrait photographer after retiring from his business, came to my office in Rockville, Maryland, one day and showed me photos of old Albanians he took during a visit to that country. They told him the rescue story, which has since been confirmed. Gershman has now released a documentary[18] narrating this little-known chapter of the Holocaust. It is titled *Besa*, and it explain that age-old Albanian custom

---

18. Gershman, *Besa*.

called *besa*, which denotes unconditional hospitality for a stranger, whom one has to protect with one's life, more so than even the members of one's own family. Thus, little-known and much misunderstood Albania became the only country in Europe—besides Sweden, who sheltered the Jews of Denmark—whose Jewish population increased rather than decreased during the Holocaust.

It should also be pointed out that some Muslims saved Jews during the Holocaust in Morocco, Tunisia, and Bosnia. When the king of Morocco was asked by the Germans to turn over his Jews, he responded that Morocco did not have Jews, only Moroccans. On a recent visit to Morocco I was impressed by the fact that this Muslim country had fond memories of its large Jewish population, most of which immigrated to Israel after the establishment of the state in 1948.

A third exception to European complicity is the case of Bulgaria. In 1941 Bulgaria entered the war as an ally of Germany. In return for its loyalty, Germany helped Bulgaria regain sovereignty over Thrace and Macedonia, which Bulgaria had lost in World War I. Germany added a condition to the deal by asking Bulgaria to deliver twenty thousand Jews from those two areas. Bulgaria complied, but was only able to come up with fourteen thousand Jews. To make up the difference, six thousand Bulgarian Jews had to be added. The vice president of the Bulgarian parliament, Dimiter Peshev, who originally supported the anti-Semitic policies of his government, refused to comply with the German policy of deportation. He was dismissed from the parliament, but his refusal to send Bulgarian Jews to their death was supported by church officials and by public opinion. Bulgaria's fifty thousand Jews who were slated by the Germans to die in places like Auschwitz and Treblinka survived the war, and most of them now live in Israel.

Dimiter Peshev is a remarkable example of how even in a country allied with Nazi Germany it was possible for one person of conscience to stand up against his own government in wartime and turn public opinion against a government decision dictated by the Nazis. Had it not been for his civic courage, most of Bulgaria's fifty thousand Jews would not have survived the war.

Once again we are reminded that while one person can cause the death of large numbers of people, the opposite is also true.

For years, Peshev lived a life of penury and anonymity. In 1973, the year of his death, Peshev was awarded the title of Righteous among the Nations from Yad Vashem in Jerusalem. He was also recognized by his country for having performed a great service to humanity during the war years.

When asked why he decided to stop the Jewish deportation, Peshev said, "My human conscience and my understanding of the fateful

# The Evolution of the Holocaust

consequences both for the people involved and the policy of our country now and in the future did not allow me to remain idle. And I decided to do all in my power to prevent what was being planned from happening; I knew that this action was going to shame Bulgaria in the eyes of the world and brand her with a stain she didn't deserve."[19]

## THE DEATH MARCHES

All told, between two hundred fifty thousand and three hundred seventy-five thousand prisoners, most of them Jewish, perished during the death marches as the Germans evacuated the camps at the end of the war. From the fall of 1944 to the spring of 1945, the SS frantically evacuated labor camps, concentration camps, and death camps to escape the Soviets in the east and the Allies in the West, and to remove any trace of the atrocities. The inmates, most of whom were in a deteriorating physical and mental condition, were made to march for miles in cold weather, mostly without food, and either perished along the way or were shot to death. This was the last killing spree before Germany's unconditional surrender. It was defined as "crimes against humanity" during the Nuremberg Trials.

This last spasm of violence marked the end of a regime that came to power with an unprecedented drive to destroy human life, and was able to have its underlings obey its orders to torture and kill until the very last moment. Instead of laying down their arms when it was clear that all was lost, they were overcome by a killing frenzy until the bitter end. In their twisted minds they were following a madman's dream of creating a brave new world, when in reality they were bringing damnation upon themselves.

## GERMAN "DELUSIONAL PRECISION"

One driving force behind such a relentlessly murderous behavior was the German virtue of precision, which under the Nazis became a lethal weapon. Germans do not like chaos and confusion, and they pride themselves on being very methodical people. They excel in science and engineering, and they have always been leaders in making precision instruments. When the Nazi regime began to implement its policy of genocide, it did two things: it began a painstaking process of building a very detailed case against the Jews and other "undesirables," and it began to keep meticulous records of its genocidal activities. Saul Friedländer writes:

19. Quoted in Bar-Zohar, *Beyond Hitler's Grasp*, 119.

> As the organized enemy they [the Nazis] were fighting was nonexistent as such, their own enterprise was to create it. Jewish organizations were identified, analyzed, and studied as part of an ever more complex system; the anti-German activities of that system had to be discovered, its internal workings decoded, it very essence unveiled.
>
> The most astonishing aspect of this system was its delusional concreteness. Very precise—and totally imaginary—Jewish plots were discovered, names and addresses provided, countermeasures taken.[20]

In the six years I worked on translating Nazi wartime documents for the U.S. Department of Justice Office of Special Investigations, I ran into many instances of what I would call German delusional precision. For example, I went over hundreds of large ledger-book sheets with handwritten entries containing the names of thousands of inmates who died in the Buchenwald Concentration Camp, their date of birth, date of death, and cause of death. It has long been established that in most instances the cause of death was bogus. In many cases, I recall, the cause of death was given as malaria or typhoid fever. I never ran into any death by execution or torture, or working someone to death, or starving someone to death, which was common practice in all the camps. It was as if the record keepers were preserving something for posterity, in which they sought to convince themselves and posterity that they were not murderous criminals, but rather custodians of "protective camps" where, unfortunately, many lives were lost because of epidemics.

Another example is the vast numbers of carefully catalogued Jewish ritual objects and Torah scrolls found in Prague after the war, taken by the Nazis from countless synagogues in order to establish a museum of the "extinct Jewish race" once they won the war. Yet another example is the photographing and filming of places like the Warsaw Ghetto, and many gruesome scenes involving the degradation and murder of the Jews by the SS and its accomplices. We should also consider the seriousness with which German doctors practiced their task of examining the racial features of so-called Aryans and so-called inferior races, and the pseudomedical tests of Auschwitz doctors like Mengele and others. In retrospect, it is hard to grasp how highly educated people in the middle of the twentieth century could engage in such absurd activities with such precision and in utter seriousness.

---

20. Friedländer, *Nazi Germany and the Jews*, 170.

On one hand, the Nazis went to great lengths to hide their crimes, but on the other hand, they must have felt a great need to document their "heroic" deeds, and to leave a legacy of their "achievements" to future generations. While it is a great virtue for a scholar or a surgeon to be very thoroughgoing, when a criminal is thoroughgoing the potential for mass murder grows exponentially.

## TECHNOLOGY IN THE SERVICE OF THE HOLOCAUST

There is only a small step between Henry Ford's invention of the assembly-line system, and the Nazi train-to-camp-to-gas-chamber-to-crematorium system. Science and technology after World War I enabled the human race to destroy life on an unprecedented scale, a fact manifested in all the stages of World War II, from the death camps to the dropping of the atomic bomb on Hiroshima and Nagasaki. Germany, one of the world's leading industrial powers, made full use of its scientific and technological resources to accelerate and maximize the "solution to the Jewish Question." It started by equipping every German home with a radio and by instituting a state broadcasting system headed by Goebbels, who, day in and day out, whipped his listeners into a frenzy of hatred against the Jewish enemy. To this Goebbels and other Nazi propagandists added hate literature, posters, plays and movies. The brainwashing process played a decisive role in convincing the public of the urgency of doing away with the Jewish threat, and of doing everything possible to disenfranchise and eventually destroy the Jews of Germany and of the rest of Europe.

Radio communications were used effectively in coordinating the activities of the various police and military forces engaged in rounding up and transporting Jews to the camps. At a time when the common man in Europe had little access to a phone, the German forces were able to communicate and take quick action. A good example is the massacre of the Jews of Kiev in Babi Yar. Those Jews did not know that a few hundred miles to the west, in places like Lvov, the Germans were mass-executing Jews. They believed the Nazi announcement that they were being relocated to the east, and they showed up by the thousands in an orderly fashion, dressed in their suits and carrying their suitcases, only to be led into the long ravine of Babi Yar where thirty-three thousand of them were massacred in two days.

The train system was another effective tool of moving thousands of people at a time to the killing sites. The death camps were built in strategic locations, easily reachable by train, and, in effect, the train was an integral part of the killing process, as it transported people from all parts of Europe to places like Auschwitz and Treblinka.

The lethal gas developed for the purpose of mass murder is yet another example of the use of science and technology to kill large numbers of people quickly and efficiently. It should be pointed out, however, that according to eyewitnesses, death in the gas chambers in many instances was not so quick and efficient. It would often take a long time for a person to die, and the suffering of many of the victims was indescribable. This, of course, was of little concern to the executioners.

In the race to develop the atomic bomb at the end of the war, Germany was a contender but did not win the race. One can only imagine what would have happened had this not been the case. It was, indeed, science and technology that dictated the outcome of the war. Man in the twentieth century had reared a monster that has been threatening its master with annihilation to this day.

As we have seen, many factors conspired in making the Holocaust the unprecedented event in human history that it was. The Jews were caught in a vise by forces that conspired against them on all sides. A death sentence was issued against them not only by a depraved German regime but also by a Europe that for the most part did not want them. The history of European Jewry is not a happy one. For centuries, the Jews of Europe were forced to live in ghettos and were at the mercy of the local ruler and the Church. The Enlightenment in the eighteenth and nineteenth centuries did not do away with anti-Semitism, and the process of becoming citizens of their country of residence was slow and difficult. In much of Europe during the Nazi era their rights were severely curtailed or taken away completely, and their civil status reverted back to the darkest Middle Ages. To this day, Europe to most Jews is a place of the past, not the future. Where large and vibrant Jewish communities once existed, now there are only small ones carrying the heavy weight of the past, and even in France, where the Jewish community grew significantly in recent times because of the exodus of the Jews and the French from North Africa, Jewish life once again has become unstable, and French Jews have begun to settle in Israel and elsewhere.

# 9

# The *Judenrat* Dilemma

In every Jewish community throughout occupied Europe, the Nazi regime forced the local Jews to select a group of representatives to form a Jewish Council (*Judenrat* in German; plural, *Judenräte*), ostensibly to keep law and order and attend to the needs of the community, but in reality to facilitate the work of "resettlement," the Nazi euphemism for extermination. In addition, the Nazi-appointed council was ordered to institute a Jewish police force to implement Nazi orders. Even in some of the concentrations camps, such as Theresienstadt, a *Judenrat* was set up. Additionally, in all camps the Nazis appointed a Jewish police force, known as kapos, to supervise forced labor and carry out administrative orders. For centuries, Jewish communities throughout Europe were self-governed by a council known in Hebrew as *kahal* or *kehillah*, and so the introduction of a *Judenrat* seemed to flow naturally from this historical continuum. But it soon became clear that the new regime was using the Jewish law enforcers as a tool to make their own genocidal work easier.

According to Hannah Arendt,

> To a Jew this role of the Jewish leaders in the destruction of their own people is undoubtedly the darkest chapter of the whole dark story. It had been known about before, but it has now been exposed for the first time in all its pathetic and sordid detail by Raul Hilberg, whose standard work *The Destruction of the European Jews* I mentioned before.

Raul Hilberg is considered the preeminent scholar of the Holocaust. His three-volume, 1,273-page magnum opus mentioned by Arendt, first published in 1961 (around the time of the Eichmann trial), is considered the seminal study of the Nazi Final Solution. In the '80s, when I worked on Nazi documentation with the U.S. Justice Department's Office of Special Investigations (which looked for former Nazis who had entered the United States with false documents), his book was routinely used as a reliable reference by the prosecutors of such cases. In this book, Hilberg writes that "truly, the Jewish communal organizations had become a self-destructive machine."[1]

In *Eichmann in Jerusalem*, Arendt goes on to say:

> The whole truth was that if the Jewish people had really been unorganized and leaderless, there would have been chaos and plenty of misery, but the total number of victims would have hardly been between four and a half and six million people. (According to Freudiger's calculations about half of them could have saved themselves if they had not followed the instructions of the Jewish Councils. This is of course a mere estimate, which, however, oddly jibes with the rather reliable figures we have from Holland and which I owe to Dr. L. de Jong, the head of the Netherlands State Institute for War Documentation. In Holland, where the *Joodsche Raad* [the Jewish Council] like all the Dutch authorities very quickly became "an instrument of the Nazis," 103,000 Jews were deported to the death camps and some five thousand to Theresienstadt in the usual way, i.e., with the cooperation of the Jewish Council. Only five hundred and nineteen Jews returned from the death camps. In contrast to this figure, ten thousand of those twenty to twenty-five thousand Jews who escaped the Nazis—and that meant also the Jewish Council—and went underground survived; again forty to fifty percent. Most of the Jews sent to Theresienstadt returned to Holland.)[2]

When Arendt's book, reporting on the Eichmann Trial, first came out in 1963, paragraphs such as the above one quoted from her book caused a firestorm in the Jewish world. To many Jews it appeared as though this highly respected German Jewish scholar was shifting the blame for the destruction of European Jewry from the Germans to the Jews. The Jewish establishment practically ostracized her. Now, half a century later, her book has been reissued as a Penguin Classic and has found a new generation of readers. The controversy started by its author, however, continues unabated. Israel's

---

1. Hilberg, *Destruction of the European Jews*, 125.
2. Arendt, *Eichmann in Jerusalem*, 125.

leading Holocaust scholar, Yehuda Bauer, has presented a counter-argument to the above text about the tragedy of Dutch Jewry.

Bauer writes,

> Hannah Arendt's conclusion that had there been no Judenräte the Germans would have faced serious problems is restated despite the fact that many of the Soviet territories had no Judenräte, and the destruction was even more efficient there than in Poland.[3]

Elsewhere, Bauer writes,

> The historical literature on the behavior of the Judenräte is voluminous, *and yet the subject is far from being exhausted.* Two basic approaches can be discerned. One is represented by Raul Hilberg, who has analyzed the Judenräte with the tools of the social scientist. He says in effect, that the moment the Jewish leadership groups accepted nomination at German hands, they became, willy-nilly, cogs in the destruction machine that the Germans developed to annihilate the Judenräte's own charges, the Jewish people. The Judenräte facilitated the murder, even when they did everything in their power to extricate themselves from that role. When they established hospitals and cured sick Jews, they made more slave workers available to toil for the Germans until the Germans decided to kill them.[4]

Bauer goes on to present his own view which he attributes to Aharon Weiss's earlier work on the subject. He writes:

> I must repeat, we know they failed. But *we* know that they had to fail; they usually knew this only when it was too late; but—did they try to protect their communities even after they knew the situation was hopeless? We judge them with hindsight, and that is always a much more knowledgeable view. So we have to ask whether in a totally immoral world they tried to maintain elementary morality, whether their strategies were designed for the common good, and not whether their actions were successful. Finally and most importantly, we have found that generalizations about their behavior put forward by Hilberg, and in a different and more extreme form perhaps by Hannah Arendt, are inappropriate, because no Judenrat behaved in quite the same way as any other Judenrat. Each Judenrat presided over a hell,

---

3. Bauer, *Rethinking the Holocaust*, 77.
4. Ibid. 128 (italics added).

and similar though these hells were to each other, they were at the same time quite different.[5]

As we shall see in the next chapter, during the Holocaust the leadership of entire Jewish world, including the leadership of American and British Jewry, and the leaders of the Zionist movement worldwide and in Palestine, failed to act in any significant way to minimize the catastrophic dimensions of the destruction of European Jewry. Those who could and should have done more did not. As for the behavior of the Jewish Councils, their Jewish police force, and the kapos doing their ghastly work in the camps, here we are dealing with the doomed being manipulated by an enemy who, as we know, was one of the most ruthless enemies the world has ever known. With a gun to their head, they could have chosen to die rather than accept the role of Judenrat member, or ghetto police, or camp kapo. How can we, in the comfort of our homes and protected by the law as we are, how can we, judge them? What would we have done? Most likely, the majority of us would have done exactly what they did. We would have rationalized that we were delaying the bitter end by our actions. Hitler could die tomorrow, or the Allies could suddenly win the war. The traditional Jewish attitude is never to lose hope. A believing Jew says, I rely on divine providence. A careful study of the various heads of Judenräte throughout Europe shows that their behavior ran the entire gamut from close cooperation and abuse of power to self-sacrifice. Let us look at some salient examples.

In the Lodz ghetto, one of the major ghettoes in Poland, the head of the Judenrat was a Jewish businessman named Chaim Rumkowski. According to Bauer,

> Rumkowski was without any doubt a brutal dictator. He handed the children of the ghetto over to the Germans. He not only knew what their fate would be; he even made a speech, which has been preserved, telling the inhabitants of the ghetto why he was doing it: if he did not, the Germans would take young people as well as the children and the old people. If the young people did not survive, there would be no hope for the future; if they did, they would give birth to new children.[6]

Taken in isolation, this true story is horrifying. But years later survivors of the Lodz Ghetto referred to what might be called the "math of death," and concluded that because of Rumkowski's actions the Lodz Getto lasted two years longer than the Warsaw Ghetto, and in the end several

---

5. Ibid., 129.
6. Ibid., 131.

thousand ghetto residents survived, which gave Rumkowski a posthumous victory over Hitler.

The Warsaw Ghetto was the largest of the Jewish ghettoes in Poland. The head of the Judenrat in Warsaw was Adam Czerniakow. In regard to Czerniakow, the distinguished Israeli Holocaust historian Saul Friedländer writes,

> In stark contrast to Rumkowski, Czerniakow's ordinariness was his most notable characteristic. Yet his diary shows him to be anything but ordinary. His basic decency is striking in a time of unbridled ruthlessness. Not only did he devote every single day to his community, but he particularly cared for the humblest and the weakest among his *four hundred thousand wards*: the children, the beggars, the insane.[7]

On July 23, 1942, as the Germans were gearing up for the mass deportation of the Warsaw Ghetto residents to the death camp, Czerniakow committed suicide. On April 19, 1943, the Warsaw Ghetto Uprising took place. It was a massive act of suicide, but it was also a message sent out to the world and in particular to the comrades of the Jewish fighters around the world and especially in the land of Israel: Jewish blood is no longer a free-for-all. Jews will no longer be led like sheep to the slaughter. The message was not lost. The Jewish world will never be the same again.

At the other end of the spectrum from Rumkowski we have Ilya Mishkin in the Minsk Ghetto, which contained eighty-four thousand inhabitants. Regarding Mishkin, Bauer writes:

> His only qualification was that he spoke German. But from the first day he collaborated with the Communist underground, led in the ghetto by a Jewish Communist refugee from Warsaw named Hersh Smoliar. How could Mishkin do both: obey German orders (otherwise he would be removed and killed) and support the underground, supplying partisans in nearby forests with medical aid, clothing and other equipment and helping to smuggle some 7,000 Jews out of the ghetto and into the forests? But he did, and when he was murdered after relying on a supposedly anti-Nazi German officer, his successor, Moshe Yaffe, a refugee from Vilna, followed an identical policy. Yaffe was killed in July 1942 because he had warned the assembled ghetto inhabitants that they were going to be murdered.[8]

---

7. Friedländer, *Nazi Germany and the Jews* (italics added).
8. Bauer, *Rethinking the Holocaust*, 134.

Bauer goes on to say: "Most of the Judenräte in Europe were somewhere between Lodz and Minsk in the degree to which they yielded to the Germans."[9] In other words, some slavishly followed the Nazi orders while others resorted to various forms of resistance, culminating in uprisings such as the one at the Warsaw Ghetto. But the great majority was somewhere in the middle, looking for ways to live another day. That meant offering the enemy workers to show that a particular ghetto had able-bodied people who could help the German war effort. It also meant preserving public health and obtaining badly needed food. In short, the story of the Judenräte is far from simple. Arendt referred to it as the "darkest chapter in the whole dark story." But I respectfully beg to differ with her. All the chapters were equally dark, yet all contained sparks of light. To condemn doomed people is immoral. We have no right to judge them. But, as we shall see in the next chapter, we do have a right to judge Jewish leaders who were outside the Nazi-occupied zone and were able to do more and did not.

---

9. Ibid., 134.

# 10

# Jewish Inaction during the Holocaust

The largest and most politically influential Jewry outside Europe during the Holocaust was American Jewry. The most militant was the Yishuv, or the Jewish community in Palestine, backed by the Zionist organizations. Both communities consisted largely of Jewish immigrants from Europe or their offspring. Both had relatives in Europe. The plight of European Jewry deeply affected the Jews in America and Palestine. Yet neither one can lay claim to having played a significant role in rescuing Europe's Jews. Here again, as I felt when I was writing the chapter titled "The Complicity of the World: A Tale of Two Conferences," I feel deep pain as I am writing these lines. More could have been done, but the Jewish leadership did not rise up to the occasion.

It could be argued that during the war American Jewry was immobilized by an American administration that was supported by the great majority of American Jews, and that fought the Nazis, but that did not actively seek to rescue Hitler's Jewish victims. The Yishuv, on the other hand, living under the British Mandate for Palestine, was immobilized by a British government that was headed by Winston Churchill who was sympathetic to the Zionist cause, and who also fought the Nazis, but whose administration did not consider allowing masses of Jews from Europe to enter Palestine a viable solution. The leadership of the Yishuv agreed during the war not to fight the British in the interest of winning the war. Only the small LEHI group (also known as the Stern Gang) that broke off from the Revisionist Zionist movement refused to cooperate, and its leader, Avraham (Yair) Stern, was assassinated by the British in his hideout in Tel Aviv. Stern sought to make an alliance with the Nazis against the British in return for having Germany enable the establishment of a Jewish state. It is hard to fault him for wanting to save Jews, but it is very doubtful that he would have succeeded.

When we look back on those years, we cannot help but ask ourselves whether, in spite of the conflict of interests with the British, the Jewish leadership in Palestine could have done more for the Jews of Europe. One major problem was the internal politics of the Yishuv. In her book about the leadership of the Yishuv during the Shoah, *Entrapped Leadership* (in Hebrew), Israeli Holocaust scholar Dina Porat writes:

> The Jews of the free world did not look upon Zionism and the Yishuv as the address for the rescue operations, and there was no other address . . . [T]here were clashes within the Zionist movement; at the top, between Ben-Gurion and Weizmann; in the ranks, among the splinter groups of the Revisionists and between them and the Left; and also among the various left movements, and between the Orthodox and the Secularists; in matters of the rescue operations, between Greenbaum and Ben-Gurion; and at a certain time also between the rescue centers in Istanbul and in Geneva.

> "Try to place the exact dates of the news of the annihilation of thousands of Jewish communities . . . and next to them the news about the divisiveness and the debates among the parties and the splinter groups, and you will see the danger for our entire future," said Dinburg.[1]

Porat goes on to say, "Indeed, when we look back today at the clashes that were mentioned, and at the internal rift and the debates at that time among the people and in the Zionist movement, then—without taking into account the question of rescue opportunities, the Germans and the Allies—we agree with every word he said, and our heart is bitter, very bitter."[2]

Dinburg, or Dinur, who served as minister of education in the early years after the establishment of the State of Israel, was a historian who was well versed in Jewish history. He knew the Talmudic view that Jerusalem fell to the Romans because of divisions and infighting among the Jews inside the besieged city. He also knew that when the Jewish people were united

---

1. Porat, *Blue and the Yellow Stars of David*, 474.
2. Ibid.

they were able to prevail. The political and religious division among Jews, particularly in present-day Israel, gives many a cause for concern. In the prestate years things were even worse. Today at least Israel has become an independent state, a major military power, and home to the world's largest Jewish community. But during the Shoah it was a community of less than half a million people, barely able to defend itself against hostile Arab neighbors, and without an official status among the nations of the world. As Porat said, it was not an address for rescue operations, as it became later on when it stunned the world with such spectacular rescue feats as the Antebbe Operation.

One can only speculate what would have happened if the leadership of the Yishuv worked as one united body with Jewish organizations in Europe and in America on a joint rescue effort, say, as early as 1938 or 1939. Sadly, in those days the Jews did not have a visionary leader like Dr. Herzl, who could see the future.[3]

The main leader of the Yishuv in those years was David Ben-Gurion, who would become the founder of Israel and its first prime minister. I would argue that Ben-Gurion was also a visionary leader, but his vision was limited to one thing—the establishment of the Jewish state. His entire life was devoted to this one goal, which he certainly accomplished. It could be argued that he had to make an either/or choice in those days, painful as it was. I am sure this point will be debated for generations.

Be that as it may, salvation did not come to European Jewry from Zion. Nor did it come from the *goldene medinah*, the golden land of America, with its five million Jews who played a major role in American politics, economy, and culture. While the British closed the gates of Palestine to Jewish immigration, the U.S. closed it gates to Jewish refugees from Europe. Neither country took joy in the Jewish tragedy, but the Americans were pulling out of the Great Depression and the British needed Arab oil. Apparently European Jewry was not such a vital commodity in a world fighting a global war. Rabbi Stephen Wise, the leader of American Jewry at that time, was a close friend of President Roosevelt, and he did plead with the chief executive to do more for the Jews of Europe. The president kept insisting that everything had to be channeled into the war effort, which took precedence

---

3. Herzl predicted in 1898 that the Jewish state would come into existence if not in five then in fifty years. It happened fifty years to the day. He also saw the coming catastrophe for the Jews in Europe. Some may argue that there was such a leader, namely, Vladimir Jabotinsky, the founder of Revisionist Zionism. Jabotinsky saw the Shoah coming with all its horrors. He traveled around Poland in the '30s and pleaded with Jewish audiences to leave Poland while there was still time. He was scorned and maligned by the Zionist establishment, and he died in New York in 1940.

over everything else. Wise relented, and was accused by American Jewish activists like Ben Hecht or Rabbi Eliezer Silver of caving in. Roosevelt had the Great Depression in his rearview mirror and the war in his "unfinished-business" file. Moreover, American soldiers were dying in the Pacific and in Europe. The hapless Jews of Europe had to await their turn. Their turn, alas, never came.

Thus, European Jewry was left to fend for itself. At that point in time the best brains in the Jewish world were in Europe. In the aggregate, this was the largest and most influential Jewry in the world. One would have expected them to be able to do more for themselves, but that was not the case. Perhaps the main reason is that there was no such thing as a coherent European Jewry. The old joke is that where there are three Jews there are five opinions. I have a letter my father's brother, Yehuda, had sent him from Chirov, their native village, or shtetl, in eastern Poland (now Ukraine), in the late '30s. It is a very sensitive letter written in beautifully classical Hebrew, in which one can feel Yehuda's yearning to join his brother in the Land of Israel. It contains a paragraph about the Jews of the village enjoying a leisurely Saturday afternoon by the river. Uncle Yehuda describes the various groups of Jews—Belzer Hasidim in black garb; Bundist socialists wearing Ukrainian shirts; members of Zionist youth organizations ranging from right-wing Betar to left-wing Ha'Shomer Ha'Tzair, with their own distinctive shirts. In other words, the village was a microcosm of Polish Jewry in prewar Poland. The believing Jews were waiting for the messiah. The socialists were waiting for a new Europe where all people are equal. Others wanted to join family members in America, but in the '30s very few East European Jews could get a visa for America. The Zionists were dreaming of Aliyah, or going to Palestine to build the Jewish homeland. A few, like my parents, fulfilled that dream. But the great majority kept putting it off until it was too late. Nearly all of them, including my father's and my mother's entire families, perished in the Holocaust.

My uncle's letter was emblematic of the condition of Polish Jewry in particular and European Jewry in general on the eve of the war. In the larger urban Jewish communities, like Warsaw, for example, things were even more complicated. Here one could find Jewish assimilationists, who sought to distance themselves from the Jewish community, as well as an assortment of Jews of nearly every ideological school. This diversity came into sharp focus during the Warsaw Ghetto Uprising. One would have expected that after the Germans crowded the Jews into enclosed ghettos which in effect were large urban prisons, appointed a Jewish council to run the internal affairs of the ghetto, and a Jewish police to keep people in line, the Jews would find ways to work together as one people facing the same mortal enemy.

More specifically, the various Zionist youth organizations in the ghetto should have been able to unite under one umbrella to find ways to survive and to plan their resistance once they realized that the Germans had no intention to let any of the Jews in the ghetto survive. But that unfortunately was not the case. Reports by survivors of the uprising tell a different story.

To begin with, there were two separate fighting organizations in 1942 in the Warsaw Ghetto, as the Germans were gearing up for Großaktion Warschau, or the mass extermination of the Jews of Warsaw. The older one, which wanted to revolt back in 1940, was the right-wing Jewish Military Union (ZZW), consisting mainly of Revisionist Zionist youth. It was smaller but better armed than the Jewish Combat Organization (ZOB), which combined several left-wing Zionist youth organizations under the leadership of the legendary twenty-four-year old Mordecai Anielewicz. The two did not trust each other and were not able to work together. To make matters worse, there were also the Bundists, the Jewish non-Zionist socialists, who did not trust either group. And then there was the Polish underground outside the ghetto walls, which had spotty relations with the Jewish groups, charged a fortune for weapons, and ran its own show. To make a long story short, when the uprising finally got going in the spring of 1943 it was chaos, and it was too little too late. It was the stuff legends are made of, like Masada or the Alamo, but it did not stop the massacre.

Jews removed from the Warsaw Ghetto after the suppression of the uprising.

That said, the Warsaw Ghetto Uprising was indeed a glorious chapter in the long history of the Jewish people. The ghetto fighters, men, women and children, held the Nazi forces at bay for four weeks, fighting armor with Molotov cocktails and inflicting losses on the invincible Germans. It greatly inspired the Polish people who subsequently rose up against their occupier. And it inspired the Yishuv, which in 1948 faced an invading Egyptian armored column in the Negev and with a handful of light weapons stopped it at Kibbutz Yad Mordecai (named in memory of Mordecai Anielewicz) and prevented it from reaching Tel Aviv.

On May 10, 1943, Szmul Zygielboim, a Jewish Bundist member of the Polish government in exile, committed suicide in London to protest the lack of support from the Allied governments. In his suicide note, Zygielboim wrote:

> I cannot continue to live and to be silent while the remnants of Polish Jewry, whose representative I am, are being murdered. My comrades in the Warsaw ghetto fell with arms in their hands in the last heroic battle. I was not permitted to fall like them, together with them, but I belong with them, in their mass grave. By my death, I wish to give expression to my most profound protest against the inaction in which the world watches and permits the destruction of the Jewish people.[4]

As a child growing up in Israel, I was raised on the concept of catastrophe and heroism. The Holocaust was the catastrophe, but there was also a narrative of heroism. In fact, in the early years of the state the emphasis was put on acts of heroism, such as the Warsaw Ghetto Uprising under Mordecai Anielewicz and his comrades, or the group of young Yishuv parachutists who were dropped behind enemy lines in Europe. It is not hard to understand why the wholesale slaughter of Jews was played down while the few isolated instances of heroic action were given such prominence. My parents' generation was building a new Jewish state after two thousand years of Jewish statelessness against enormous odds. We, the native Israelis, were raised to be a new breed of Jew: proud and fearless, the opposite of the cowardly Jews portrayed by the anti-Semites and particularly by the Nazis.

I am not trying in any way to minimize Jewish heroism, particularly during the Holocaust. On the contrary, I believe that any Jew who managed to live another day under Nazism was a hero. But unfortunately the heroic acts that have become part of the official narrative were mostly symbolic. There is no escaping the pain-filled words of Porat and Dinur. Particularly because they also apply to American Jewry during that time, as well as to

---

4. Zygielboim, "Last Letter."

European Jewry, the victims themselves. All come up short when we consider the Jewish responses, which played into the hands of the enemy. It was by no means one of the glorious chapters in Jewish history.

One could only wish that there would have been much more resistance against the Nazis. Yes, there were Jewish partisans who fought in the woods. There were uprisings in several ghettos. There were Jews fighting in all the Allied Armies, and there was even a Jewish brigade in the British Army. But none of this prevented the Germans from decimating the Jews of Europe. To stop the Germans from mass-murdering the Jews two things were needed: much more Jewish resistance, and support from the Allies. The Allies had their own agenda, in which saving the Jews was not a high priority. Furthermore, the Jewish groups lacked unity, duped by the connivance of the Nazis, who decimated them in stages and tricked them with false hope, and, like Hamlet asking himself "To be or not to be," they became, for the most part, incapable of action.

Far be it from me to sit in judgment of Jewish inaction during the Holocaust. I was not there, and I have no way of knowing whether I could have done any better. But in trying to understand the unfathomable scope of the Catastrophe, we Jews must take a hard look at our own part in attempting or failing to attempt to prevent what befell us. In the second part of the book I will make an attempt to further clarify this point.

## THE RESISTANCE OF THE DOOMED

Those of us who, thank goodness, did not experience the Nazi hell-on-earth known as The Camps, cannot begin to understand what it was like to live another day and, if you were lucky enough, to survive those camps. Many did go on living under totally dehumanizing conditions, which robbed them of any semblance of human dignity, and thousands did survive, especially in the last stages of the war. This did not happen by accident. Here we encounter a phenomenon that negates the common belief that Europe's Jews simply went like "sheep to the slaughter." No one has brought this to our attention better than an American college professor by the name of Terrence Des Pres. In his book *The Survivor: An Anatomy of Life in the Death Camps*—a book too painful to read yet a must for anyone who is seriously interested in delving into the horror known as the Holocaust. Des Pres draws his conclusions from many testimonies of survivors, some of whom I have known personally, who let us into their secret world of the close camaraderie among Holocaust survivors—that shared part of their lives which is their common experience in those torture and death centers that made them different from the rest of us, which taught them lessons the rest of us have never learned, and which made them value life in a way we will never be able to understand.

Perhaps the main point of the book is that those inmates who sought to survive by only looking after themselves did not, for the most part, survive, while those who became involved in cooperative action or even in networks of clandestine and passive resistance survived in much greater numbers. The author explains how under the most dire conditions people on the verge of starvation, exhaustion, and death, began to find inner strength and began to realize that those who had made themselves lords and masters over their lives were the actual subhumans who were making every effort to prove to themselves that the inmates were subhuman or worse. It became clear to them that they had to make every effort to survive, use every last ounce of physical or mental energy to remain alive, and resort to any action or stratagem that would enable them to live another day, keep outwitting their tormentors, and reach the day when the Germans were finally defeated by the Allies and the gates of places like Buchenwald and Bergen-Belsen and Auschwitz were flung wide open, enabling them to return to the land of the living and begin the process of healing their bodies and minds.

Des Pres provides concrete examples of such behavior. There were many instances in the camps where the healthy nursed the sick back to health; where, under the noses of the SS guards, prisoners developed intricate networks of bartering food for cigarettes and many others improvised items such as sewing needles and work tools; of sharing news about the progress of the Allies on the battlefield, which, especially toward the end of the war, was vital for survival; of celebrating Jewish holy days, which helped uplift the spirits of those living only a step away from death, and reminded them that they were morally and spiritually superior to their tormentors and executioners. It was not necessarily altruism or compassion that guided those actions. It was rather a realization that, facing a highly organized enemy, the only way to fight back is by becoming "organized," a term which, as the author explains, was common in the camps and had a variety of meanings, from smuggling to coordinating an uprising, as had happened in Auschwitz and Treblinka.

How many acts of kindness and common decency took place among inmates whose lives were at constant risk we will never know. But over the years I learned that Holocaust survivors, and especially camp survivors, have had a strong common bond that has not diminished since the end of the war. To the contrary, it has grown stronger with each passing year. Many of those survivors who have done well financially have contributed generously to help those less fortunate than they, and to commemorating the Shoah in such places as Yad Vashem and many Holocaust museums and memorials around the world. Many have written their memoirs, and whether they rose to high positions and have been overachievers or whether they remained ordinary citizens, there is a certain resilience of the spirit about them and a certain human dignity that I have always admired. Needless to say, there were more than a few Jews who turned on their fellow Jews to survive. A starving person or a person with a gun held to his head cannot think rationally. What is remarkable is that there were many who did not give in to the depredations and were able to carry on and even help others.

I recall as a young child growing up in the new State of Israel in the early years following World War II, survivors began to arrive in my hometown of Haifa. I remember the green numbers tattooed on the forearms of the camp survivors. I remember how many of them were emaciated, their cheeks sunken, their eyes receded in their sockets, their gestures nervous and suspicious. I recall how they were objects of pity to us native-born children of the Land of Israel. We didn't quite know what to make of them. Were they really the same as us? Would they prove themselves on the battlefield when we had to stop Arab armies from invading our land? Were they emotionally maimed for life? And always the nagging question: Why was it so easy to slaughter millions of them? Why did so many go passively to their death, "like sheep to the slaughter"?

Now, years later, as I recall those distant days, I am filled with shame for myself and my contemporaries. It took a long time for us to start to understand what they had been through, and what it took for those remnants to survive. In fact, we often resented their survival, because many of our own relatives had not survived. We suspected that they did things they shouldn't have done to survive. And they knew how we felt, and God only knows what they had to go through to overcome all that prejudice and misunderstanding. In the early years after the war, they did not talk about their past. Not in Israel, not in the U.S., and not in the rest of the world. The world was not ready for it. The enormity of the Holocaust was too overwhelming. They were busy rebuilding their lives, and the world was busy emerging from the worst war in all of human history. Fortunately, those days are behind us. Slowly, it all began to sink in. With each passing year we and the rest of the world have learned that they are indeed the ultimate witnesses of man's inhumanity, and at the same time a living testimony that the human spirit cannot be destroyed, not by a Hitler and not by aStalin and not by any other tyrant, past or present. The human race, despite all the calamities that have befallen it, continues to rise from the ashes, and the tyrants of the world continue to fall. We are still a long way away from utopia, but we are infinitely better off than we were during those years of seemingly endless darkness.

## THE GNAWING QUESTION: WHY DID IT HAPPEN?

We have now looked at the Holocaust from all sides, and yet, we are still left with the gnawing question: Why was such a horrendous event possible? Why did centuries of human civilization, why did people who call themselves Christians, why did the most civilized continent in the world, sink to the bottom of human depravity and commit crimes the like of which the world had never seen before?

The *why* of the Holocaust is not limited to the Holocaust. It reaches down to the very essence of human existence. It makes us wonder what else can go wrong in the future. I am an optimist by nature, but I must ask with Primo Levi, what is man? Is man indeed hopeless? Are we doomed to destroy ourselves? Is the world run by dark forces?

We will leave these thoughts to the second part of the book, where we deal with the ultimate questions of life. Here we will consider the measurable causes of the Shoah, which we have discussed in the previous chapters. They all lead to one inescapable conclusion.

*The magnitude of the Shoah is due to the fact that it was a perfect storm in which everything conspired against the Jews of Europe, leaving them no way out.*

If we look back across centuries of Jewish history, it becomes clear that during the worst catastrophes in that long and harsh history there was always a way out. When Jerusalem was destroyed by the Babylonians and again by the Romans, a certain portion of the vanquished Jews in both instances was allowed to continue to live on their land while another portion was exiled. Both groups found ways to carry on, and Jewish life continued to flourish. The same happened in the ensuing centuries, during which Jews were expelled from several countries and always found a new home elsewhere. The most notable example is the expulsion of the Jews (and the Muslim Moors) from Catholic Spain in 1492. On July 30 of that year, the entire community of some two hundred thousand souls, a community that excelled in almost every field of human endeavor, was given an order to leave the country. Spanish Jewry found refuge in other European countries such as Holland and Italy, in North Africa, Turkey, and the Middle East, and eventually in Germany, Poland, and the rest of Eastern Europe.

When Hitler's Germany turned on the Jews in the mid-1930s, something unprecedented in human history happened. A policy was set in motion that turned Germany and then the rest of Europe into a death trap from which no Jew was to escape. From the day in 1935 when Nazi Germany introduced the Nuremberg Laws, which stripped the Jews of the Reich of their citizenship rights, to the day in 1945 when Germany was finally defeated, everything imaginable conspired against the Jews of Europe, leaving them no way out. With the exception of the open city of Shanghai in the Far East, all doors around the world were closed to them. Only a few managed to get out of the Nazi-occupied parts of Europe. The rest were hopelessly trapped from 1939 to 1945 in what was a murderous war zone. They were cut off from the world, surrounded by hostile populations with a long history of anti-Semitism and with long-standing personal and national agendas. They were slated to die by a powerful regime that had espoused an extreme ideology that considered its people to be racially superior and having a license to kill off so-called inferior races. This regime was emboldened by the apathy displayed by the Western democracies, and by the fact that it faced a formidable foe, namely, the Soviet Union, which was also ruled by a ruthless dictator who also showed little regard for human life.

The Holocaust happened because Nazi Germany came under the spell of a leader who was able to convince masses of Germans that there was a world Jewish conspiracy against them, which explained why Germany lost the First World War. Hitler's oratorical power cast a spell on millions of Germans (see George Steiner's remark about Hitler's command of the German language[5]), many of whom followed him as if he were their savior. Indeed, there was something mystical about Nazism, a blind faith that had turned its back on two millennia of Judeo-Christian morality, and espoused the Barbarian ethos of the Teutonic ancestors of the Germanic people. It mocked and manipulated its own Christian heritage, and it applied the laws of the jungle—"might is right" and the "survival of the fittest"—to human affairs. Under the various totalitarian regimes in Europe at that time human life became expendable, and the rulers of those regimes played God by deciding who would live and who would die. In the case of Nazi Germany, the Jews had to die for the Germanic people to rise and become the rulers of Europe and perhaps the world as well. In the famous words of Dostoevsky in his novel *The Brothers Karamazov*, "In a world without God, anything goes."

The Germans who perpetrated the Holocaust were the parents and grandparents of Germans I know personally, interact with, and have great respect for. I do not find them to be different from anyone else. A few years ago I was serving as a cruise rabbi on a ship sailing through the Red Sea.

---

5. See Rosenbaum, *Explaining Hitler*, 303; for a quotation from that interview, see ch. 13 in this volume, 151.

There were a fair number of German passengers on the ship, mostly in their seventies and eighties. But there was also a young German couple in their forties, whom my wife and I befriended. I noticed that they did not associate too much with their older compatriots. As we were crossing the Suez Canal, I was standing on the deck watching the sights. The young German woman approached me and began to tell me that her father served in the Wehrmacht and fought under Rommel in North Africa. She then proceeded to let me in on her feelings of guilt and sorrow for what her parents' generation had done to the Jews. She said that the Holocaust haunted her and her generation. Since then, I have heard similar comments from other Germans of various ages. And so I find it difficult to comprehend the bottomless hatred of Jews that typified the Third Reich as compared to my own present-day experience with German people.

In looking for an answer I recall the 1959 play *Rhinoceros*, in which the French-Romanian playwright Eugène Ionesco sought to explain how people who are otherwise kind and considerate can be transformed overnight into zealots who would go to all extremes to achieve their goals. He describes a small village in France where one day a local man becomes a rhinoceros. Soon more people become rhinos, and the town is divided between humans and nonhumans. More and more people begin to justify the transformation of humans into rhinos, and eventually everyone, except for one man, becomes a rhino.

This play has been interpreted to be a commentary on such pre–World War II movements as fascism, communism, and Nazism, which sought to bring about an extreme transformation of society, in which the individual person had little value, while the society is transformed into a faceless and uncaring autocracy that ignores the laws of civilization. There are many testimonies of people who lived under one of those regimes—or even of outsiders who happened to visit one of them—in which the person was swept up by the ecstasy of a mass rally where thousands were cheering their leader, whereupon one found oneself cheering along for someone one did not believe in.

Whether or not Ionesco had Nazi Germany specifically in mind when he wrote *Rhinoceros*, it certainly captures what happened in Germany in the '30s. The evils of the time—anti-Semitism, racism, Germany's wounded nationalism, the complicity of other nations, and the failure of the world's democracies to take a stand against totalitarianism—all conspired to produce a radical transformation in Nazified Germany that affected the judgment and behavior of sufficient numbers of Germans to bring about the disaster known as the Holocaust. What is particularly scary about all of this is that by the mid-twentieth century Europe had reached the apex of human civilization. In his book *Green Hills of Africa*, published in 1935, Ernest Hemingway says in a conversation that America does not have a writer of the caliber of the German novelist Thomas Mann. Like many young American writers of the World War I generation, Hemingway went to live in Europe to become part of the cultural and artistic scene of Europe, which set the standard for the rest of the world. This was true of almost any field of human endeavor. I have already mentioned Jewish scholarship. I have also mentioned giants of science like Albert Einstein, and seminal thinkers like Sigmund Freud. To think that Europe, which had become the beacon of human civilization could commit such atrocities makes us wonder whether what we consider a civilized person is actually a wolf in sheep's clothing, as was observed by the ancient Romans who coined the phrase, *homo homini lupus est* (man is a wolf to his fellowman).

We are left with a choice: we can argue that the Holocaust happened because humans are capable of bottomless evil of which the Holocaust is the supreme example, or we can say that the Holocaust was a perfect storm, in which a group of criminals who took over a major state were able, under a most unusual set of circumstances, to carry out a misguided yet satanic plan which resulted in the death of millions of innocent people. Unfortunately, there is enough guilt to go around in the case of the Holocaust to incriminate almost everyone—victimizers for what they did; victims for what they failed to do; those who stood by and did nothing; and finally, Jewish leaders around the world who could possibly have done more but did not.

# 11

# Righteous Gentiles

The Talmudic sage Hillel the Elder used to say, "In a place where no one behaves like a human being, try to behave like one."[1]

One of the best things the authorities of the Yad Vashem Holocaust Memorial Museum in Jerusalem did was to establish a special section designed to commemorate and honor those non-Jews who saved Jews during the Holocaust, known as Righteous Gentiles. Many of them will forever remain anonymous, but thousands have already been discovered and honored either in life or posthumously. These men and women, ranging from foreign diplomats to farmers and representing the entire human race, are shining examples of the nobility of the human spirit and the abiding hope that in the end good will always triumphs over evil.

A special place among those Righteous Gentiles is occupied by the Polish resistance fighter and later professor at Georgetown University in Washington DC, Jan Karski (1914–2000). When he was recognized by Yad Vashem in 1982 as a Righteous Gentile, the decision read as follows:

> Although he had not saved individual Jews, The Commission for the Designation of the Righteous decided that he had risked his life in order to alert the world to the murder. He had incurred enormous risk in penetrating into the Warsaw ghetto and a camp, and then committed himself wholly to the case of rescuing the Jews. Karski's case is quite exceptional in many ways. While other rescuers had taken the difficult decision to

---

1. Mishnah, *Sayings of the Fathers (Pirqe Avot)* 2:5.

leave the side of the bystanders, not to remain silent and to stand up and act, Karski, after he reached the West, brought this dilemma to the doorstep of the free world's leaders.[2]

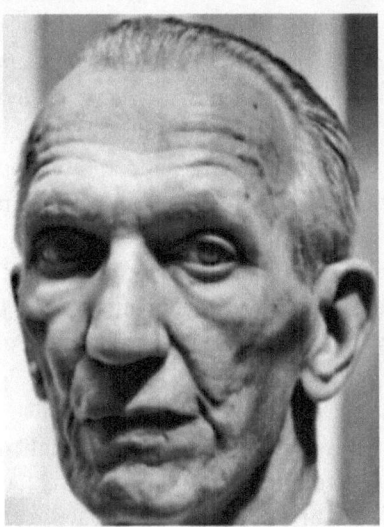

Jan Karski

While Karski failed to persuade the leaders of the free world, primarily President Roosevelt, to take timely action to stop the murder of millions of Jews and non-Jews, he moved heaven and earth to shame the Allies into action by bringing the atrocities committed in the Warsaw Ghetto, and the ongoing transports to the death camps to their attention. Like a biblical prophet, he pursued his mission relentlessly, but his words kept falling on deaf ears. What compelled a Polish Catholic underground fighter to risk his life time and again, and to espouse the cause of the doomed Jews of Poland and Europe is not altogether clear. But one can say that here was a man who represented the best in the character of the Polish people, a true Polish Christian and humanitarian, a man who was willing to die to save the lives of millions of innocent people, despite the centuries-long divide that existed in Poland between Jews and Gentiles, as we pointed out earlier in the book.

Karski's life, which became intertwined with the fate of the three million Jews of Poland, also embodies the fate of Poland under the German and the Soviet occupations. Born to a working class family in Lodz in 1914, Karski excelled in his university studies and was destined to become

2. An outstanding website depicts Karski's story: "Jan Karski (1914–2000); Humanity's Hero."

a leading Polish diplomat when the Nazis invaded Poland in September of 1939. As an officer in the Polish army, he was captured by the Red Army and taken prisoner. When it became clear that the Soviets intended to execute the officer class of the Polish army while sparing the enlisted men, Karski exchanged his officer's uniform for a private's and managed to return home, which was now under German occupation. The Soviets subsequently massacred thousands of Polish officers, mainly at the Katyn Forest, one of the most tragic events in Polish history. In the German-occupied part of Poland, Karski joined the Polish underground and became a courier between the underground's headquarters and the Polish government-in-exile, first in France and then in England. To reach those destinations he had to assume many different identities and risk his life. At one point he was denounced and captured by the Gestapo. Severely tortured, he tried to commit suicide in jail. He was hospitalized and managed to jump out of a hospital window and reach safety.

Resuming his courier activities, Karski met two Jewish leaders in a suburb of Warsaw in the summer of 1942, at the height of the extermination of Polish Jewry. They told him about the fate of the Jews of Poland. Karski was struck by their despair and overwhelming sense of hopelessness. They expected the Allies to win the war, but, by that time, three million Polish Jews would all have perished. In his book, *Story of a Secret State*, Karski reports what they told him:

> You other Poles are fortunate. You are suffering too. Many of you will die, but at least your nation goes on living. After the war Poland will be resurrected. Your cities will be rebuilt and your wound will slowly heal. From this ocean of tears, pain, rage and humiliation your country will emerge again but the Polish Jews will no longer exist. We will be dead. Hitler will lose his war against the human, the just and the good, but he will have won the war against the Polish Jews. No—it will not be a victory, the Jewish people will be murdered.[3]

The Jewish leaders suggested that Karski go to London and to Washington and convince Western Jewish leaders to go on a hunger strike, indeed, to put their lives on the line to awaken the conscience of the world to the plight of Poland's Jews. Karski was shaken to the core. He became obsessed with the terrible fate of his country's Jewish citizens, and saw it as his mission to bring their tragedy to the attention of world leaders in the West. At the same time he realized he was an insignificant Polish underground fighter who could be easily dismissed by those leaders as an alarmist. He made

---

3. Karski, *Story of a Secret State*, 322.

the bold decision to smuggle himself into the Warsaw Ghetto and become an eyewitness to the extermination process. Risking his life, he visited the ghetto and was horrified by the condition of the starving and dying Jews in Poland's largest ghetto. Subsequently, he visited a German transition camp disguised as a Latvian guard and witnessed the brutal treatment of Jews piled on trucks to be sent to the death camp at Treblinka.

Equipped with this horrific knowledge, Karski made his way through France, Spain, and Portugal, until he reached London. Here he met with Szmul Zygielboim, a Jewish Bundist member of the Polish government in exile, and told him what the Jewish leaders in Warsaw suggested, namely, for Zygielboim and other Jewish leaders to go on a hunger strike and be willing to die for their people. As I mentioned earlier, Zygielboim was deeply affected by what he was told, and later on committed suicide. Karski was devastated. He blamed himself for causing Zygielboim to take his own life. He was now fully aware of the enormity of the task he had undertaken, and while at first he despaired of being able to do anything to save the Jews, he began to rally and started visiting key leaders in England and in America, hoping to get them to take action to stop the Nazi murder machine in Poland.

Karski went to the White House to see President Roosevelt. He was granted a meeting of one hour and twenty minutes. The American president wanted to know about the general condition in Poland, assuring Karski the U.S. was a loyal friend of Poland and would not abandon it. Finally, Karski was allowed to turn to his main topic, namely, the Jewish genocide. Roosevelt told Karski that action would be taken in due time. It became clear to Karski that the great man was in no rush to help those who were on their way to the gallows.

At an International Liberators' Conference in 1981 Karski said,

> The Lord assigned me a role to speak and write during the war, when—as it seemed to me—it might help. It did not. When the war came to its end, I learned that the governments, the leaders, the scholars, the writers did not know what had been happening to the Jews. They were taken by surprise. The murder of six million innocents was a secret, a "terrible secret" ... Then I became a Jew. But I am a Christian Jew. I am a practicing Catholic ... My faith tells me the second Original Sin has been committed by humanity: through commission, or omission, or self-imposed ignorance, or insensitivity, or self-interest, or hypocrisy, or heartless rationalization. This sin will haunt humanity to the end of time. It does haunt me. And I want it to be so.[4]

---

4. Quoted on a post by Berenbaum, "Jan Karski."

Karski, a deeply religious man, did not lose his faith either in people or in God. But he did lose his faith in governments and in leaders. He learned a bitter lesson that in the moment of the greatest human emergency, so-called great leaders and so-called great political and nonpolitical organizations are slow to come through, and usually act after the fact, when it is too late. But Karski knew how to heed Hillel's dictum, "In a place where no one behaves like a human being, try to behave like one." For generations to come, he will continue to serve as a shining example that even in the heart of hell some people do not forget that they were created in the image of God.

When, in 1994, Karski was awarded by Israel an honorary Israeli citizenship, he said in his acceptance speech,

> This is the proudest and the most meaningful day in my life. Through the honorary citizenship of the State of Israel, I have reached the spiritual source of my Christian faith. In a way, I also became a part of the Jewish community . . . Since the early years of my school in Lodz, I have been getting understanding, friendship or help from the Jews; and now, they took me in; and now, I, Jan Karski, a Pole, an American, a Catholic, have also become an Israelite! Gloria, Gloria in excelsis Deo. Our Lord revealed himself to many nations in His own ways, but always with the same commandment, Love your neighbor . . . He endowed us with a free will. We have infinite capacity to do good, and an infinite capacity to do evil. We are all schizophrenic.[5]

One is inclined to add that if we only had more Jan Karskis in this world, it would be a much better world.

---

5. Quoted in Paldiel, *Saving the Jews*, 43.

**Varian Fry**

As a child, I was enchanted by the paintings of Marc Chagall, the Russian Jewish artist, and affected by the novel *The Forty Days of Musa Dag*, written by the Austrian Jewish writer Franz Werfel, which described the genocide committed against the Armenians by the Turks. What I didn't know until much later was that, during the Nazi occupation of France, an American scholar named Varian Fry volunteered to go to France, recently defeated by the German Reich, for the purpose of saving luminaries like Chagall and Werfel and others from the clutches of the Nazis. Many of them subsequently found their way to the United States and elsewhere and greatly enriched American and world culture.

Like Karski, Fry was a man who was not afraid to go against the grain, and while the world shut its eyes to the plight of the Jews of Europe, he grasped early on the terrible fate awaiting them and all those in Europe who believed in freedom and justice. In 1935 he was sent to Germany as a young writer working for a magazine that covered foreign affairs to report on the situation in that country, now under Nazi rule. While in Berlin, Fry witnessed the harsh treatment of the Jews by the local Nazis. In a coffee shop on the elegant Kurfürstendamm Boulevard he witnessed Nazis, members of the SA, running a knife through the hand of a Jewish customer into the table. His observations on Hitler's Germany appeared in the *New York Times* that year. Like Karski, Fry tried to shake the world out of its apathy and, like Karski's, his words fell on deaf ears. Fry, a non-Jew, a Harvard graduate, and an American who was far removed from the gathering storm in Europe, was more sensitive to the fate of Europe's victims of Nazism than most Jewish American writers, intellectuals, artists, and public officeholders at that time.[6] He was ready to do something to help the potential victims of Nazi persecution. The question was what.

The opportunity presented itself when a group of American intellectuals met in New York and formed an Emergency Rescue Committee for the purpose of rescuing prominent European artists, writers, and intellectuals trapped in Vichy France, which was under a French administration that collaborated with the Germans. When it became clear that the Germans were out to arrest those leading lights of European culture and send them to the concentration camps, the committee met with First Lady Eleanor Roosevelt, who was staying in her New York Apartment at that time, and pleaded their case. Mrs. Roosevelt called her husband in their presence and urged him to issue a limited number of visas. The president was reluctant to grant entry visas into the United States at a time when The U.S. maintained friendly relations with Vichy France and when the quota system was strictly enforced by the State Department. Eleanor would not give up. She told her husband the committee was ready to take action that would embarrass the government. Roosevelt finally relented and agreed to instruct the State Department to issue 200 visitor visas to a select group of people. Fry, a soft spoken, well dressed intellectual who knew Europe and spoke French, was picked for the mission.

One may wonder whether Fry had carefully considered what he was getting himself into. Since he was going to work against the policies of the Vichy government, he had to engage in clandestine work, in which he had no experience. The State Department had begrudgingly granted those two hundred visas, but otherwise it did not look favorably upon the kind of work he was doing. There were quite a few American officials and diplomats in those days who were sympathetic to the Germans, and were by no means friends of the Jews. Many of them believed that Hitler was the best buffer in Europe against the spread of communism, and they played down the brutality of his regime. The Jews in France at that time lived under a reign of terror—both French Jews and the vast number of refugees from Germany and Austria and the rest of Europe who were staying in France. When I was in Paris in 1956, I stayed at the home of friends of my mother's from the old days in Poland. They told me that during that time they had left Paris, which was occupied by the Germans, and looked for refuge in Marseilles,

---

6. See Hecht, *Child of the Century*. In a meeting of writers in Hollywood, mostly Jewish, during the height of the Shoah, Ben Hecht was chastised by them for playing up the Holocaust.

on the Mediterranean coast, where Fry had opened his office. They were sitting in a restaurant one day having dinner when German and French police came in looking for Jews. My host, Monsieur Fisch, did not panic. He took a serving towel from a waiter who was standing by, wrapped it over his arm, and started to pick up dishes, pretending he was an employee of the restaurant. He and his wife were one step away from being identified and sent to Auschwitz.

Once Fry installed himself in Marseilles, his life changed forever, and his story became one that continues to be told in books and movies. Along with a volunteer staff, he began to process hundreds and finally thousands of refugee applications on his own cognizance with the stern disapproval of the State Department, issuing false passports and other bogus documentation, creating false identities, establishing escape routes through Spain and Portugal to other parts of the world. By May 1941 his office had processed some fifteen thousand applications, carefully screening every case and providing assistance to approximately four thousand people. Among the Jews Fry helped to smuggle out of France were a number of well-known personalities, such as Hannah Arendt, Marc Chagall, Jacques Lipchitz, Siegfried Kracauer, Franz Werfel, Lion Feuchtwanger, and many others. Years later many of them would pay tribute to him for saving their lives. Some leading German Jews, like the philosopher Walter Benjamin and the writer Stefan Zweig, committed suicide at that time. Betrayed by their country, they did not have the moral strength to carry on. The rest started a new life in America and in other parts of the world, and they continued to make major contributions to world culture.

As was to be expected, the French authorities came after Fry and began to harass him, finally issuing an order for him to leave the country. He returned to the United States where the authorities considered him a renegade, and where many of his own friends shunned him. J. Edgar Hoover put him under the surveillance of the FBI as a subversive subject for excoriating the State Department, and he ended up until his premature death in 1967 at age fifty-nine as a Latin teacher at a boys' school.

In his book *Saving the Jews*, Mordecai Paldiel writes:

> It is perhaps not too surprising that Varian Fry's activity should have greatly irritated the French, considering their policy of collaboration with Nazi Germany. However, for the United States—Fry's home country, and the proud self-vaunted "Arsenal of Democracy"—to have been a partner in the hounding and harassment of Fry, not because of any pronounced anti-American activity on his part, but simply because of his commitment to a

strictly humanitarian endeavor—this, even in hindsight, is hard to swallow; it is frankly shocking.[7]

Shortly before his death, the French government awarded Fry the Chevalier of the Légion d'honneur. Streets have been named after him in France and in Germany.

In 1994 Fry was awarded the title of Righteous among the Nations by Yad Vashem. Varian Fry's son planted a tree in his honor at Yad Vashem in 1996. The ceremony was attended by U.S. Secretary of State Warren Christopher, who on that occasion apologized for the State Department's abusive treatment of Fry during the war years.[8]

**Chiune (Sempo) Sugihara**

Chiune (Sempo) Sugihara (1900–1986) was the Japanese consul in Kaunas, Lithuania, in 1940, when he defied the orders of his superiors in Tokyo and issued visas to Jewish refugees who had nowhere else to turn for help, as the world was shutting its doors to the Jews of Europe. In his book *In Search of Sugihara*, Hillel Levine estimates that Sugihara saved as many as ten thousand Polish and Lithuanian Jews by issuing those visas.[9] The risk Sugihara took was enormous. He was a low-level Japanese diplomat. Imperial Japan was an ally of Nazi Germany. He was putting his life and the lives of his wife

---

7. Paldiel, *Saving the Jews*, 67.

8. Ibid., 73.

9. The number ten thousand which Levine uses in his subtitle, is in dispute, but according to all estimates it was in the thousands. See the Yad Vashem site, http://www.yadvashem.org/yv/en/righteous/stories/sugihara.asp.

# Righteous Gentiles

and children at risk. He had no connection whatsoever to Jews, but he felt empathy for fellow human beings in their greatest hour of need. In his book, Levine quotes him as saying,

> You want to know about my motivation, don't you? Well. It is the kind of sentiments anyone would have when he actually sees refugees face to face, begging with tears in their eyes. He just cannot help but sympathize with them. Among the refugees were the elderly and women. They were so desperate that they went so far as to kiss my shoes, Yes, I actually witnessed such scenes with my own eyes. Also, I felt at that time, that the Japanese government did not have any uniform opinion in Tokyo. Some Japanese military leaders were just scared because of the pressure from the Nazis; while other officials in the Home Ministry were simply ambivalent.[10]

According to the Jewish Virtual Library,

> For 29 days, from July 31 to August 28, 1940, Mr. and Mrs. Sugihara sat for endless hours writing and signing visas by hand. Hour after hour, day after day, for these three weeks, they wrote and signed visas. They wrote over 300 visas a day, which would normally be one month's worth of work for the consul. Yukiko also helped him register these visas. At the end of the day, she would massage his fatigued hands. He did not even stop to eat. His wife supplied him with sandwiches. Sugihara chose not to lose a minute because people were standing in line in front of his consulate day and night for these visas. When some began climbing the compound wall, he came out to calm them down and assure them that he would do his best to help them all. Hundreds of applicants became thousands as he worked to grant as many visas as possible before being forced to close the consulate and leave Lithuania. Consul Sugihara continued issuing documents from his train window until the moment the train departed Kovno for Berlin on September 1, 1940. And as the train pulled out of the station, Sugihara gave the consul visa stamp to a refugee who was able to use it to save even more Jews.[11]

Before he died in 1986, Sugihara was honored by the State of Israel as a Righteous Gentile. He was also honored by Lithuania and Poland, and by Jewish and Japanese communities in the United States. Two years later he died in Japan. Today he is considered a hero in Japan.

10. Quoted in Levine, *In Search of Sugihara*, 259.
11. Jewish Library, "Chiune Sugihara,"

Other diplomats in Nazi-occupied Europe who put saving human lives ahead of their careers were Raoul Wallenberg of Sweden and Aristides de Sousa Mendes of Portugal. Wallenberg has been honored all over the world as one of the greatest heroes of humanity during its darkest hour. Streets and schools have been named after him around the world, and monuments have been erected in his honor in many countries. His story in a way parallels Sugihara's story, but its twists and turns resemble a Greek or a Shakespearean drama.

**Raoul Wallenberg**

Wallenberg, an architect and a businessman in his early thirties, was sent by Sweden to Hungary in July 1944, as a special envoy to work on rescuing Hungarian Jews. It was a highly risky mission, as the trains under Eichmann's supervision were in full swing of deporting the Jews of Hungary to Auschwitz. At that time, over four hundred thousand Jews were being deported to the death camp, with the collaboration of the Hungarian fascist Iron Cross Party which came to power in October 15 of that year. Wallenberg was able to issue protective passports for tens of thousands of Hungarian Jews, which identified them as Swedish subjects and kept them off the trains. He rented apartment buildings in Budapest, which came under Swedish jurisdiction and provided a shelter for those Jews. He knew he was pursued by the Iron Cross and by Eichmann's agents, and he had to sleep each night in a different house to evade his pursuers.

On January 17, 1945, during the Siege of Budapest by the Red Army, Wallenberg was detained by Soviet authorities on suspicion of espionage and subsequently disappeared. He was later rumored to have died in 1947, while imprisoned in the KGB's Lubyanka Prison in Moscow. The motive for death remains a mystery to this day and has given rise to a great deal of speculation.

**Aristides de Sousa Mendes**

Aristides de Sousa Mendes, the Portuguese consul general in Bordeaux, France, during the Nazi invasion in 1940, like his colleague, the Japanese vice consul Sugihara in Lithuania, also defied his government's instructions not to issue visas to refugees fleeing the Nazi onslaught. He was contacted by a Jewish refugee, Rabbi Haim Kruger, who asked him to issue visas for some ten thousand Jewish refugees. Mendes told the rabbi he could issue a visa for him and his family, but if he went any further he would be risking his career and the lives of his family members. The rabbi replied that he would not leave his fellow Jews behind. Mendes did a great deal of soul-searching, and finally decided that he had to answer to a higher authority, disregard his own interest, and rescue as many people as he could. He set up an improvised office in the consulate and, with the help of two of his sons and several Jews who were waiting nearby, began to issue entrance permits. Sousa Mendes toiled for three days and three nights, allowing himself not a moment's rest and collapsing in exhaustion once the job was done. Between June 15 and June 22, 1940, Sousa Mendes issued a total of 1,575 visas. In some cases he personally helped the refugees cross the border into Spain and sent them off to safety. Mendes was dismissed from the diplomatic service of his country and became a persona non grata in Portugal. He died a broken man, and his family had to be supported by a Jewish relief agency.

Eventually, a democratic regime in Portugal recognized him as one of the heroes of his country, and he was honored by Israel as a Righteous Gentile.

People like Sugihara, Wallenberg, and Sousa Mendes, besides saving thousands of doomed people, also provide proof that even within bureaucracies there are individuals who follow their conscience rather than bureaucratic dictates and are willing to take great risks to save human lives. That the world honors them today speaks well for the post-Holocaust world.

But there were also thousands of ordinary people who put their lives at risk to save one person or one family. The Nazis and all their accomplices could not extinguish the spark of humanity that exists in the hearts of people who could tell right from wrong. A few examples will suffice.

In Berlin, under the noses of the Nazi leadership, the wife of a Wehrmacht soldier sheltered a Jewish woman in her apartment. In 1999 they became the subject of a German film, *Aimee and Jaguar*. Aimee was the nickname of the German woman, Elisabeth Wust. Jaguar was the nickname of the Jewish woman, Felicie Schrader, whose real name was Rachel Schragenheim. The story ended tragically, with Rachel-Felicie caught at the end of the war and taken to a concentration camp where she perished. Aimee-Elisabeth managed to shelter three more Jewish women, all members of a lesbian community living secretly in Berlin. After the war one of her sons submitted her name to Yad Vashem in Jerusalem and she was accorded the title of Righteous Gentile.

In Boryslav, located near Lviv, formerly in Poland and now in Ukraine, the Weiss family was hidden on the farm of a Ukrainian neighbor named Yulia, whose son Yuzek joined the Nazis' Ukrainian police that rounded up local Jews to be sent to their death. The son did not know that his mother was hiding a Jewish family. The family survived, and when the war ended, and the victorious Soviets were hunting for Nazi collaborators, Yulia asked the Weiss family for a special favor: to hide the son who would have sent them to the gas chambers. They agreed. One of the Weiss sons, Shevah Weiss, became a political leader in Israel an Israel's ambassador to Poland.

In France, a Catholic priest helped my mother's relatives escape across the border to safety in Switzerland. The entire family survived. Their son, Dr. Mordecai Paldiel, became the director of Yad Vashem's Righteous Gentiles Section. He helped process many righteous gentiles' applications until his recent retirement, including those of Oskar Schindler, of *Schindler's List* fame, and that of Schindler's wife, Emilie.

The saga of the Holocaust continues. A day does not go by without news of some new discovery related to one of its many facets. Almost every day we come across a review of a new book published somewhere in the world that strives to shed new light on one of its aspects. With each passing year, the number of Holocaust survivors shrinks, but the enormity of the event does not diminish. Of all the things Hitler was wrong about, his greatest miscalculation was that killing large numbers of Jews would elicit little response from the world. The world does not want to forget the Holocaust, or perhaps it does but is not able to. The mystery of why the Nazis did what they did remains a mystery. The existential questions it raises refuse to go away. Before long a century will have gone by since those ghastly events took place. But time does not seem to matter. The questions continue to press on, and people need answers.

In this first part of the book we have looked at the various human aspects that conspired in making the Holocaust the "perfect storm." One question we are left with here is, was the Holocaust inevitable, or was it just a cruel accident of history?

My conclusion is that the Holocaust was avoidable. There were several critical moments when it could have been stopped, but the will of the world was not there, and the forces of darkness prevailed. It could have been stopped before it ever started if previous twentieth-century genocides, particularly the genocide perpetrated by the Turks against their Armenian population had caused an outcry in countries like Britain or the United States. It could have been stopped if Winston Churchill had been the prime minister of the UK in 1938 instead of Neville Chamberlain, who let Hitler grab Czechoslovakia and then proclaimed "peace in our time." It could have been stopped if the Évian Conference had resulted in Walter Mondale's idea of each of the democracies taking in seventeen thousand Jews from the Reich. Millions of Jews and others could have been saved if the railroads to Auschwitz and other death camps had been bombed, something which was doable but never took place. I could go on and on.

In the Holocaust the Jews became the sacrificial lamb of the world. Let it be made clear. It was not the first time in history the Jews were made to pay for no other reason than being a vulnerable minority in a cruel world. Feeling the pain of my people, I have to exert great self-control not to want to give up all hope for the human species. The Bible tells me, "Choose life," and so I have to internalize the pain and opt for optimism. What Europe did to my people during the Shoah is something that will never go away, until the end of time. But rather than dwell on the atrocities committed by so many misguided people, and the apathy of so many others, I choose to think of people like Jan Karski, and Varian Fry, and Sempo Sugihara, and Raoul Wallenberg, and Aristides de Sousa Mendes, and if I could, I would kiss their feet, for they are the ones who give us a glimmer of hope for the future.

# Part 2

# The Problem of Faith

### RABBI LEVI YITZHAK OF BERDICHEV CALLS GOD TO JUDGMENT[1]

Good morning to You, Master of the Universe,
I, Levi Yitzhak, son of Sarah of Berdichev,
I come to You to put You on trial for Your people Israel.
What do You want from Your people Israel?
What do You demand of Your people Israel?
For everywhere I look it says, "Say to the Children of Israel."
And every other verse says, "Speak to the Children of Israel."
And over and over, "Command the Children of Israel."
Father, sweet Father in heaven,
How many nations are there in the world?
Persians, Babylonians, Edomites . . .
The Russians, what do they say?
They say that their Czar is the only ruler.
The Prussians, what do they say?
They say that their Kaiser is the supreme ruler.
And the English, what do they say?

---

1. Origin unknown; attributed to Rabbi Levi Yitzhak of Berdichev.

That King George is sovereign.
And I, Levi Yitzhak, son of Sarah of Berdichev, say,
"*Yisgadal v'yiskadash shmei raboh*—
Magnified and sanctified be Your Name."
And I, Levi Yitzhak, son of Sarah of Berdichev, say,
"From my stand I will not budge
And from my place I shall not move
Until there be an end to all this suffering.
"*Yisgadal v'yiskadash shmei raboh*—
Magnified and sanctified is only Your Name."

## A CENTURY LATER

In a few years the events discussed in this book, beginning with the Nazis' rise to power in 1933, will become a century old. There is little chance the enormity of the evil we call the Holocaust will recede into the past when that milestone is reached in 2033. These events have already affected every aspect of life and culture on this planet, and as the years pass their impact continues to grow. In explaining the Holocaust, it is not enough to discuss the historical events of those years of darkness. We need to take a look at life now, as the new century unfolds, and see what progress has been made decades after one of the most advanced nations in the world committed history's greatest crime. Has the world learned the lesson? Are we in a better place than we were then? Can we continue to go about our life as if it were "business as usual"?

After the freeing of the slaves in the United States as a result of the American Civil War, it took nearly a century for the goal of granting the freed slaves equal rights to become a reality. The defeat of Nazi Germany and its allies in World War II set in motion a new world order where institutionalized racism and racial supremacy were no longer acceptable. But it also resulted in a Cold War, dividing the world into two camps engaged in a nuclear arms race, with the threat of a nuclear holocaust hanging over the heads of humankind during most of the second half of the twentieth century. Not unlike the threat of Nazism, this new threat was also ideological. It was the result of two diametrically opposed ideologies, namely, communism and capitalism, saying in effect to each other, "This world is not big enough for the two of us. It's either you or we." With the demise of the Soviet Union, the Cold War and the threat of a nuclear holocaust seemed to have ended. But international conflicts, international terrorism, totalitarian regimes, and, worst of all, genocides, have not ended.

It can be argued that the post-Holocaust, post–Cold War world is suffering from an ideological crisis. On a recent visit to Vietnam, which is still a communist country, our guide in Saigon (yes, they call it Saigon again, not Ho Chi Minh City), said to our group, "We are not really communists. We call ourselves 'red capitalists.'" Similarly, to soften the selfish nature of right-leaning capitalism, a recent U.S. president tried to put into currency the term *compassionate conservatism*. It can be further argued that the major religions of the world, especially in the West, are also undergoing an ideological crisis. Jews, Christians, Muslims and others are facing a crisis of faith. The tectonic plates of organized religion are shifting. Much of it is happening under the surface, but there are signs everywhere. In this second part of the book let us take a look at the problem of faith in the post-Holocaust world.

Faith needs to be looked at in the broadest sense of the word—not only faith in God but also faith in people, not only religious faith but also faith outside religion. As a student of religions, I am aware of a dual process taking place around the world today. On the one hand, masses of people, from the former Soviet Union to Africa and Latin America, are turning to religion. On the other hand, masses of people everywhere are turning away from religion. This process is not new. It predates the Holocaust. But in the post-Holocaust world it takes on a new urgency. It puts in question both faith and the lack of faith. How can one believe in either God or people after Auschwitz? Conversely, how can one, to paraphrase the Holocaust thinker Emil Fackenheim, hand Hitler a posthumous victory by giving up faith?

The Holocaust teaches us a dual lesson. It teaches us that man is capable of great evil, but it also teaches us that man is capable of great good. Even in that hell on earth created by the evil occupiers of Europe, there were many people of all nationalities and creeds, as we have seen in the chapter on the Righteous Gentiles, who risked their lives to rescue the doomed. The Yad Vashem Holocaust Memorial Museum in Jerusalem deserves much credit for honoring and perpetuating their memory.

The other lesson it teaches us, as was so aptly pointed out by another important Holocaust thinker, namely, Irving Greenberg (more on him later), is that by dehumanizing certain groups of people, the perpetrators rejected the precept that all people were created equal. If there is any hope for the future of human life on this planet, then the concept of human equality must be fully implemented everywhere. This equality includes the right of every man and woman on the planet to choose to believe or disbelieve as he or she sees fit. In spite of the great progress in this area that has been made in some parts of the world in recent years, there is still much prejudice and discrimination today affecting millions of people everywhere. What is needed is a process of reexamination of traditional teachings and mental habits that exclude and discriminate. Above all else, the concept of "I am my brother's keeper," namely, I, as a member of the human race, am responsible for the welfare and the well-being of others, has to be brought home to everyone, young and adult.

The Holocaust started in Germany because the German people failed to take responsibility for the results of the actions of a criminal regime that turned the teachings of traditional Christianity on their head and replaced Christian values with the law of the jungle. Germany has come a long way since then. The recovery started with the Nuremberg Trials and the process of Denazification that was implemented by the Allies at the end of the war, and was taken over by the West German authorities. Because of the enormity of this task, involving millions of former members of the Nazi Party and Nazi institutions, the process was far from perfect. It was followed by Chancellor Konrad Adenhauer's policy of paying reparations to the victims of Nazism whose property was stolen by the Nazi state. Germany today continues to make every possible effort to own up to its past and to ensure that what happened during the twelve years of Nazism will never happen again. The same cannot be said of other countries in Europe, such as Austria, Croatia, and, yes, the Netherlands, who carry a heavy share of the guilt of their collaboration with the Nazis yet pretend to be victims rather than victimizers.

In his book *The Holocaust Is Over: We Must Rise from Its Ashes*, former Knesset speaker Avraham Burg argues that Germans and Jews today are joined at the hip as victims and victimizers, and both are suffering the consequences of this dual tragedy. It has been my personal experience in recent years as a rabbi working on cruise ships to run into German passengers who were born after the war and who carry the guilt of their parents and grandparents. Many have opened up to me and made it clear they were looking for answers. They feel that the guilt had been passed on to them, and they need to find a way to posthumously atone for the sins of the fathers. It is in everyone's interest to forgive those who seek forgiveness, yet never to forget the millions who perished because of the victimizers' inhumanity to their victims.

12

# A Brief History of Jewish Martyrdom

Not everyone believes in God. As a rabbi, it has been my experience over the years, particularly in working with young children in religious schools, that people are either born with a "God gene" or without it.[1] It doesn't seem to matter whether one is born into a believing community or not. There are people who belong to strict faith communities and yet they live their lives going through the motions of religious practice without really feeling the presence of God in their lives. And there are those who live among secular or free-thinking people and yet have a strong sense of God. I once heard the great American poet Robert Frost say that even those who call themselves atheists can also be believers, because the word *atheist* contains the word *theist*, or "believer." Over the years I have heard people ask the question over and over again, where was God during the Holocaust? I have even heard people say, I don't believe in God, but if there is a God, where was God during the Holocaust?

---

1. The God gene hypothesis was presented by geneticist Dean Hamer in his 2005 book *The God Gene: How Faith is Hardwired into Our Genes*. It argues that a specific gene, VMAT2, is responsible for spiritual predisposition. This theory is based on behavioral genetic, neurobiological and psychological studies. It posits that the God gene has a positive effect on one's life both physically and psychologically. Without necessarily endorsing this hypothesis, I mention it here solely to illustrate my long experience as rabbi and religious educator with faith or its absence in young and adult.

Where was God between 1933 and 1945? Certainly not in Germany, or in most of Europe, for that matter. When my mother wanted to leave Europe in the late '20s and go and live as a *halutza*, or pioneer, in Palestine, her father told her she had to stay in Poland, where God was. My grandfather believed that God was in exile along with his people. He prayed every day for the messiah to come and take his people back to the Promised Land. He believed that an eighteen-year-old Jewish girl had no business going off on her own and living with those godless pioneers, who were not patient enough to wait for the messiah and instead were forcing God's hand. Thank goodness my mother had a mind of her own and did leave Europe in time. The messiah never came, but Hitler did.

When I think now about those years and ask myself, where was God at that time? I cannot help but feel that God grew tired of being in exile, and went elsewhere. Demonic forces stepped in and took over. Those who demonized the Jews betrayed their own Christian God and made a pact with the devil. What is so difficult to understand is not that opportunistic anti-Semites took control of much of Europe, but that so many of the leaders of the churches in Europe reverted back to the darkest Middle Ages and betrayed their Savior. This was the case in Spain under Generalissimo Francisco Franco; but at least Franco embraced the church as a counterforce against the Left. Hitler and his gang disavowed their Christian faith and made it clear they had little use for its clergy and its institutions. This, however, did not prevent both Catholic and Lutheran church leaders in the Reich from enthusiastically supporting Nazi policies. Nor, for that matter, did it prevent the wartime pope, Pius XII, from accepting Hitler as a legitimate head of state and a Catholic, instead of excommunicating him.

Whether one is a believer in God or not, everyone is forced to confront the question of good and evil, and everyone has to have a moral code, regardless of how one defines the source and the nature of morality. Over the years, I have heard more people than I can count say, "I am a good person. I don't have to believe in God to be a good person. All that really matters in this life is to be a good person and do what's right. The rest is something that gets in the way and causes problems. There are too many people who call themselves believers, who pray to God and go through the motions of their religious faith, but they still manage to cheat and lie and behave badly."

My parents were not religious Jews. They were secular Zionists, and they believed in self-reliance. But there is no doubt in my mind that deep in their hearts they believed in the God of their ancestors, and they were good people who did not put their self-interest ahead of the needs of others. I never heard them ask the question, where was God during the Holocaust? In their youth, growing up among anti-Semitic Poles and Ukrainians, they knew that God was not there. And so they left. They left for the land that, according to the teachings of the Jewish faith, God had promised to Abraham and to Isaac and to Jacob. They knew hardship and hunger and danger. But they loved that land: the land in which more Jewish blood was shed over millennia than any other place in the world, a land referred to in the Bible as "a land that devours its inhabitants" (Num 13:32).[2] And yet that land loved them back, and to them it was the gift God gave them after God took away their families in Europe.

So I learned early on that there are many ways to God, and they do not all pass through the synagogue or the church or the mosque. And because I was born with a "God gene" in a place where no one professed to be religious, I have never wavered in my faith, nor have I ever believed that my faith was better than anyone else's. I believe there are good Christians and good Muslims and good Jews. And as a believer who found faith on his own, I do feel the need, as do so many people to this day, to ask the question, how does God fit into this catastrophe we call the Holocaust?

In this second part of the book, I shall attempt to examine several aspects of the question regarding the role of God or the absence of God in the Holocaust. I would like to look at it from the Jewish, the Christian and other sides, since the faith of all comes into play in this unprecedented human tragedy. Holocaust historians have paid much attention to the part played by the Christian churches, and Holocaust theologians have grappled with the questions of faith after the Holocaust. But nowhere have I seen an attempt to examine the events from all sides so as to form a cohesive understanding of how man can relate to God in today's world in our common human quest to put an end to genocides and establish a peaceful world order.

What we call into question here is the morality of human culture, human religion, and human belief as seen through the prism of the Holocaust. At the dawn of the twentieth century there was great optimism in Europe, a belief that the new century was going to bring great human progress and even world peace. Science and technology were going to solve the problems of the human race, do away with hunger, disease, and human conflicts. The English writer H. G. Wells, who wrote *The Outline of History*, predicted that in the new century nationalism would decline and a world government would be established. Then came the Great War and the rise of extreme ideologies on the Left and on the Right, which resulted in the next, most devastating war of all time. Unlike past wars, World War II was not fought for the greater glory of God. It was initiated and fought by a secularized self-aggrandizing state that turned its back on God, morality, and even culture.

---

2. All Bible translations are my own.

It was fought by a megalomaniac dictator and his cohorts, who decided to play God, and who legitimized murder as a political tool and issued a death sentence for an entire people. It was not the first time in human history this has happened. But its scope was unprecedented.

We are now well into the twenty-first century, but it is a century that did not start with euphoria but with the September 11 attack by Islamist terrorists on the United States. It is also a century of bloody conflicts in Africa and the Middle East and other parts of the world. Are we living in a godless world? Are we doomed to live in constant conflict, in which we can expect the worst? All those questions point back to the question, where was God during the Holocaust? By attempting to answer this question we can hope to begin to understand the world we live in today and dedicate our best efforts to finding our way out of the darkness that still linger on from those harrowing times.

## JEWISH MARTYRDOM THROUGH THE AGES

Jewish martyrdom began 3,800 years ago with the sacrifice of Isaac. While God spares Isaac's life at the last moment, there is no escaping the question why would God select Abraham to be the father of a "great nation" (*goy gadol*) in whom all "the families of the earth" would be blessed, and then, in his advanced old age, Abraham is told to take the first and only son his wife Sarah gave birth to in her advanced old age, bind him on an altar and commit a holocaust that would have put an end to that future nation by offering Isaac as a burnt offering, or *holocaustum*.

Here we have the paradox of Jewish existence. Here questions about divine justice begin. Abraham's faith, we are told, was being tested. How far was Abraham willing to go in obeying God's command? But what about the pain and suffering of an old man who is told by God, "Take your son, your only son, the one you love, and sacrifice him"? Would a just and loving God do this to someone whom he took away from his family and from his land so that he may fulfill God's will and bring the knowledge of God to the world? (Christians could ask the same question about the crucifixion, which could be seen as a foil to the story of the binding of Isaac.)

No easy answers here. Abraham did no wrong, and Isaac certainly did no wrong. Why are they being punished? Does God punish the ones God loves for no good reason?

God has been testing the faith of Abraham's descendants for millennia, and still does. This, at least, is how we can view the story of Jewish martyrdom through the prism of the biblical narrative. If we choose to dismiss the validity of the biblical text, then the whole affair becomes simply the story of a very unusual small nation going against the grain of a cruel world and paying the price. This view takes God out of the equation and leaves us exposed to our fate in a godless world where danger lurks on all sides and the strong rather than the just always prevail. I for one find this view to be wanting, because according to this view that small nation should have long disappeared. Its survival through nearly four millennia of martyrdom flies in the face of the belief in "power always prevails."

The first time this yet-to-become nation defies the laws of history and the predominance of a great power is the revolt of the Hebrew slaves led by Moses against the Pharaoh four hundred years after the time of Abraham's grandson, Jacob. We are told that Jacob's son, Joseph, saves Egypt from a severe famine. But after Joseph dies, "a new Pharaoh arose in Egypt who did not know Joseph." This Pharaoh proceeds to commit genocide against the Jews who, according to the biblical text, were multiplying at a rapid rate and were threatening his crown. The new Pharaoh decrees, "All the newly born males you shall cast into the Nile, and all the females you shall spare." The newly born Moses is taken to the Nile, but instead of being drowned, Moses is put in a basket, and sent down the river. He is found by Pharaoh's daughter, who takes him to the king's palace and raises him.

As slaves of the Pharaoh, the Hebrew tribes are property of the state and have no rights. But even after generations of slavery they refuse to assimilate into the Egyptian polytheistic culture. They maintain their faith in the God of their ancestor, Abraham, and continue to give their children Hebrew names and speak their native Hebrew language. They survive Egyptian bondage and narrowly escape extermination.

Now begins the forty-year trek through the desert as the liberated slaves make their way to the Promised Land. In the desert a mortal enemy, the Amalekites, keeps attacking the weary and the weak, killing them indiscriminately. When the tribes settle in the land of Canaan they are set upon by numerous enemies and are constantly under attack. The list is long: Canaanites, Edomites, Moabites, Ammonites, Midianites, Philistines, to name a few. But at the top of the list once again we find the Amalekites, who dwell in the Negev desert, and come north as marauders without any provocation. The biblical text keeps singling out the Amalekites as an enemy in a class all by itself. A decree is issued from on high: "Root out Amalek! Don't leave any of them alive! Make them disappear from the face of the earth!" This decree is repeated several times over a period of some three hundred years, from the time of Moses to the time of King David. One could argue that the Israelites are being ordered by their God to commit genocide, which may give pause to many a reader, particularly a Jewish reader. Once again, as in the story of the binding of Isaac, one may wonder: Is the God of Israel a loving and compassionate God?

The question of the decree against Amalek has been discussed throughout time, and is still being discussed. Once again, there are no easy answers. An Orthodox rabbi recently tried to explain it as follows: There was a fundamental difference between Amalek and all the other enemies of Israel at that time. In all the other cases, there was a reason for the conflict, be it territorial, economic, strategic, and so on. In the case of Amalek there was no reason. It was nothing but blind hatred and vicious behavior. It was killing for the sake of killing by a bloodthirsty enemy who over a long period of time was out to commit genocide against the Israelites. It had reached the point of "them or us." If the new nation was going to survive, it had to root out this implacable enemy.[3] We might add that the entire history of the ancient Near East is the history of one tribe or nation exterminating another, or a regional power such as Assyria, Babylonia, or Egypt doing the same thing (as in the case of what the Pharaoh sought to do to the Hebrew slaves). The Amalekites are one of many of the local people of that time that disappeared from the pages of history centuries ago. Indeed, the same story has been repeated all over the world, and still is.

The Amalekites become synonymous in Jewish history with all those who sought to exterminate the Jewish people. In the story of Esther centuries later, Haman, the second to the king of Persia who looks to annihilate the Jews, is considered a descendant of Amalek. That would make another Persian in our time, namely, Ahmadinejad, former president of Iran, also a descendant of Amalek. And, quite naturally, one cannot miss the connection between Nazi Germany and Amalek. As was pointed out in the beginning of the book, what sets the Holocaust apart from all other genocides of history is that the Germans had no rational motive for exterminating the Jews. Here again we have blind hatred and killing for its own sake. If history does anything, it certainly repeats itself.

Following the death of David, Israel's greatest king, the kingdom of Israel only lasts for three hundred years before the next great national catastrophe takes place. The year is 722 BCE. The kingdom has now split in two—the northern kingdom of Israel and the southern kingdom of Judah. In that year the Assyrians show up in the north, destroy the northern kingdom, and exile the ten tribes of Israel eastward to the vast recesses of their empire. We never hear from them again, and to this day the mystery remains as to what ever happened to the Ten Lost Tribes. Assyria was one of

---

3. http://www.biu.ac.il/jh/Parasha/vayikra/kle.html/; Yanklowitz, "Genocide and the Torah."

## A Brief History of Jewish Martyrdom

the most brutal empires of antiquity. It conceived of a plan that might have inspired the Nazis centuries later, namely, forcibly exiling entire populations and having them lose their culture and their national identity. This was actually the least of its acts of brutality. Even at a time when brutality was common everywhere, the Assyrians were known for excelling in torture and mayhem. It is safe to assume that not much was left of the ten tribes after the fall of the northern kingdom.

About 136 years later the southern kingdom of Judah falls as well. This brings us to the year 586 BCE, the time of the prophet Jeremiah and King Zedekiah, when King Nebuchadnezzar of the empire that brought down Assyria, namely, Babylonia, lays siege to Jerusalem and after a protracted battle conquers the city, destroys the Holy Temple, and exiles the Judeans to Babylon. While Nebuchadnezzar is seen in Jewish history as an arch-villain, in some ways he was quite an enlightened ruler, who gave the restive kingdom of Judah several chances to come around; but in the end had no choice but to come over and lay down the law.

Now, for all good ends and purposes, the end of the Jewish people was in sight. No nation in all of antiquity ever came back from destruction and exile. But Jewish history always appears to operate according to a set of rules totally different from the rules of world history. Following the fall of Babylon and the rise of the Persian Empire, the Persian emperor Cyrus allows the exiled Jews to return to their land, rebuild their house of worship, and establish an autonomous province run by the priestly class. The Jews enjoy political autonomy and religious freedom for the next three centuries, until the Hellenistic period, which follows in the wake of the spectacular conquests of Alexander the Great. Alexander's successor, King Antiochus of Syria, seeks to commit a spiritual holocaust against the Judean province by replacing the faith of Israel with Greek paganism. The Jewish population resists, and martyrdom follows. Here we have the story of Hannah and her seven sons, who refuse to give up their faith and are killed one by one. And here is where the heroic Maccabean brothers take up the fight of the few against the many and prevail. For a century their dynasty rules over Israel, until, in the last century before the Common Era, the province of Judea comes under the rule of Roman-appointed kings such as Herod the Great, whose tyranny leads to the great uprising against Rome in the first century of the Common Era. This uprising results in the second destruction of Jerusalem and the Holy Temple in the year 70 CE, and in the beginning of the dispersion of the Jews around the ancient world.

Sixty years after the destruction of Jerusalem, in 132 CE, the Jews rebel again against the Roman rule. Led by the heroic Bar Kokhba, they overthrow the Romans and establish a free state for two and a half years. But the

Romans are not about to give up. The Roman Emperor Hadrian sends his best legions to put down the revolt, and what follows is a horrendous series of massacres in which between four hundred thousand Jews (according to the Jewish count) and six hundred thousand Jews (according to the Roman count) perish. This would be comparable to the killing of six million Jews in the Holocaust. Moreover, Hadrian razes Jerusalem and the Temple and changes its name to Aelia Capitolina. On the site of the Temple he erects a statue of Jupiter. He forbids the practice of Judaism under threat of death, and seeks to put an end to the Jewish people.

Once again, the attempt fails. Not only do the Jews refuse to disappear from the stage of history, a Jew crucified by the Romans around the year 33 CE named Yeshu, or Jesus, gives rise to a new religion that will overtake the Roman Empire. Judaism itself enters a new era in which the center of Jewish life shifts from the Holy Land to the Diaspora, first in Babylon and then in Spain.

By the seventh century, the Jews will begin to live under the cross in the west and under the crescent in the east. Two daughter religions emerge from Judaism—Christianity and Islam. The two will be fighting each other to this day. On balance, the Jews will fare better under Islam than under Christianity. It is in Muslim Spain that the Golden Age of Iberian Jewry will flourish. Here the greatest Jewish religious philosopher, Maimonides, and the greatest Medieval Hebrew poet, Judah Halevi, will emerge, as well as many other Jewish luminaries who will enrich Jewish and world culture. This is not to say that Jews always lived in peace under Islam—quite to the contrary. But it is Christianity, and particularly the Catholic Church, that is accountable for Jewish martyrdom, directly and indirectly, from the Middle Ages to the twentieth century. It all begins with the Crusades, which were aimed against the Muslim world but took an enormous toll on the Jews of Europe and even of the Middle East, and it culminates with the Holocaust, which was not committed by the Catholic Church or the Protestant churches, but which had its roots in church teachings. Furthermore, during the Holocaust, the churches *for the most part* were either passive bystanders or active participants. It is this painful history that we will need to return to and do some deep probing into in this part of the book.

First, I return to the Crusades. The Crusades were a holy war fought by Christian Europe against the Muslim "infidel" who ruled the land holy to Christians and controlled its Christian holy places, which had to be returned to their rightful custodian, namely, the Church. On the way to their destination, the Crusaders came across another "infidel," namely, Jewish communities across Europe, who were an easy target for brutalizing and looting. While the Crusades were blessed by popes like Urban II, it was not the intention of the Church to exterminate the Jews. In some cases the papacy defended the Jews against the Crusaders. But the long-term impact of the Crusades on Christian-Jewish relations has been profound. The Crusades drove a wedge between the two faiths, and the two communities began distancing themselves from each other and demonizing each other, with the expected result that the dominant one began to persecute the subordinate one as things continued to escalate during the Middle Ages and down to our own time.

In Jewish historiography it is common to describe the history of the Jews in Christian Europe as the story of the persecutors and the persecuted. Rather than look objectively at both sides, Jewish chroniclers and historians down to our own time have presented us with a litany of Christian persecution and of Jewish suffering. This is perhaps the way history in general has been written from the standpoint of the weak. In today's Jewish historiography we have seen a shift towards much greater objectivity. A good example is the book *Exclusiveness and Tolerance: Studies in Jewish-Gentile Relations in Medieval and Modern Times* by the late Hebrew University professor Jacob Katz. The author analyzes Christian-Jewish relations during those two eras as an interactive phenomenon in which both sides have input; it's not that one side is active and the other passive. In the section of this volume on Polish Jewry during the Holocaust, we saw how the masses of Jews and Gentiles before and during World War II had little if any social contact with one another. This social and cultural separation between the two communities during history throughout most of Europe was the rule rather than the exception.

While Jews were forced into ghettos in medieval Europe, they also chose to live separately from their Gentile neighbors. Whereas the Church looked down on Judaism as a failed faith, the Jews for their part looked down on their Christian neighbors as the heirs of the pagan world, while they, the Jews, were the only ones who had the true faith. While Christians called Jews by derogatory names, Jews did the same in referring to Christians. The distrust, the alienation, and the contempt were mutual rather than one-sided. There was only one difference. The Christians had the power and the Jews did not. The Jews lived in Christian lands and were at the mercy of the authorities of their country of residence. Until the nineteenth century, the Jews of Europe did not have citizen rights and were aliens living in someone else's country. All this needs to be said so that when we return later to this discussion, we can begin to look for future solutions rather than dwell on the woes of the past.

One of the inglorious chapters in the history of the Church in Europe was written by the Spanish Inquisition after the defeat of the Moors. To this day, the Spanish Inquisition, which was sanctioned by Rome, is synonymous with evil wrought by religion. Medieval Spanish Catholicism was one of the most extreme manifestations of religious fanaticism, which resulted from the direct conflict between Christian Europe and Muslim Spain. As the Muslim empire retreated in the late fifteenth century, both Jews and Muslims were expelled from Spain. The Grand Inquisitor who presided over the expulsion of the Jews from Spain and did the bidding of Spain's monarchs, Ferdinand and Isabella (*los reyes católicos*) was Torquemada, a descendant of Jews who had converted to Catholicism. More than once in European history, the most vicious Jew haters were former Jews or descendants of Jews. We have discussed the case of Reinhard Heydrich, the original architect of the "Final Solution."

Here again we have a precedent for the Nazi drive to make the Third Reich *Judenrein*, free of Jews and other undesirables, which today we refer to as ethnic cleansing. As far as the Church in Spain was concerned, there was only one true faith in the world, the Catholic faith, and everything else was heresy. Unlike the Nazis, the Church gave "nonbelievers" the option to join its ranks. Many Jews and non-Jews converted under duress, but only outwardly. Jews known as *conversos* or converts or by the pejorative name *maranos* ("swine") continued to practice their Judaism in secret. The Church responded by establishing a "religious police" under the auspices of the Inquisition, which came after the offenders, arrested them, and subjected them to extreme torture that often ended in forced confessions or condemnation to be burned alive in an *auto da fé*, a religious ceremony that posed as the will of God when in reality it was more like the will of the devil. Spanish Jewry, one of the most illustrious Jewish communities the world has ever known, was scattered throughout Europe, North Africa, and the Middle East. The proud Jews of Spain vowed never to return to that land. They became active in the affairs of host countries like the Netherlands and England, and helped bring down the Spanish Empire in the New World and elsewhere by facilitating the rise of the Netherlands and particularly of England as the new powers. The expulsion of the Jews from Spain was yet another major example of Jewish martyrdom, which the Jews once again overcame as they found new places and new ways to survive and even prosper. In the Netherlands they would give rise to one of history's greatest philosophers, Benedict or Baruch Spinoza.

In his book *Ulysses*, James Joyce has a famous conversation between the book's main character, Stephen Dedalus, who is a schoolteacher in Dublin, and the school's headmaster. Did you know that Ireland is the only country in Europe that has never expelled the Jews? the principal asks the young teacher. He goes on to answer his own question: Because we never

## A Brief History of Jewish Martyrdom

let them in the first place.[4] The history of the Jews in Europe is one long litany of dislocation and peregrination. My father's family was originally from Hungary. From there it moved to Czechoslovakia and from there to what used to be Poland and now is Ukraine. At a young age my father left Europe and became a pioneer in the Land of Israel. His story is by no means unique. It is the story of a great many Jews in our time.

The Jews who left Spain and Portugal first migrated to central and northern Europe and then found their way to eastern Europe. Poland became a main center of Jewish life, which also included what today would be Lithuania, Belarus, and western Ukraine. At first Jews fared well in the kingdom of Poland, where they were welcomed as a merchant class, which was very useful for the nobility in what was an agrarian country. But in mid-seventeenth century they came under attack by the Cossacks under Bohdan Khmelnytsky. The Cossack uprising claimed the lives of a vast portion of the Jewish population, and plunged European Jewry into despair, giving rise the a large messianic movement in Europe that followed the Jewish false messiah Sabbatai Zvi, who took large numbers of Jews with him to the Land of Israel, occupied at that time by the Turks. The messianic journey ended in disaster as the Turkish sultan forced the would-be messiah to convert to Islam, leaving many of his followers stranded, and plunging European Jewry into even greater despair.

What follows in Europe and later in America in the eighteenth century is the Age of Enlightenment which sees the beginning of the emancipation of the Jews of Europe. After the French Revolution in 1789 and the Napoleonic Wars, Jews in Europe begin to receive citizenship for the first time in France and in other European countries. At first it seems that at long last Jews have finally arrived and were to become accepted as equals in a new emancipated and enlightened Europe. But the euphoria did not last long. Anti-Semitism remained the order of the day. By the late nineteenth century we have the Dreyfus Trial in France, in which the only Jewish officer of the French General Staff is falsely accused of treason to cover up for other French officers, and a young Austrian Jewish journalist named Dr. Theodor Herzl realizes that the future of Jewish life in Europe is dim. He starts the Zionist movement in an attempt to establish a Jewish state in the historic land of Israel. As the Zionist movement takes it first steps in the closing years of the nineteenth century, a new century dawns with great promise of a world at peace and unprecedented progress. It is not to be. In 1914 the Great War breaks out, and Europe is devastated. Here we link up with the earlier part of the book in which we discuss Germany before and after World War I. The stage is set for the greatest catastrophe in the history of

---

4. Joyce, *Ulysses*, 47.

Jewish martyrdom, namely, the Holocaust, or the destruction of European Jewry by the hands of the Nazis and their willing collaborators throughout Europe. Now the millennial story of Jewish martyrdom has come full circle. What started with the binding of Isaac, now culminated in the gas chambers and crematoria of Auschwitz.

One may wonder: Why did the Jewish people cling to their ancestral faith through such a harsh history? Why did the Jewish people continue to believe that God was good, that God was on their side, that they were chosen from among all the nations for a higher purpose?

In reality, not all of them did. Many left the fold. Many felt that their Jewishness was a liability rather than a blessing. During the Enlightenment in Germany, the leader of German Jewry, Moses Mendelssohn, advocated being a Jew at home and a German in public. His grandson, Felix Mendelssohn, became a Christian in order to pursue his musical career in an anti-Semitic Germany. So did the great German Jewish poet Heinrich Heine. So did, later on, the Austrian Jew Gustav Mahler. And so did many others, in and out of Germany, including Benjamin Disraeli, England's illustrious prime minister, who was once asked by Queen Victoria whether he was a Jew or a Christian. Disraeli, a man of superior intelligence and wit, responded: Your Majesty, I am the blank page between the Old and the New Testament.

Others became secular or cultural Jews, and turned their backs on their forebears' religious faith. Here we have the socialists, the Bundists, and most of the Zionists. All of them had despaired of the old belief in a messiah who would miraculously appear and redeem his people. They did not give up their identity as Jews, but they did give up the belief in a supreme being. Among the several parties that emerged in the Zionist movement in the twentieth century, only one or two were religious Zionists. All the others, on the left and on the right, were secular Jews. To this day, the majority of the Jews in the State of Israel are not religious Jews.

But the Jewish belief in God did not disappear. Even the non-theistic Declaration of Independence of the State of Israel contains the words the "Rock of Israel." Underneath the secularism or the "free thinking" of many a so-called secular Jew lurks a still small voice that says, as Moses said when the voice of God first addressed him, *hinneni*, here I am. God has not disappeared, and people today, especially Jews, whether they are actively religious or not, want to know, where was God during the Holocaust?

If we learn anything from this brief history of Jewish martyrdom over the ages, it is that this history offers no easy answers to this question. Jews could have raised the same question on several occasions in antiquity, in the Middle Ages, and in modern times. In antiquity people believed that if they were defeated by their enemies and have lost their land, their god or gods

## A Brief History of Jewish Martyrdom

were also defeated and ceased to have any power. They would accept the god or gods of their conquerors and become absorbed into the victorious belief fold. The expansion of the Christian faith around the world is a case in point. But this did not happen to the Jews. Not after the destruction of the First or the Second Temple and not after the Holocaust. One may ask why, and a whole range of answers may be offered. I only have one answer.

My answer is the Bible. The Jews have a book that remains valid to this day. Even nonbelieving Jews recognize its importance. The Jews have always known that in the Bible they find a message that comes to them from somewhere beyond human understanding. That message makes them realize that they have been given the answer, hard as it may be to grasp, and that there are no other answers.

In other words, God operates beyond human knowledge. We don't know why Auschwitz happened. And we do not know what God's plan is or was. But we do know that we cannot blame Auschwitz on God. We, the human race, have to take responsibility for it, and that includes the Jews as well. We do not know why God chose to try Abraham's faith when God told him to sacrifice his only son. And we do not know why we have suffered so much martyrdom. But we do know that God has always given us a choice, as we read in the book of Deuteronomy: "Behold, I have given you today life and good and death and evil . . . therefore, choose life" (Deut 30:19). After Auschwitz, we Jews must heed our contemporary Jewish philosopher, Emil Fackenheim, who has told us to add a 614th commandment to the 613 we have in the Torah, namely, "Do not hand Hitler a posthumous victory." In his book *After Auschwitz*, Richard Rubenstein quotes Fackenheim as follows:

> We are, first, commanded to survive as Jews, lest the people of Israel perish. We are commanded, second, to remember in our guts and bones the martyrs of the Holocaust, lest their memory perish.
>
> We are forbidden, thirdly, to deny or despair of God, however much we may have to contend with Him or with belief in Him, lest Judaism perish. We are forbidden, finally, to despair of the world as the place which is to become the kingdom of God lest we help make it a meaningless place in which God is dead or irrelevant and everything is permitted. *To abandon any of those imperatives, in response to Hitler's victory at Auschwitz, would be to hand him yet other posthumous victories.*[5]

In other words, do not give up your faith, which is what the Nazis would have liked you to do. Choose life, a life guided by the teachings of the Torah and by good deeds.

---

5. Rubenstein, *After Auschwitz*, 180 (italics added).

# 13

# A New Language of Faith

According to Buddhist teachings, all religion evolves, and Judaism is no exception. The language of religion is enshrined for all time in its sacred scriptures. Jews still speak of the Covenant. Christians still speak of Salvation. Muslims still speak of the Day of Judgment, and so on. But over time, the sacred language evolves as humans gain more experience, overcome more adversity, and acquire new knowledge. A good example in the history of the Jewish faith is the biblical verse "An eye for an eye and a tooth for a tooth." The original intent of this verse was *lex talionis*, or retribution. It literally meant punishing the offender who deliberately deprives someone of an eye or a tooth by inflicting the same injury. The intent was to limit the extent of the retribution, since revenge often meant causing greater injury or even death. By the first century BCE, however, as the biblical era ended and the rabbinic era began, this dictum underwent a major transformation by the leading sage of the day, Hillel, who reinterpreted it to mean that one had to provide a monetary compensation to the victim commensurate with the value of that organ, rather than repay injury with injury.[1]

---

1. Biblical law is seen by many as antiquated and often barbaric. This is due to the fact that one judges life centuries ago by today's standards. A good example is the so-called bitter-water test in Num 5:24, in which a woman suspected of adultery is ordered by the priest to drink "bitter water" as a pregnancy test. In ancient Israel, the mere suspicion could have resulted in the death of the presumably adulterous woman. By letting the priest take charge of the situation, the decision of the case was taken out of the hands of the jealous husband and the woman's chance to be cleared of the charge was much improved.

But quite often religion becomes frozen and does not keep up with the changing times. The prime example is the reaction of the Church in Italy to Galileo's astronomical discovery that the earth rotates around the sun rather than the other way around. *E pur si muove* (and yet it moves), poor Galileo murmured after the Inquisition forced a confession out of him to the contrary. For some religious literalists, I suppose, be they Christians or Jews, who refuse to accept the fact that Holy Scriptures always require human explication and interpretation, the sun still rotates around the earth.

A key tenet of both Judaism and Christianity is the idea of sin. Since Jews have always believed that God is just, when a major national catastrophe befell them they would take responsibility for their actions and say that God had punished them for their sins. On Yom Kippur and on other solemn occasions we find a prayer that refers to the destruction of the Holy Temple and the exile by stating, "Because of our sins we have been exiled from our land." This is very much in keeping with the teachings of the biblical prophets who predicted destruction and exile because of the people's sins. After the Holocaust, traditional Jewish leaders such as the Satmar Rebbe have argued that the Jews of Europe were punished for the sins of those Jews who had turned their back on the Torah and followed in the ways of the Gentiles. When asked why did close to two million observant and pious Jews perished among the six million, the answer the Satmar gave was that when the Evil One is unleashed in the land he kills indiscriminately. This view stands at the total extreme of the many views that have been offered since the end of the war. There is nothing original or innovative about it, and for most Jews it is unacceptable.

The problem with the Satmar's response is that it is based on a belief system that is frozen in time. It does not speak to the reality of today's world. The time has come to take a new look at the language of the Jewish faith, even as post-Holocaust Christian thinkers, both Catholic and Protestant, have begun to think of a new Christian language of faith.

Let us consider the Hebrew word for sin, namely, *het*. It is derived from a Hebrew root which means "to miss the mark." It does not mean deliberately committing an evil deed. Thus, it is quite different from the Christian concept of sin, which begins with the so-called original sin, committed by Adam and Eve, who betray God. In Christian traditional belief, man is born in sin, and only baptism and the accepting of Jesus as the savior can save man from that original sin. In Judaism man is born as a *tabula rasa*, neither good nor bad. As he grows up he may become a *rasha'* (an evil person) or a *tzaddik* (a righteous person). Most people are *beynoniyim* (in the middle). Yes, there are those who commit grievous crimes, but they are not sinners but rather criminals.

Seen in this light, the Jewish narrative tells that the Jews were not exiled from their land because they were so evil, but because they had missed the mark. The 70 CE uprising against Rome, as well as the one sixty years later under Bar Kokhba, were ill-conceived, because the little province of Judea did not stand a chance against the mighty legions of Rome. The Romans could not afford to have little Judea whip their mighty army, and pulled out all the stops in both instances. It is clear that it was a mistake—one that was repeated—and the Jews paid the price. This brings us to the Holocaust. The million and a half Jewish children who were brutally murdered in the Holocaust were neither sinners nor evil. Rather, as we have seen in the first part of the book, they lost their lives because so many people on all sides missed the mark. It is futile to say "because of our sins we have had a Holocaust." It had nothing to do with sin in the traditional Jewish sense or the Christian sense. It had to do with human evil, and with the inability of those on the other side of the equation to act and do what needed to be done.

Another word in the Jewish language of faith that needs complete overhauling is the word *messiah*. The messiah my mother's father waited for in Poland did not come to Poland, and certainly not to Auschwitz. How long are the Jews expected to wait for the messiah to come? They have waited now for two thousand years. Are they to wait for another two thousand years? If the Satmar Rebbe had his way, they would have never founded the State of Israel, which he considers illegitimate, but instead would have continued to live, like the Satmar Hasidim do, in small ghetto-like enclaves on the margins of Christian and Muslim society, a pitiful remnant of what an anti-Semitic English poet once referred to as "a hopeless faith, a homeless race." One would have to take leave of one's faculties to pursue such existence.

I am not proposing to do away with the messianic idea and the messianic hope, only with the messiah as a miraculous person. I do believe that the human race must work towards a messianic era in keeping with the vision of Isaiah and Micah, when, in the end of days, "nation shall not lift up sword against nation, nor shall they learn war anymore" (Isa 2:4; Mic 4:3). This is a worthy cause for all people to strive for. Waiting for a miracle worker to redeem the world through supernatural means is an entirely different matter and in our time it has caused much more harm than good.

Yet another key term of Jewish faith that needs revisiting is the idea of the Second Isaiah of the people of Israel as a "light to the nations." Traditionally, it has meant that the small nation of Israel was destined to spread the knowledge of the one God among the people of the world. Judaism never spread around the world as a mass religion like the other two monotheistic faiths. What became widely accepted after the Holocaust is that the Jew is

God's witness to the world, a witness who is not necessarily welcome but who nevertheless plays a crucial role in humanizing the world. This role of witness also needs to be revisited. The post-Holocaust world is no longer the same as the pre-Holocaust one. It requires a new role for the Jewish people and for other people who are concerned about the direction in which the world is moving. The "light to the nations" needs to be shared by many other people around the world.

There are many other key words in the Jewish language of faith that need overhauling, but this is the subject of another book. What I would like to show in the ensuing chapters is that religions in our time need to redefine and reform themselves, as they have done in the past during times of enlightenment, and have failed to do during times that the Jewish philosopher Martin Buber has referred to as the "eclipse of God."

## THE LANGUAGE OF POST-HOLOCAUST JEWISH THINKERS

When the Holocaust came to an end in 1945, there were some acclaimed European Jewish thinkers who survived and continued to write. Some of the best known were Martin Buber, Leo Baeck, and Abraham Joshua Heschel. They were all products of the pre-Holocaust world, and their fame grew after the war. Buber and Baeck were German Jews, while Heschel was a Polish Jew who studied in Germany. They were shining examples of what I would term the Golden Age of German Jewry. While the Satmar Rebbe and others Jewish fundamentalists may cast them in a negative light, for world Jewry and for the world in general they were revered teachers. I remember reading Buber's *I and Thou* in Spanish in South America in the late '50s. Buber escaped Germany before the war and became a professor at the Hebrew University in Jerusalem. When Eichmann was captured in Argentina and brought to Israel to stand trial, Israel faced the grim decision of performing the only execution in the state's history. Prime Minister David Ben-Gurion went to see Buber to consult him on what to do.

Before the war, all three were believers in the nobility of the human spirit. But during and after the war they had to begin to introduce a new vocabulary of faith. The world they once knew was gone. The people among whom they had lived and thrived had betrayed them. Worse yet, those people had betrayed themselves by desecrating the image of God in which they, as Christians, were created. Buber, who wrote not only about Judaism but also about Christianity, had to take a second look at what he had written and titled his postwar collection of essays about the crisis of faith in Europe *Eclipse of God*. He went back to his source of faith, the Hebrew Bible, and borrowed a concept from the prophet Isaiah about the "hidden God." In other words, there are times when God disappears from human affairs, and the Shoah was such a time. Unlike his concept of I-Thou/I-It, which still resonates with many people, myself included, the "hidden God" idea barely seems to address the enormity of the Holocaust. It is simply not a good enough explanation. In his book *To Mend the World*, Emil Fackenheim writes in responding to Buber's theory about the hidden God: "This answer, arresting and thought-provoking in many ways, is, in one sense, no answer at all."[2]

Rabbi Leo Baeck was a saintly man. He was the leader of German Jewry when the Nazis came to power. He could have left Germany but chose to stay. They did not dare harm him. Instead, they interned him in the showcase concentration camp at Theresienstadt, which they used for propaganda purposes to fool the world about torture centers like Dachau, and about death camps like Auschwitz. Baeck survived the war and started a new life in the West. While at Theresienstadt, Baeck secretly wrote a book on pieces of toilet paper, later titled *This People Israel*. In this book he has the following paragraph:

> For only if the punishing Judgment of God would fall on all these *masters and servants of blasphemy*, only then would those lands once again become pure and free and wide, so that humanity would be able to live there. It is anger, often fiery anger, which speaks here, but humanity's yearning and conscience seek expression in it. It contains more true humanness then is found in many a sweet song of man.[3]

*Masters and servants of blasphemy* is part of the new language of faith Baeck had to articulate as a camp inmate and as someone who represented the goodness in both the Jewish and the German people that was now being trampled upon. But a careful reading of this passage shows that even though he was an inmate, Baeck's faith in God and in man remained unshaken, as he continued to believe that humanity was going to overcome the blasphemers and recover from the blight of Nazism.

Baeck's faith and his absence of bitterness have baffled many a postwar Jewish thinker. He stands at the exact opposite end of the spectrum from such a Holocaust theologian as Richard Rubenstein, for whom the logic of the Jewish faith died at Auschwitz. And then there was Heschel. Born in Poland and educated in Germany, Heschel addresses the Holocaust

---

2. Fackenheim, *To Mend the World*, 197.
3. Baeck, *This People Israel*, 11 (italics added).

## A New Language of Faith

in Albert Friedlander's book *Out of the Whirlwind* but does not offer any new language that may help us deal with man's bottomless evil and God's absence. As a religious writer, Heschel excels in rhapsodizing the beauty and glory of Judaism with his peerless poetic language. He makes us fall in love all over again with the treasures of the Jewish people, such as the prophets and the Sabbath and the Land of Israel. He was a passionate civil rights activist in the U.S. in the '60s and marched with Dr. Martin Luther King Jr. in places like Selma, Alabama. But the Holocaust was not at the center of his theology, and he too like Buber was not able to encompass its enormity and offer us some new language to help us deal with it.

But perhaps I am being unfair to these giants of the Jewish spirit. They were too close to the events to be able to fully assess them. They were all victims of the Holocaust, and they did not have the perspective we have now, seventy years later. They all refused to yield to despair, and they had to hold on to something, and that something was the prewar world they knew so well. Buber and Heschel were steeped in the lore of classical Hasidism, which they reintroduced to the Jewish world as a movement of Jewish renewal known as Neo-Hasidism. They brought the tales and the wisdom of Hasidism to the rest of the Jewish world and beyond. Baeck was steeped in German philosophy and liberal German Jewish thought but was too old by the time he was liberated from the Nazi hell to start all over again.

These three towering figures were followed by a new generation of Jewish scholars and thinkers and historians around the world. Some are well known and others are less known. But what seems to be common to all of them is the near-desperate struggle to grapple with the enormity of the Holocaust and its theodicy, and their search for a new language of faith that would enable them to articulate a new viable Jewish belief system where one can say yes to God without being torn by the questions we must confront when we deal with the Shoah. Later we will see that the same holds true for Christian and other thinkers in our time who have taken the time and trouble to confront the same questions.

Let us look at some of them.

We have mentioned Richard Rubenstein several times. When his book *After Auschwitz: Radical Theology and Contemporary Judaism* first appeared in 1966, it caused quite a stir and made the phrase "after Auschwitz" part of the new language of faith (or loss of faith), which resonated with many. It came out during a short period in American Christian thought in the '60s that gave rise to several "death of God" theologians, including Paul Van Buren, Thomas Altizer, and others. *Time* magazine on April 8, 1966, profiled this radical phenomenon; the following words were emblazoned on its cover: *Is God Dead?* In the tumultuous '60s it was all the rage, but the movement did not last long. Apparently the consensus in America was that God was still alive after all. Rubenstein, who had jumped on the "death of God" bandwagon, caused a great controversy in the Jewish community. He became the enfant terrible of post-Holocaust Jewish theology, which propelled him to further alienate himself from the Jewish establishment. All the while, Rubenstein continued to affirm his position as a rabbi and a Jewish scholar, and he refused to abandon his faith despite the absence of God. Rubenstein's argument ran as follows: If God is present in human history, then God controls human affairs. God, therefore, bears responsibility for the Holocaust. To Rubenstein, a God who allowed an Auschwitz to happen is a God who has abandoned the covenant with the Jewish people and could no longer be followed.

In 1992, twenty-six years after the book first appeared and the "death of God" movement was a thing of the past, Rubenstein issued a second edition of his book. This time the subtitle read: "History, Theology, and Contemporary Judaism." The term "radical theology," which appeared in the first edition, was gone. Rubenstein was now sixty-eight years old and had mellowed somewhat. He rewrote many sections of the book, and added new sections about late twentieth-century issues, such as the Israeli-Palestinian conflict. In the new edition of the book Rubenstein revisits the "death of God" movement of the '60s. He writes:

> Nevertheless, *I believe that radical theology errs in its assertion that God is dead.* Such an assertion exceeds human knowledge. The statement, "God is dead," is only significant in what it reveals about those who make it. It imparts information concerning what the speaker believes about God; *it reveals nothing about God*. I should like to suggest that, since this information has strictly phenomenological import, *we ought to formulate it from the viewpoint of the observer*. It is more precise to assert that *we live in the time of the death of God* than to declare "god is dead." The death of God is a cultural fact. We shall never know whether it is more than that.[4]

Here the older and wiser Rubenstein comes to terms with the realization that "it reveals nothing about God," because the whole idea of God dying is alien to Judaism. Maimonides makes it clear in his Thirteen Articles of the Jewish faith: He has no corporeal attributes; he was, he is, and he will always be. The death of a god is a pagan idea. It appears in Greek mythology, and in a way it is borrowed by Christianity where the deity in the human form of Jesus dies and is later resurrected. It was given prominence at the end of the

---

4. Rubenstein, *After Auschwitz*, 250 (italics original).

nineteenth century by the German philosopher Friedrich Nietzsche, who rejected traditional Christianity as a "slave religion" that needed to be replaced by a new secular belief system centered on what Nietzsche called the *Übermensch*, translated into English as "Overman" or "Superman." Clearly, a fine Jewish scholar such as Rubenstein came under the sway of Christian theology in the radical '60s and went along for the ride. At the same time he sought to remain within the Jewish fold. He could not, however, have it both ways. It simply doesn't work. In the end, it didn't even work for the Christian theologians since Americans, more so than Europeans, are not ready to turn their backs on their faith.

Another Jewish writer who got on the "death of God" bandwagon in the '60s is Elie Wiesel. In his celebrated memoir *Night*, Wiesel also makes his mark on the post-Holocaust language of faith in the famous paragraph in which he witnesses the execution by hanging of a Jewish child in Auschwitz. Wiesel tells us that it took that child half an hour to die on the gallows. Wiesel goes on to say:

> Behind me, I heard the same man asking:
>
> "Where is God now?"
>
> And I heard a voice within me answering him:
>
> "Where is He? Here He is—He is hanging here on this gallows."[5]

The book first came out in English in 1960. Originally, Wiesel wrote it in Yiddish and later in French, but it was in the U.S. in the '60s that his star began to rise. I knew Wiesel in the early '60s before he became famous. He lived in a small apartment on the west side of Manhattan and worked as a reporter for an Israeli paper. I visited him in 1964 and asked him whether he still believed that God died at Auschwitz. Wiesel answered me as follows: According to Maimonides, certain questions can only be answered with silence. Subsequently, I read several of his books and I did not feel that he really believed that God had died. It was clear to me that he was extremely angry at God. In those days when I knew him, he seemed extremely lonely, as if he had no one in the world. Holocaust survivors used to stop at his place and seek some comfort from his experience and his wisdom. Once he became an American celebrity, he seemed to have changed. He finally got married, had a child, and started to live a comfortable life. Since I am equally at home in the U.S. and in Israel, I noticed that while he was lionized in America, in Israel he was not too popular. Some leading Israeli writers even referred to him as the "contractor of the Holocaust." I wasn't quite sure

---

5. Wiesel, *Night*, 62.

whether it was jealousy due to his material success, or that they did not feel he was a genuine voice of the Holocaust from their perspective. As for myself, I have always found Wiesel to be more effective as a public persona than as a writer. As for his contribution to the post-Holocaust language of faith, certainly the mainstream Jewish world has rejected his assertion that God had died at Auschwitz. Beyond that, Wiesel has not offered a language of faith that allows a way back to God after Auschwitz.

Another literary figure of our time who has confronted the enormity of the Holocaust and the question of language as it relates to human evil has been George Steiner, the cosmopolitan scholar born to Austrian Jewish parents, who is considered one of the greatest intellects of the postwar era. I once met Steiner at an international translators' conference in Washington DC, at the Library of Congress, and I was dazzled by his knowledge and eloquence. By that time I had read some of his seminal books such as *Language and Silence*, *In Bluebeard's Castle*, and *After Babel*. A few years later he published a work of fiction titled *The Portage to San Cristobal of A. H.* The premise of the book is that A. H., or Adolf Hitler, does not die in the bunker at the end of the war, but rather escapes to South America where he lives quite comfortably. Reminiscent of the Mossad's hunt for Eichmann and Mengele, here too Hitler is hunted down by Israeli agents who capture him and take him away. They run into difficulties and decide to improvise a trial for him in the rainforest. The last part of the book is a long speech by A. H. who speaks in his own defense. The defendant argues that he borrowed the idea of the master race from the Jews, who considered themselves the "chosen people," and was saving the world from Jews such as Moses, Jesus and Marx who were forcing a moral code on the world which the world did not want. The last point A. H. makes is that he may very well be considered the messiah the Jews had always waited for, because he enabled the Jewish state to come into being as a result of the Holocaust.

Needless to say, the book and the play based on the book caused a great uproar, especially among Jews. Truth be told, more than a few Jews believe that had it not been for the Holocaust, the State of Israel would not have come into being. But it may be the kind of a painful truth that many people today are not quite ready to accept, be they Holocaust survivors, Israelis, or others.

Yet it is not Steiner's take on Hitler that is of particular interest here, but rather the prominence of his extensive discussions in the aforementioned books and in much of the rest of his oeuvre regarding the nature of human language, and particularly the impact of the Holocaust and World War II on human culture and language. In his book *Explaining Hitler*, Ron Rosenbaum dedicates a chapter to an extensive interview he conducted

# A New Language of Faith

with Steiner as part of his research for his book. The interview focuses on Steiner's *A. H.* book and provides many insights into the tormented soul of this highly complex scholar and his inner struggle and inner conflicts as a displaced Viennese Jew, a cosmopolitan intellectual disenchanted with Western civilization, and simply as a man, to paraphrase Rosenbaum, who is too smart for his own good. Yet perhaps Steiner's main contribution to our discussion is his own great insights into the nature of human language. In the interview, Steiner says about Hitler:

> He [Hitler] is one of the greatest masters of the language. As are [Martin] Luther's pamphlets asking that all Jews be burned. *German language has—all languages can have it—but in the German language, Hitler drew on a kind of rhetorical power which, in a way that is perhaps peculiar to German, allies highly abstract concepts with political, physical violence in a most unusual way* ... And [Hitler] was easily a genius at that, absolutely no doubt about it.[6]

Steiner, the consummate literary scholar, is intoxicated with the power of language more as a cultural and political phenomenon than as a vehicle of faith. He shows little or no interest in the Jewish faith or the meaning of Jewish history. To him, his Jewishness is an accident of birth, an accident which for his hypersensitive soul is a terrible burden. In this respect he is very similar to other European luminaries such as Freud, Zweig, or Werfel, who were thoroughly European but only peripherally Jewish. And yet his insights into the nature of language can teach us a thing or two about the language of faith. What emerges from his interview with Rosenbaum is the terribly destructive power of language as utilized by the Nazis. One is reminded of the Talmudic dictum: "He who insults his friend in public is like one who committed murder." The Nazi onslaught started and was sustained by the rhetoric of Hitler, Goebbels, and the whole Nazi propaganda machine that whipped an entire nation into a murderous frenzy for a period of some twelve years, a period that would change the course of history forever.

Thus, over against the language of faith we have here the language of anti-faith, not only anti-Jewish faith but *anti-* the entire concept of faith, morality, and human dignity, replaced by the law of the jungle and by total reversal of language to the point where, to paraphrase George Orwell, hate is love, war is peace, and so on. We are indebted to Steiner for taking us deeper into the dark places of human language than anyone before him, but there is nothing we can learn from him about the new language of faith.

---

6. Rosenbaum, *Explaining Hitler*, 303 (italics added).

Part 2: The Problem of Faith

During the decades following the time of Buber, Heschel, and Baeck, many a Jewish scholar across the entire spectrum of Jewish belief (or lack thereof) has grappled with the issue of the language of faith after Auschwitz. By and large, not much progress was made in creating such a language. In calling his book *To Mend the World*, Fackenheim is pointing us in the right direction, which acknowledges that the world is broken and needs mending. But aside from his famous admonition to add a new commandment to the existing 613 biblical *mitzvoth*, he does not provide a new language of faith. The same applies to the rest of those who have written or spoken on this subject. The most common denominator among many of them is that they look to defend their own personal stance as a Jew or as a person in dealing with this subject. A good example is Melissa Raphael's book *The Female Face of God in Auschwitz: A Jewish Feminist Theology of the Holocaust*, in which Raphael seeks meaning for Jewish feminism in a new understanding of God's presence or the *shekhinah* during the Holocaust.[7]

Another good example is Ignaz Maybaum's theory of the Shoah. Maybaum, a European Reform rabbi imbued with the idealistic view of classical Reform Judaism regarding the progress of the Jew in the modern world, wrote a little-known book titled *The Face of God after Auschwitz*, which was published in 1966, the same year Rubenstein's well-known book *After Auschwitz* was first issued. In this book Maybaum presents a thesis diametrically opposed to Rubenstein's, but also radical in its own way. Unlike Rubenstein, who originally saw Auschwitz as the end of the road for Jewish faith, Maybaum saw the exact opposite. The Holocaust, according to his thesis, was a necessary event for the renewal of Jewish life and faith. He groups it together with the destruction of the First Temple in the days of Nebuchadnezzar (the first *Churban* or destruction), and the destruction of the Second Temple by the Romans six centuries later (the second *Churban*), whereby the Holocaust becomes the third *Churban*. Obviously, Maybaum's thesis did not play well in the Jewish world and has remained obscure to the public. But the case he is making for the idea of the three destructions is very forceful and compelling. He goes to great lengths to show how the destruction of Jerusalem in 586 BCE completely transformed the Judeans from a tribal and territorial people to a new breed of people able to survive as a community of faith living in the shadow of a pagan world power in Babylon, and in the process to begin spreading the knowledge of the one God to the rest of the world. The second destruction in the year 70 CE ended the animal-sacrifices cult in the Jerusalem Temple and made Judaism

---

7. Raphael, *Female Face of God in Auschwitz*.

a religion of the word, which has sustained the Jewish people for nearly two millennia until our time.

Regarding the third destruction, namely the Holocaust, Maybaum writes with great passion that once again God sacrificed the Jewish people for their own good and for the good of the world. According to his argument, the Jewish people in Europe, and particularly in eastern Europe, where the greatest numbers perished, had reached a dead end. They had continued to live in the Middle Ages in the middle of the twentieth century, rather than in the modern world. Hitler, as the rod of God's "creative destruction," destroyed the Middle Ages in Europe and as a result both the Jews and the world finally have fully entered the modern world. As an analogy, Maybaum uses the example of the crucifixion, in which God, according to Christian belief, sacrifices the only begotten son to save humanity. Thus, the Jews in the Holocaust did not die for their sins but for the sins of the world—for the good of the world and for their own good.

Maybaum's thesis was quite radical in 1966 and remains radical now, half a century later. But I am not ready to dismiss it out of hand, as I have dismissed the thesis of the so-called "death of God." To do so is to invalidate the words of the biblical prophet Jeremiah regarding the first *Churban*. In our search for the new language of faith, we need to reinterpret both the words of Jeremiah and the words of Ignaz Maybaum. It is very clear to me that Maybaum was overly optimistic about what he calls the "modern world," and that his optimism is rather wishful and reflects the prewar optimism of many Europeans, including many German and Austrian Jews. But Maybaum, like Fackenheim, may be pointing us in the right general direction where we need to go in order to find the new language of faith, namely, back to our roots and the great lessons of the past as seen through the prism of the Shoah.

Rubenstein, Wiesel, Steiner, Fackenheim, and Maybaum all represent non-Orthodox Jewry. The majority of the world's Jews are not Orthodox, partially because of the Shoah. To non-Orthodox Jews, the proposition of a new language of faith is perfectly understandable. It is somewhat different with Orthodoxy. Here the traditional liturgy, the traditional interpretation of the Holy Books, and the dictates of Jewish law or *halacha* remain rather fixed in time. And yet it appears that the Shoah was such a *tremendum*, to borrow Arthur Cohen's term, that even among many Orthodox thinkers and writers there has been a sea change regarding the meaning of Jewish faith after Auschwitz. Here we meet scholars like Irving (Yitz) Greenberg, Eliezer Berkowits, Sha'ar-Yashuv Cohen, and many others who, while remaining loyal to their Orthodox beliefs, have ventured beyond the Orthodox party line and have explored the realms of the new language of faith.

In my opinion, the most remarkable member of this group is Irving Greenberg. I met him thirty-five years ago when I worked as the education director for the B'nai B'rith International youth organization (BBYO) in Washington DC. He came to give a seminar to the headquarters staff on the condition of the Jewish world. He was an affable, tall, lanky young Modern Orthodox rabbi who spoke very eloquently, and he told us about a new era in the history of the Jewish faith and about the need for a new language of faith. I recall agreeing with him and being somewhat surprised to hear an Orthodox rabbi speak like that. Looking back, I realize I did not fully understand in what context he was speaking. As I became more familiar with his work and his writings, I began to understand the impact the Holocaust had on his thinking. It is only now that I have begun to fully appreciate his seminal contribution to the full spectrum of the issues that confront us. Specifically, he has looked at the human and the God-based aspects of the Shoah from both the Christian and the Jewish perspectives, and has had some important things to say about both. We shall return to this aspect of his writing later. He has dealt with the historical and theological implications of the Shoah vis-à-vis the emergence of the Jewish State in a compelling way, and has looked at the universal implications of the great tragedy that befell the Jews of Europe. He writes:

> We also face the urgent call to eliminate every stereotype discrimination that reduces—and denies—this image in the other. It was the ability to distinguish some people as human and other as not that enabled the Nazis to segregate and destroy the 'subhumans' (Jews, Gypsies, Slavs). The ability to differentiate the foreign Jews from the French-born Jews paved the way for the deportation first of the foreign-born, then of native, French Jews. This differentiation stilled conscience, stilled the church, stilled even some French Jews. The indivisibility of human dignity and equality becomes an essential bulwark against the repetition of another Holocaust. It is the command rising out of Auschwitz.
>
> This means a vigorous self-criticism, and review of every cultural or religious framework that may sustain some devaluation or denial of the absolute and equal dignity of the other. This is the overriding command and the essential criterion for religious existence, to whoever walks by the light of the flames. Without this testimony and the creation of facts that give it persuasiveness, the act of the religious enterprise simply lacks credibility. To the extent that the religion may extend or justify the evils of dignity denied, it becomes the devil's testimony. Whoever joins in the creation of the rehabilitation of the image of God is therefore practicing in 'restoring to God his scepter and

crown.' Whoever does not support—or opposes—this process is seeking to complete the attack on God's presence in the world.[8]

Thus, while Orthodox scholars are generally more particularistic and non-Orthodox are more universalistic, Greenberg, in my opinion, has exceeded all others in his understanding of the universal reach of the Holocaust in the above passage, in which he articulates some very critical points about the future language of faith.

Another Orthodox rabbi who has weighed in heavily on this discussion is Rabbi Eliezer Berkovits, author of the book *Faith after the Holocaust*. His conclusions are not nearly as far-reaching as Greenberg's. Rather, his is a more mainline Orthodox stance, which shifts the responsibility for the Holocaust from God to man. Berkovits puts great emphasis on the concept of free will, according to which man is accountable for his own actions, for otherwise man will no longer be human. He couples this concept with the Buberian concept of the hiding God, which is borrowed from the prophet Isaiah and therefore has biblical legitimacy. According to Berkovits, God was hiding during the Shoah, but was still present, suffering along with the victims. Berkovitz also turns to the book of Job as an example of the inexplicable suffering of the innocent. For Berkovitz, Job is an example of a righteous man who finally has an encounter with God and reaffirms his faith.

It is hard to find any new language of faith in Berkovits. As I suggested in writing about Buber, the idea of God hiding does not seem to provide great consolation for those like myself who lost so many family members in the Holocaust. It is a convenient way of giving God a free pass, so to speak, but it does not move us beyond the horrendous events of the years of darkness.

Another writer who talks about the hiding of God is Sha'ar Yashuv Cohen, the former chief Orthodox rabbi of my native town, Haifa. Cohen is a religious Zionist, and he sees the establishment of the State of Israel as the beginning of the coming of the messiah. He therefore takes to task those Orthodox, or rather ultra-Orthodox or Haredi, Jews such as the Satmar Rebbe who blame Zionism for the Shoah. Cohen counters their argument by positing that the failing of Diaspora Jewry to heed the call of the Zionist movement to live in Israel is what led to the Shoah. Thus, Cohen's position is not different from those he criticizes because he too sees the Shoah as a divine punishment. Nevertheless, Cohen does point us in a new direction, namely, he points to the need for a national home for the Jewish people after so many years of anti-Semitism, discrimination, and persecution. While he is waiting for the traditional personal messiah whereas I am waiting for a

---

8. Greenberg, "Cloud of Smoke, Pillar of Fire," 44.

messianic age, I have no quarrel with him. I firmly believe that our world, as Fackenheim has pointed out, needs mending, for the forces of evil in the world are alive and well. To sum it all up, voices all across the spectrum of Jewish thought and belief have struggled with the meaning of God and the Holocaust, and constructive ideas have come from all sides.

I would like to return to the issue of the new language of faith later in the book, after we have examined the import of the Catastrophe in light of Christian and other non-Jewish thought, and in light of both the dynamics of Jewish history and the rebirth of Jewish sovereignty in the land of Israel.

# 14

# Christianity and the Holocaust

Christianity was born around the time when the Jewish people lost their independence, lost their Holy Temple, lost their holy city, and began their two-thousand-year history known as the *galut*, the exile, the dispersion of the Jewish people around the world, mainly in Christian and Muslim lands. As Christianity became Europe's dominant religion and would eventually become the dominant religion of the world, Judaism shrank in numbers and lived on the margins of its host countries. There were brief periods during which Judaism was respected and was able to contribute to the common welfare and even to produce some of history's leading minds, but for the most part Jews led a precarious existence which was given a comic twist in the musical *Fiddler on the Roof*, in which the rabbi of the village of Anatevka in czarist Russia is asked what is the blessing for the czar, to which he responds: "May God bless and keep the czar—far away from us."

The Holocaust was the culmination of centuries of Jewish existence in a Christian world. As we saw in the first part of the book, the Holocaust was a perfect storm in which the Christian world on all sides of the conflict known as World War II assumed different roles by either perpetrating the annihilation of the Jews or standing by and letting it happen. In either capacity, the Christian world committed history's gravest crime, a crime not only against the Jewish people but also against itself. For during the Holocaust the Christian world lost its soul, and now—decades later—it is yet to find it. It is no wonder that adherence to the institutions of Christian faith in Europe is at an all-time low.

Historical anti-Semitism fostered by Christianity for nearly two millennia made the Holocaust possible. It gave the Nazis and their collaborators throughout Europe a spiritual license to kill Jews with impunity, and it gave the world's Christian democracies a justification not to hasten to the rescue of those who were "different." To this day, there are more than a few people in the world who consider themselves "good Christians" yet are sorry that Hitler "did not finish the job." Over the years, I have heard those words spoken, and seen them in print, in different parts of the Christian world.

But this is not where the story begins and ends. The Holocaust refuses to recede into the past and be consigned to the dustbin of history. In about two decades from now we will observe the centennial of the Nazis' rise to power, and whether you are a Jew or a Gentile you feel as though it only happened yesterday. New generations have now been born since those evil times, but the old questions are still being asked by both Jew and Gentile, only with greater intensity. The world can never go back to "business as usual" when it comes to religious belief. One can pretend the Holocaust never happened, as those known as "Holocaust deniers" do, but ignoring reality does not change it in any way, it only diminishes those who deny it.

Christian scholars and theologians around the world have begun to ask the hard questions. There has been much soul-searching, and it seems that this process will continue for years to come. Most important, the prevalent view today among those Christian thinkers across the entire spectrum of Christianity who, so to speak, look to recover the soul of their faith, is that the time has come for a major overhauling of the Christian faith so that it may be able to confront the realities of the post-Holocaust world and become the force for good it was meant to be.

This process began in the Catholic Church in 1962 under the auspices of Pope John XXIII with the Second Vatican Council, also known as Vatican II, which addressed relations between the Roman Catholic Church and the modern world. This Council, which lasted until 1965, marked a historical turning point in the annals of the Catholic Church. Among other things, as a clear result of the Holocaust, during which time Pope John XXIII did a great deal to rescue Jews, it redefined the attitude of the Church toward to Jews. The Council stated,

> True, the Jewish authorities and those who followed their lead pressed for the death of Christ; still, *what happened in His passion cannot be charged against all the Jews, without distinction, then alive, nor against the Jews of today*. Although the Church is the new people of God, the Jews should not be presented as rejected or accursed by God, as if this followed from the Holy

Scriptures. All should see to it, then, that in catechetical work or in the preaching of the word of God they do not teach anything that does not conform to the truth of the Gospel and the spirit of Christ. Furthermore, in her rejection of every persecution against any man, *the Church, mindful of the patrimony she shares with the Jews and moved not by political reasons but by the Gospel's spiritual love, decries hatred, persecutions, displays of anti-Semitism, directed against Jews at any time and by anyone*.[1]

This is not to say that the Church changed overnight and all its followers became tolerant towards and accepting of Jews and their faith. As is well known, the Catholic Church, the most powerful Christian religious body in the world, is beset today by many problems, and since Vatican II there has been much going forward and backward on many issues. One such issue is the canonization of Pope Pius XII, who is denounced by Holocaust scholars as one who failed to speak out against Nazi atrocities. Pope Benedict XVI moved him closer to canonization in 2010, eliciting much protest from Jewish groups. Nevertheless, one cannot deny that the Catholic Church has finally taken a stand against anti-Semitism and against all the ills that plagued the Church for centuries in its dealing with the Jews. Most important, in *Nostra Aetate* the Vatican finally recognized the validity of the covenant between God and Israel, alongside the validity of God's new covenant with the Church.

One writer who has chronicled the history of the Church's attitudes towards the Jews since its inception is the former Catholic priest James Carroll, author of the celebrated book *Constantine's Sword: The Church and the Jews*. Carroll's honesty and passion are remarkable indeed. One seldom comes across someone who is devoted to his own faith yet is not afraid to be critical of it where it deserves criticism. In praising Pope John XXIII for his accomplishments, Carroll quotes the great theologian Hans Küng as saying, "What he achieved for the Catholic Church was unforgettable too. In five years he renewed the Catholic Church more than his predecessors had in five hundred years . . . Only with John did the Middle Ages come to an end in the Catholic Church."[2]

The following two paragraphs from Carroll's book deserve to be quoted at length, remarkable as they are:

---

1. Second Vatican Council, *Nostra Aetate*, sec. 4, paras. 6-7 (italics added), http://www.vatican.va/archive/hist_councils/ii_vatican_council/documents/vat-ii_decl_19651028_nostra-aetate_en.html/.

2. Küng, *Reforming the Church Today*, 66-67; quoted in Carroll, *Constantine's Sword*, 550.

> The examination of conscience for which John XXIII had called required more than was possible at the time, probably even more than he envisaged . . . to eliminate the contempt of Jews that lives not only in the hearts of prejudiced Christians but in the heart of "the Church as such" requires fundamental changes in the way history has been written, theology has been taught, and Scripture has been interpreted. Indeed, in this context, the very character of Scripture as sacred text becomes an issue . . . So, yes, the reforming impulse of Vatican II fell far short of what was needed, and yes, in the years since, the authorities of the Church have done their best to dampen any return of that impulse within Catholicism. How, given this history could it have been otherwise?
> 
> But the reforming impulse refuses to die, even in the Church, because the event that set it moving has only continued to grow in force in the conscience of the West. This is what it means that, at the most basic level, Pope John XXIII was responding to the Holocaust. The Final Solution refused to remain unadjudicated in institutions everywhere. In Bayer, Swiss banks, the Louvre, owners of apartments in the Eighth Arrondissement, the Ford Motor Company, the U.S. Treasury Department, and the *New York Times* are made to confront their relationship to this unfinished business of the twentieth century, so with the Catholic Church . . . As a Catholic I have been raised with the intuition that such moral reckoning is essential to the life of conscience, whether the individual's or the community's. I now understand better than I did before that Church history is itself the record of such moral reckoning, if accomplished in fits and starts.[3]

Carroll goes on to draw the following conclusion:

> The time has come for a gathering of those invested in the future of the Church, which, as is clear by now, means a gathering more broadly defined than any in Church history. Centrally Catholic, it will also include Jews and Protestants, people of other faiths and of no faith, clergy and laity, and, emphatically, women. The time has come for the convening of Vatican Council III.[4]

In the concluding section of *Constantine's Sword*, Carroll discusses the need for the Catholic Church to fully come to terms with Jews and others by thoroughly revising the traditional Catholic understanding of the message of the Christian Savior as an inclusive rather than an exclusive message.

3. Ibid., 554–55.
4. Ibid., 558.

According to his understanding of the current state of the Church, the Church is still evolving and looking to perfect itself, rather than to lay claim to perfection and completion. Carroll's concern for the Church is not limited to the historical problem of the rejection and vilification of the Jews, but encompasses all aspects of the Church, including issues such as celibacy and contraception. In other words, he is looking for a thorough revision of the old ways to allow the modern world to finally find fulfillment in the Church.

It has been my experience over the years in working with Catholic priests and scholars, especially in the United States, that there is a great deal of goodwill and openness on their part as they reach out to Jewish clergy and scholars like myself in a sincere attempt to build bridges and enter a new era of mutual respect and understanding, not merely because of self-interest, but because of the realization that after Auschwitz they need to make a common cause with Jews and others if religion is to become a force for good in this world. In this respect, we have progressed by light-years since the time of my grandparents in Poland when the local rabbi and the local priest had absolutely nothing to do with each other, and we all know what eventually happened. I personally welcome this new reality, and it gives me hope as I will attempt to explain in greater detail when I will draw my own conclusions about the role of faith in finding a meaning in the Holocaust.

Here are some examples of Catholic scholars speaking about the impact of the Holocaust on their religious thinking. The first is that of Harry James Cargas, author *of Shadows of Auschwitz: A Christian Response to the Holocaust*:

> To call myself a Roman Catholic is to describe my spiritual development incompletely. It is more honest for me to say at this time in my life that I am a post-Auschwitz Christian in the wider context of Western Christianity. The Holocaust event requires my response precisely as a Christian. *The Holocaust is, in my judgment, the greatest tragedy for Christians since the crucifixion.* In the first instance, Jesus died; in the latter, Christianity may be said to have died. In the case of Christ, the Christian believes in resurrection. Will there be, can there be, a resurrection for Christianity? That is the question that haunts me . . . Can one be a Christian today, given the death camps that, in major part, were conceived, built, and operated by a people who called themselves Christians?
>
> . . . Jesus should be recognized as a link between Jews and Christians . . . Too often Jesus has been offered as a stumbling

block between Christians and Jews, as a rationale for mutual exclusion.[5]

Another example is quoted by Michael McGarry, author of *Christology after the Holocaust*, from a joint report sponsored by the National Council of Churches and the National Conference of Catholic Bishops:

> The Church of Christ is rooted in the life of the People of Israel. We Christians look upon Abraham as our spiritual ancestor and father of our faith . . . The ministry of Jesus and the life of the early Christian community were thoroughly rooted in the Judaism of their day, particularly in the teaching of the Pharisees. The Christian church is still sustained by the living faith of the patriarchs and the prophets, kings and priests, scribes and rabbis, and the people whom God chose for his own. Christ is the link . . . enabling Gentiles to be numbered among Abraham's 'offspring' and therefore fellow-heirs with the Jews according to God's promise.[6]

Yet another example is the words of David Tracy, author of "Religious Values after the Holocaust: A Catholic View":

> In a real sense, this [reexamining the gospel] has begun to occur powerfully among Christian theologians . . . who have begun to recognize the profoundly Jewish character of Christianity itself. The Christian God is none other than the God of Israel, the God of Abraham, Isaac and Jacob. Our Christ is none other than Jesus the Jew of Nazareth. Our sacred texts are none other than the Hebrew Scriptures, which also serve as our Old Testament, and the apostolic writings—the apostolic writings of the early Jewish Christians, which we call the New Testament.[7]

Gregory Baum, the noted Canadian Catholic theologian of German origins, writes in "Rethinking the Church's Mission after Auschwitz":

> After Auschwitz the Christian churches no longer wish to convert the Jews. While they may not be sure of the theological grounds that dispense them from this mission, the churches have become aware that asking the Jews to become Christians is a spiritual way of blotting them out of existence and thus only enforcing the effects of the Holocaust . . . *for after Auschwitz*

---

5. Cargas, *Shadows of Auschwitz*, 160–61 (italics added).

6. Quoted from "Statement to Our Fellow Christians," in McGarry, *Christology after Auschwitz*, 57–58.

7. Tracy, "Religious Values after the Holocaust," 95.

*and the participation of the nations, it is the world that is in need of conversion.* The major churches have come to repudiate mission to the Jews, even if they have not justified this by adequate doctrinal explanations. We have here a case, frequently found in church history, where a practical decision on the part of the churches, in response to a significant event, precedes dogmatic reflection and in fact becomes the guide to future doctrinal development. Moved by a sense of shame over the doctrinal formulations that negates Jewish existence, the churches have come to recognize Judaism as an authentic religion before God, with independent value and meaning, not as a stage on the way to Christianity.[8]

Here Baum speaks not only for the Catholic Church but for all of Christianity. His words are reinforced by Paul Tillich, the great German theologian of the twentieth century, who says in an interview with Albert Friedlander: "this [converting the Jews] is something that I cannot accept. I have never tried to convert Jews; we have a common task, and synagogue and church must work together."[9]

All the above statements point to a sea change in the post-Holocaust Catholic Church. As Carroll and others have emphasized, this process is far from completed. Much still needs to be done, especially at the lay level. But what should become clear is that the Catholic Church has embarked on an irreversible course that can only go forward. Jews had to pay a horrible price, but a new era has dawned on Catholic-Jewish relations.

The Catholic Church is not the only institution in the Christian world that has been grappling with the Holocaust and has done something about it. Voices are being heard from all corners of the Christian world, and they all have a similar tone—they are overwhelmed by the *tremendum* of the Holocaust, and they are looking for an answer.

The noted Christian theologian Paul Van Buren, who became well known in the '60s with the "death of God" movement, writes:

> For Christians there is a revealed relationship between God and His creatures more nearly in line with Jewish Halachic faithfulness than with our idea that all that happens does so solely by God's action. If we are to continue to speak of "by grace alone," then we shall need to allow for the fact that, by the grace of Creation, the grace of Sinai and the grace of Jesus Christ—all and each unfinished events—God has really turned over into

---

8. Baum, "Rethinking the Church's Mission after Auschwitz," 113 (italics added).
9. In Friedlander, *Out of the Whirlwind*, 520.

our hands the Way into the future which He has promised. We can move ahead in hope, but it will be a hope that calls us to cast our efforts into God's plan for the world. Redemption has been promised. The creation shall be completed. *But this is something that will not happen apart from the efforts of God's people and God's Gentile church.*[10]

In this passage van Buren points out to something I would like to examine in greater detail when I begin to draw my own conclusions about the role of faith in finding a meaning in the Holocaust.

The Uruguayan liberation theologian Julio de Santa Ana, writes in "The Holocaust and Liberation":

> The theology of the Holocaust should be replaced by a theology of solidarity, through which the Jewish people would give a full expression to their universal vocation. The emphasis should be on the expression of faith, and not on its exclusivity. This practice of solidarity begins with those who are closest. The other, the Palestinian, calls for recognition, dialogue, life with open relationships. This is what is written in the *Torah*. More than a Jewish liberation theology, it is a challenge to the Jewish people to develop a profound practice of liberation. Solidarity, beginning with the Palestinians, will be indelible proof that bitterness has been overcome. And, let us not forget, the Holocaust was a horrifying expression of bitterness—something that should never be repeated, not even by the Jews.[11]

Here again there are some points I would like to come back to later.

The Catholic German theologian Johann Baptist Metz writes in this book *The Emergent Church: The Future of Christianity in a Postbourgeois World*:

> The question whether there will be a reformation and a radical conversion in the relations between Christians and Jews will ultimately be decided, at least in Germany, by the attitudes we Christians adopt toward Auschwitz and the value it really has for ourselves. Will we actually allow it to be the end point, the disruption which it really was, the catastrophe of our history, out of which we can find a way only through radical change of direction achieved via new standards of action? Or will we see it only as a monstrous accident within this history but not affecting history's course.

10. Van Buren, *Discerning the Way*, 180–81 (italics added).
11. Santa Ana, "The Holocaust and Liberation," 44–45.

## Christianity and the Holocaust

> We Christians can never again go back behind Auschwitz: to go beyond Auschwitz, if we see clearly, is impossible for us of ourselves. *It is possible only together with the victims of Auschwitz.* This, in my eyes, is the root of Jewish-Christian ecumenism ... To confront Auschwitz is in no way to comprehend it. Anyone wishing to comprehend in this area will have comprehended nothing.[12]

As I mentioned before, Irving Greenberg, a modern Orthodox rabbi and a noted Holocaust scholar, did much to clarify the issues that emerged from the Holocaust for both Christians and Jews. In "Cloud of Smoke, Pillar of Fire," Greenberg universalizes the experience of the Holocaust to include all people. He says,

> We also face the urgent call to eliminate every stereotype discrimination that reduces—and denies—this image in the other. It was the ability to distinguish some people as human and others as not that enabled the Nazis to segregate and then destroy the "subhumans" (Jews, Gypsies, Slavs). The ability to differentiate the foreign Jews from the French-born Jews paved the way for the deportation first of foreign-born, then of native, French Jews. This differentiation stilled conscience, stilled the church, stilled even some French Jews. The indivisibility of human dignity and equality becomes an essential bulwark against the repletion of another Holocaust. It is the command rising out of Auschwitz.[13]

Why is it so important to bring Christianity into the conversation of what is a patently Jewish topic, namely, the Holocaust?

As a political system, National Socialism, or Nazism, thank goodness, is dead. In the world today there are still neo-Nazis, white supremacists, and latent Nazis, many of them hiding in the shadows and waiting for an opportunity to reemerge. But Christianity, with all its problems, and with all due respect to Nietzsche, is far from dead. The same is true of Judaism and also of God. And certainly Islam and Buddhism and the other religions of Asia, are far from dead. Even now when at long last the Jews have their own sovereign state, Jewish life, like it or not, continues to be linked in every possible way to Christian nations and Christian people who run the gamut from nominally Christian to devout Christian. Most Jews know very little about Christianity, and the little they know is often inaccurate and distorted. The reverse is equally true—the ignorance is mutual. And

---

12. Metz, *Emergent Church*, 18 (italics added).
13. Greenberg, "Cloud of Smoke, Pillar of Fire," 44.

ignorance, as should be clear by now, is at the heart of all human conflict. Considering the fact that we Jews continue to be a tiny minority in a vast Christian world, it should be clear to every thinking Jew that Jews have a much greater interest in building bridges of understanding and trust with Christians than they do with us. The typical Jewish attitude towards the Christian world, which is part traditional and part post-Auschwitz, is that of an aggrieved party vis-à-vis an aggressor. In reading the foregoing views of several Christian scholars, it is quite clear that nearly all of them accept this prevailing Jewish attitude and try to work with it as best they can. But therein lies the problem. It is my contention that it is not in the best interest of the Jewish people to continue to play the role of victims and let Christians and others do all the heavy lifting. The time has come for us Jews to reach out to Christians and to members of other faiths and cultures and to find a common language that will enable us to take our rightful place in the family of nations as an important player in the process that has already been started by the Catholic Church and by the other churches in seeking new ways of working in harmony towards mutual goals that will enable humanity to move on to a better place.

## GOD REDEFINED

The time has come for religion—all religion—with its new language of faith, to redefine God. Quite obviously, to many Christians, their Savior stands for "them and us." To many Jews, the God of Israel stands for "them and us." And to many Muslims, Allah stands for "them and us." This is what is known in religious parlance as triumphalism. This attitude does not allow for any progress in intercultural and interfaith relations, and does not build bridges for the future. Words like *heretic* or *infidel* have no place in the new language of faith. Man is not the judge of another man's faith or belief. All the major religions profess to be living by the Golden Rule, which proclaims "love others as you love yourself." This is the only rule that allows God to enter the human sphere, and if one would rather not believe in God, then this is the only rule that offers human existence the possibility of peace and understanding.

I agree with those Jewish and Christian religious thinkers like Greenberg and Santa Ana and others who maintain that in our search for an answer to Auschwitz and in our search for faith after Auschwitz we have no choice but to become universalists rather than sectarian. Christians believe that what happened to Jesus affects the entire human race. Jews believe that the God of Israel is the God of the universe. And Muslims believe the same about Allah. What this really means is that no matter what our particular path to God or to the possibility of God happens to be, we all believe in the same universal truth or in the possibility thereof, and therefore we are all responsible for one another, and the time has come for all of us to realize that life is not about "them and us"; it is about one small planet inhabited by one small species facing universal problems that cry out for solutions that can only be achieved by global human cooperation and goodwill.

The conflict among the faiths can no longer be ignored. It requires all parties to dedicate time and resources to build badly needed bridges across the abyss of ignorance and prejudice, and to stop the bloodshed everywhere on the planet.

# 15

# The Problem of Jewish Victimhood

For over eighteen centuries, from the Bar Kokhba rebellion against Rome in 132 CE to the establishment of the State of Israel in 1948, the Jewish people were stateless. They lived in host countries, which more often than not tolerated them (at best) but often turned against them and even expelled them or, as happened in the Holocaust, sought to exterminate them. It is little wonder, then, that over the centuries the Jews, who, while living in their land in the days of the Davidic dynasty or later in the days of the Hasmonean period and then under Roman rule, were a warrior people; and that after the Bar Kokhba rebellion, which was brutally suppressed by the Romans and resulted in the death of some half a million Jews, the Jews became a passive people, turning inward and becoming a faith community that relied on a supernatural force or a messianic figure to redeem them and bring them back to their land. At the same time, the Jews developed a sense of victimhood that has persisted to this day, and, in fact, after the Holocaust, became magnified among those Jews who feel that the whole world is against them, that their existence in this world continues to be precarious, and that they must guard against all enemies, real and imagined, at all cost.

This sense of Jewish victimhood has become a two-edged sword for the Jewish people. While the main lesson of the Holocaust for the Jewish people today is that without a land of their own and without the means to defend this land the Jews are at the mercy of evil regimes that may look to

## The Problem of Jewish Victimhood

repeat the Holocaust, there is a second lesson that is equally important: The Jewish people of today are not the Jewish people of the pre-Holocaust world. There comes a time in the life of a people when their attitudes and actions cannot and should not be informed primarily by fear. President Franklin D. Roosevelt understood this during the Great Depression when he said in his famous radio speech, "We have nothing to fear but fear itself." This was also understood by President John F. Kennedy, who said during the height of the Cold War, "We should never fear to negotiate, but should never negotiate out of fear." Roosevelt went on to deal with the Depression, and the United States got back on track. Kennedy's successors, particularly President Ronald Reagan, were not afraid to push their agenda of a freedom-loving world, and put the Soviet Union out of business.

The Germans of today are no longer the Germans of the 1933–1945 Nazi era. The Jews in today's world no longer face the threat of extermination. And, most important, in regard to Israel, the Arab League, in spite of its famous statement not so long ago enunciating the famous triple no, which rejected any accommodation with the Jewish state in its meeting at Khartoum in the Sudan, has changed its tune. Both Egypt and Jordan have signed peace agreements with Israel that have now lasted for some time. Despite the bluster of Iran's former president, Mahmoud Ahmadinejad, Israel's security in the Middle East has never been stronger.

And yet opportunistic Israeli politicians will have us believe otherwise. They play the fear card for all its worth to push their own agenda, which is based on the sense of Jewish victimhood, misusing the experience of the Holocaust for their own political ends. By doing so, they are handing Hitler a posthumous victory. He may not have succeeded in annihilating the Jewish people, but he may have succeeded in having many Jews live in fear now, nearly a century after he took power in Germany in 1933. This, as any thinking person should realize, is not in the best interest of the Jews. I remember Israel's former foreign minister Abba Eban once saying—and I am quoting from memory—"The United Nations expects the State of Israel to lie down with its ear to the ground and listen to any gripe expressed by any country. To me, lying down with your ear to the ground is neither dignified nor productive."

I remember when I took my granddaughter recently on a safari in the Serengeti, how the gazelles were constantly perking up their ears to listen for an approaching predator. If Jews were gazelles during the Holocaust, they certainly are not gazelles today. The people, including my parents, who founded the State of Israel, turned their backs on the mentality of what they called the Exile Jews, and became the pioneers who gave birth to the first generation of free Jews known as Israelis. As a native born Israeli, I do not consider myself to be a victim. Rather, I am a person who counts his blessings and is driven by the desire to see a new Middle East emerge out of centuries of colonialism and tyranny and obscurantism. I am very concerned about the plight of the Palestinians, with whom I grew up and whom I never considered to be my enemy. And I am equally concerned about Arabs living under oppressive regimes, particularly in countries like Syria. As a Palestinian-born Jew, I know that the best thing that can happen to Israel is full peace and harmony with the Palestinian Arabs, and a progressive Middle East. I realize this may not happen overnight, but the first rays of the Arab Spring have flickered with the fall of tyrants like Gaddafi and the push for democracy in Egypt. The Middle East has been a bad neighborhood for too long, and this has not benefited the people of the region, who continue to experience oppression and poverty and ignorance. Here Israel can and should take a more proactive role for its own sake and for everyone's sake. To do so, Israelis first must get rid of their complex of victimhood and start realizing that the whole world is not against them, and that they were put on this earth to do something not only for themselves but also for the world. This was the vision of the founders of Israel from Herzl to Ben Gurion and from Ahad Ha'am to Jabotinsky. Yes, it is easier to hide inside one's shell and shut out the world. But this is a road leading nowhere. The time has come for Jews to shed their shell of Jewish victimhood. They will do themselves a great favor if they do.

# 16

# The State of Israel as Sign and Wonder

The State of Israel was founded three years after the Holocaust ended. Hardly ever, if ever, in the history of humankind, did a people experience a genocide of such proportions followed in such a short time by the fulfillment of this people's age-old dream to become "a free people in their land." On the face of it, it was a political event. But to look upon it as merely another political event among many is to completely miss the point. It was a sign and a wonder, similar to the signs and wonders that freed the Hebrew slaves in Egypt thirty-three centuries earlier. It continues to be a sign and a wonder, as the small state continues to grow and flourish and take its place in the family of nations as a leader in many fields of human endeavor.

*Israel* is the keyword in the new Jewish language of faith. If the Holocaust had not been followed by the birth of the State of Israel, then the post-Auschwitz remnants of world Jewry would have withered away and either would have disappeared by now or would have become a pitiful vestige of what once was. The six million who died in the Holocaust were not just one-third of world Jewry. They were the heart and soul of the Jewish people. If the State of Israel did not follow Auschwitz, then it would have been safe to say that God died at Auschwitz.

The State of Israel carries an enormous responsibility on its shoulders. It is not just another state among many. First, it is responsible for the legacy of the six million. It is their *yad vashem*, namely, their memorial and the keeper of their name. Because there is a State of Israel, their death at least has some meaning. Most of them dreamed of it all their lives, whether in earthly terms or in a supernatural way. Many of them simply called it *eretz*, or land. Are you going to *eretz*? a Jew would ask his friend in Poland or in France or in Hungary. And the other Jew knew exactly what it meant. It did not mean, Are you going to America? Or to Australia, or anywhere else. There was only one 'eretz for the Jews, namely, 'eretz 'avoteinu, the land of our fathers. When Dr. Theodor Herzl, the founder of political Zionism, convened the Sixth Zionist Congress in Basel, Switzerland, in 1903, he had an offer from the British government to establish a Jewish state in Uganda, then a British colony. He waved the piece of paper with the offer enthusiastically before the congress delegates and expected them to approve it by acclamation. As an assimilated Jew who did not understand the depth of Jewish attachment to the ancestral land, he thought Uganda might be a viable solution. The Russian delegation, made up of East European Jews imbued with Jewish tradition, was in a state of shock. Among them was Ahad Ha'am, the Russian-born founder of Cultural Zionism. Ahad Ha'am later wrote an essay titled "Those Who Cried." Indeed, the East European delegates gathered in an adjacent conference room and cried. Herzl, the great visionary who was also extremely pragmatic, immediately reassessed the situation and came back to the congress with his famous pledge. He raised his right hand and said, "If I forget you O Jerusalem, may my right hand forget its cunning. May my tongue cleave to the roof of my mouth if I remember you not, if I do not put Jerusalem above my greatest joy" (Psalm 137:5–6). It became clear then and there that there was only one place in the world Jews considered their national home, and that place is called Zion.

During the '50s and the '60s and beyond, whenever Jews landed at the airport in Lod they would applaud, and some would even kiss the ground. Every Jew knew it was not only he or she who arrived in that land of dreams. It was generations of people through the many years of *galut*, or "exile," who never lived to fulfill that dream, and they were all arriving there with them. Whether consciously or unconsciously, there always seemed to be a sense of peoplehood. You do not arrive alone. You arrive with millions, including the six million, who did not make it. And you hear the beat of the wings of the *shekhinah*, the divine presence, whether you are a believer or not. This, perhaps, is the most important responsibility of this state.

Israel is also mindful of all Jews living around the world. If Jews are killed in Mumbai in a terrorist attack aimed at India, it is the responsibility of Israel to attend to it by making sure that the victims are taken care of and that justice is done. If Jews are taken hostage and are flown by terrorists to Uganda, Israel has to mount a rescue operation and bring them back from the heart of Africa. If Argentinian neo-Nazis, in retaliation for the kidnapping by Israeli agents of Adolf Eichmann, torture a young Argentinean Jewish girl, Israel has to take justice into its own hands, knowing that the Argentinian authorities will look the other way. Never before in human history has there been anything quite like it.

Second, the State of Israel happens to be home to the holiest places in the world for Jews as well as Christians, and it is also the second holiest place in the world for Muslims, second only to the Arabian peninsula. Israel the political entity cannot ignore this reality. Like it or not, the State of Israel is the custodian not only of Judaism's holiest places but also of Christianity's, and some of Islam's. When I walk down the Via Dolorosa in Jerusalem, I cannot help but hear the footsteps of the Christian Savior and of the Roman soldiers on their way to Golgotha, the field of crucifixion. When I enter the Omar Mosque on the Temple Mount and I see Muslims at prayer, I feel the depth of their faith and the sincerity of their prayers. When I stand at the Temple's Western Wall I hear the prayers of many generations of Jews, going back to the days of King Solomon. It couldn't be more real. When I touch the Jerusalem stones in all those venues, I know I touch eternity. I feel it in my bones: there lies the fate of the human race, for good or for ill.

On a visit to the Vatican, the main center of the Christian faith, I felt something similar, although not quite the same. On a visit to Jeddah in Saudi Arabia, Mecca's seaport, I wanted to visit's Islam's holiest city, but not being a Muslim I was not allowed to go there. I am sure I would have felt the spirituality of that place as well.

Needless to say, the gap in ecumenism between the Muslim world and the other two is vast. While Christianity in all its varieties is struggling to catch up with the modern world and articulate a new language of faith, Islam throughout the Arab world and in countries like Iran is held hostage by a fanatic fringe that does not allow for any religious tolerance and acceptance. This is also true in Israel and in the Palestinian territories. In another decade or so, given present trends, there will be few if any Christians living in Bethlehem, the birthplace of Jesus. The same is true of Nazareth where Jesus grew up, and even of Jerusalem where nearly 600 historic churches still stand . . .

What happened? Why has there been a great—and little reported—Christian exodus from the Middle East, with some two million fleeing in the past twenty years alone? Why have perhaps fully half of all Iraqi Christians clandestinely emigrated in the last ten years? Why have hundreds of thousands of Egyptian Copts left their homeland, with the famous Antioch community collapsing from fifteen thousand Christians a couple of decades ago to a mere handful today? The single greatest cause of this emigration is pressure from radical Islam.[1]

These estimates are alarming. They also raise a red flag for Israelis. But this does not change the fact that Israel is located in the Middle East, not in Europe, and must find ways to coexist with the Muslim Arab world. Christianity, for its part, needs to move beyond the historical conflict between itself and Islam, and reverse the trend in the Middle East of Christians leaving this part of the world.

In late life, the founder of Israel, David Ben-Gurion, told his people that Israel could not afford to be just another political entity. It was founded for a reason, and it had a mission. In many ways, Israel has already begun to live up to its mission. When Haiti was devastated by a major earthquake, Israeli medical teams were among the first to extend help to Haitian victims. In my recent travels around the world, I have found Israeli drip-irrigation systems used for farming in arid areas in countries like Chile and Ecuador and even Jordan. The list goes on and on. Technologies developed in Israel are benefiting people around the world in areas like medicine and agriculture. This is certainly a spectacular beginning, but it needs to extend beyond technologies into areas such as conflict resolution, religious pluralism, human rights, and other social activities designed to improve relations among nations and cultures around the world.

Obviously, it is not fair to expect one small country, no matter how advanced, to carry such an awesome burden on the world scene. Israel, after all, has its own internal problems. Although it enjoys a high standard of living, the cost of living is high, and young people—as is the case even in the U.S.—are not able to afford good housing and make ends meet. I am sure that many of them who may be reading my assertions will react with skepticism. They think of themselves as young people do all over the world. They want to live a good life and have a good future. I remember as a young boy growing up in Israel right after the Holocaust, the main desire of people around me was to be *k'khol ha'amim*, "like all other people." There was a general consensus to break away from the image of the Diaspora Jew, the Jew as seen by the anti-Semites: a coward, a person afraid of his own shadow, a person one can push around. We were taught to stand up for our rights, and we were taught to fight back if necessary. And rightfully so, because otherwise we would not have survived. And yet the Old Man (as we used to call Ben-Gurion in those days) knew better. He knew that the Jewish people have always had a destiny different from other nations, as it is clearly spelled out in the Bible. Individuals and nations do not choose their destiny.

---

1. Swain, *Great Silence in the Land*, 108–9.

## The State of Israel as Sign and Wonder

It is something they are born into, and they can either meet the challenge or forfeit what President Franklin D. Roosevelt used to call their "rendezvous with destiny."

The State of Israel is only in the initial stages of embracing its rendezvous with destiny. It needs to take a good look at itself, particularly in terms of its role in the world. It has been said many times that the world has double standards when it comes to Jews and to Israel. The Arabs can get away with a great deal, but Israel is often scrutinized under a microscope. This indeed is true, and quite often it is a matter of anti-Israel attitudes. But whatever the intent, the world, it seems, expects more from Israel, and rightfully so. Particularly in a post-Holocaust world, Israel, which was born out of the ashes of the Holocaust, is a sign and a wonder to the world. During the earlier years of the state, British Prime Minister Anthony Eden said that he wished Britain were more like Israel, because it once had Israel's drive and can-do mentality. Despite the fact that many countries often vote at the United Nations against Israel for all sorts of reasons, Israel is greatly admired around the world, even among educated Arabs. I know it because I have heard it from some of them. The most defeatist Israeli attitude is the one that says that "the whole world is against us." This is patently not true. To millions around the world Israel is a sign and a wonder. We can frame it in religious terms, or we can frame it any way we want, and it will still come out the same. The remarkable thing about the rebirth of Israel is that Israelis do not need to ask themselves whether or not they believe in God. They pray with the tools they use to bring the land promised to Abraham and to Isaac and to Jacob back to life, and they answer Auschwitz with the biblical imperative of "choose life." Golda Meir used to say, "What bothers me most is not that Arabs kill our children, but that they force us to kill theirs." As a child growing up in the new State of Israel, I was never taught to hate Arabs or to wage war against them. Moshe Dayan, Israel's greatest general, put it very succinctly in his *Sinai Diary*: There is no point in us killing Arabs. There are too many of them, and it can only make matters worse.[2] He and others like him made it clear that the objective of the new state was to find a way for everyone in the region to live in peace.

Peace, or *shalom*, the most beautiful word in the Hebrew language, is also a key word in the new Jewish language of faith. There is no higher command than to make peace. The Holocaust was made possible because of the devastating war during which it was perpetrated. Genocides can only be committed through violent conflict. Where there is peace there are no genocides.

---

2. This is my paraphrase.

Israel as the sign and wonder that followed the Shoah is a good point of departure for reencountering God. To find God in Auschwitz alone is not possible. Israel opens the door for us in looking for the answer. But there is much more to the answer than only the physical State of Israel. We will have to look for it beyond the confines of one small nation. The answer must be global.

The Jewish philosopher Abraham Joshua Heschel spoke of having a sense of *awe and wonder* as a prerequisite for experiencing the presence of God in the world. In his book *Israel: An Echo of Eternity*, Heschel discusses the rebirth of Israel as an affirmation of God's presence. This can only be understood by experiencing that sense of awe and wonder one encounters in understanding the role Israel is called upon to play in the world at large. What at first may seem to be an unbearable burden, will turn out in the end to be a privilege and a blessing.

## 17

## The Universality of Faith

In the second half of the twentieth century religion around the world, notably in the Soviet Union and China, was being replaced by political systems that took on a messianic aura and promised a better world of justice and equality for the human race. The religious traditions of Christianity, Judaism, Islam, and Buddhism, and other religions of the East and of the West, were suppressed and persecuted as the enemies of progress and of human welfare. In some places, such as Cambodia under the Khmer Rouge, the ferocity of this assault on traditional values resulted in the brutal death of millions. In China, Mao's Cultural Revolution, which targeted the country's Confucian traditions, achieved similar results. But nothing came close in the scope of human suffering and the loss of human life to the decades of Stalinist rule in the former Soviet Union, where the estimates of the loss of human life run higher than anywhere else in the twentieth century.

Still, the Holocaust stands apart from all of this. Tyrants like Stalin and Mao and Pol Pot espoused Marxism with its secular gospel of economic equality and solidarity among nations, none of which came to fruition. Marxism, while it did not accomplish its ultimate goals, at least liberated a major portion of the human race from centuries of imperial oppression under the Russian czar and under the pre-Mao rulers of China, when the life of the lower classes was practically worthless. The Nazi assault on the Jews, on the other hand, had absolutely nothing redeeming about it. It was nothing but insane and irrelevant brutality against segments of Europe's population who had nothing to do with the German national interest yet were systematically exterminated like some plague-carrying bacteria. And yet, as we look back on the second half of the twentieth century, we are compelled to see a link between the Holocaust and all the other mass killings and genocides perpetrated upon the human race since 1945 and up to the present, as was alluded to by the Orthodox Jewish thinker Greenberg.[1] The common denominator among all of them is the unprecedented scope of human suffering inflicted by man against man.

Redemption, as all religions teach, comes out of suffering. The cumulative suffering of the human race around the world in the past one hundred years, since World War I, has been unprecedented. The questions of good and evil and the meaning and purpose of life have not become less, but rather more, urgent. The secular ideologies have failed to provide the answers. Nor do science and technology have the answers to the ultimate questions of life. The questions are left to each person to figure out for him- or herself, and to the traditional religions.

According to an article dated March 3, 2013, on the website foreignpolicy.com/,

> From Muslims in Europe to evangelical Christians in Africa, it is religious believers who are shaping the early twenty-first century. Charismatic movements are sweeping throughout the Southern Hemisphere, while high birth rates among immigrants are provoking soul-seeking in the historically Christian West. For this List, FP looks at the fast-growing faiths that are upending the old world order.[2]

The article goes on to show how religions across the globe are growing at a steady rate. What I find particularly remarkable are the inroads made by Christian denominations such as Mormons, Seventh Day Adventists, Jehovah's Witnesses, and Pentecostals—to mention only a few—both in traditional Catholic countries within Latin America and in the non-Christian Far East, mainly in South Korea. At the same time, Islam is growing throughout the Arab world and also in Europe. Those two trends have far-reaching implications for the near future and for the long term.

Those countries around the world that have a multireligious and multicultural population—and Israel is one of them—have an obligation to cultivate religious pluralism and peaceful coexistence among the various belief systems. This is the key to peaceful coexistence worldwide. Notable examples of countries that have more or less achieved religious pluralism

---

1. In his essay "Cloud of Smoke, Pillar of Fire," Greenberg shows how all genocides are interrelated.

2. *Foreign Policy*. "The List: The World's Fastest-Growing Religions."

## The Universality of Faith

and peaceful coexistence are the United States, Great Britain, France, Russia, India, Indonesia, Malaysia, Egypt, and South Africa. Such societies have the opportunity to promote interaction through their educational systems and their social life among the various faiths so as to bring down the barriers of mistrust, discrimination, and prejudice. In the final analysis, all faith systems strive for the same thing. All have embraced the Golden Rule. All seek to live ethically, to create a community that cares for all its members, and to achieve well-being and tranquility. All, in the final analysis, believe in the same God, who embodies the ultimate reality of the universe and offers a counterpoint to the limitations of human life.

There are those who will argue that achieving such harmony among the world's religions is impossible. They will point to all the wars that have been fought in the name of religion; they will accuse religion of creating barriers among people; they will pit science against religion and argue that while science is precise and reliable, religion is based on superstitions and fanciful ideas that have no basis in reality. Moreover, they will cite the centuries of conflict between Christianity and Islam and between those two and other religions, notably the centuries of persecution of Jews in both Muslim and Christian lands. Such views and attitudes are very common in the twenty-first century, for very obvious reasons. Disillusionment with the human condition and distrust in the ability of individuals and societies to overcome their differences are common, especially among sophisticated and well-informed people. But this kind of an attitude leaves no room for hope. It condemns the human race to perpetual conflict which, in this day and age of advanced technologies—particularly nuclear technology—can only lead to self-destruction on a global scale, to the end of life on the planet as we know it. This attitude posits that religion is incapable of regeneration and of solving conflicts. It looks upon religion as a negative force, an aberration of the human mind, something man needs to overcome and leave behind. In other words, it reverts to the attitudes towards religion that were displayed by the failed ideological movements of the twentieth-century, movements such as communism, National Socialism, anarchism, nihilism, and so on.

My answer to all those people, among whose ranks are dear friends of mine and many highly intelligent people, is that all those other ideologies have been tried and have failed. If religion has also failed, it is not because the teachings of Moses and Jesus and Muhammad and the Buddha and all the other founders of the world's religions espoused evil or injustice. Quite the opposite: It has been the failure of those who professed to follow those teachings yet distorted them to suit their purposes, and in the name of morality and justice committed immoral and unjust acts. The teachings of those great teachers of humanity, if heeded by their followers, have the power to redeem the world. For this to happen, people of faith must begin by respecting the beliefs of other people of faith and must accept the basic premise that there are many paths to God, that God does not belong to any particular group, that all people are equal in the eyes of God, and that all religions are human interpretations of the will of God. In short, no one religion has a monopoly on the truth, and no one religion is infallible, that is, free of error. Enlightened members of all the major religions, as we saw in the case of Vatican II, have come to accept this basic premise. Those who believe the opposite—and they can be found in all religions—are arrogating unto themselves more knowledge and power than they actually possess. They put into question one of the basic tenets of all religion, namely, humility.

In both classical Greek and Hebrew thought, considering oneself superior to others is seen as a major human failing.[3] The time has come for all people everywhere to understand that we humans are fellow travelers on a small and fragile planet; that all the knowledge we possess is the cumulative result of all human effort everywhere throughout the ages; that the time has come to put a stop once and for all to prejudice and to conflict and to genocides, and to make every effort to reduce human violence everywhere. This goal deserves every effort and every sacrifice, for the future of human existence on this planet depends on it. The world must unite to abolish all weapons of mass destruction everywhere, and channel all the resources that have been wasted since World War II on such weapons to be used for social and economic programs designed to abolish hunger and poverty everywhere so that a peaceful world may emerge at long last.

Whether or not one believes in God, people of faith—of all faiths—and particularly their spiritual leaders, are the ones who hold out hope for making peace in the world. Politicians are people of expedience; spiritual leaders are or at least are expected to be exemplars of moral behavior. They must all leave their comfort zone and reach out to one another across all the divides and work together for the common goal they all profess to believe in.

## CIVIL RELIGION

Millions of people in the world today do not believe in God and do not practice the religion into which they were born or any other religion. Some call themselves atheists, some agnostics, and some do not even bother to label their lack of religious faith. Yet even those who consider themselves

---

3. See the Greek concept of hubris and the teachings of the prophet Isaiah about human pride.

godless believe in something, live by a certain set of rules, and engage in ceremonial and communal activities that repeat themselves every year on a given date. They are part of what has become known as the "civil religion" of present-day society. The symbol of the civil religion is the national flag of one's country. The holidays celebrated by that religion are the national holidays. The prophetic figure is the founder or liberator of the country. Some of the outstanding successors of the founder become part of the pantheon of great people of that common faith. A belief in a deity may or may not be incorporated into this belief system. In some countries it is and in other countries it is not. But each society has its laws, its social system, and its cultural heritage. In each society there is a consensus regarding the validity of all those structures that bind together the members of the society in much the same way a theistic religion does.

The term *civil religion* was coined by the French philosopher Jean-Jacques Rousseau in his book *The Social Contract* (1762), describing what he regarded as the moral and spiritual foundation essential for any modern society. For Rousseau, civil religion was a broadly defined system that provided the state with a quasi-sacred authority and enabled it to function as a cohesive organism. Needless to say, the term is vague and manifests itself in many different ways. But the intent is clear. In order for society to function, it needs what Rousseau refers to as a "social contract," which in many ways resembles the precepts and rituals that an organized religion expects its adherents to follow.

One does not have to believe in a supreme being to follow civil religion. Nor does one have to consider oneself a believer to be a moral person. But inasmuch as one finds the answers in civil religion, one thing should be emphasized: civil religion cannot answer the ultimate questions of life, nor is it a substitute for traditional religion. Moreover, when civil religion respects the rights of the individual member of society, it can be a great force for good. But when civil religion, as has happened in Nazi Germany, gives up its civil rights and allows a leader to become the master of life and death, one can expect the worst.

18

# The Possibility of Faith after the Holocaust

As I pointed out in the beginning of this second part of the book, some people naturally grasp the existence of God in the universe and some do not. For those who don't, the issue of God allowing the Holocaust to happen is a nonissue. They are left to puzzle over humanity's bottomless capacity for evil. To borrow the words of the new pope, Pope Francis, "Who am I to judge?" Who am I to question their disbelief? No book ever convinced me to believe or not to believe in God. In elementary school my teachers, who were secular Zionists, taught me that when the biblical prophets tell us that God spoke to them, what they really mean is that they were hearing the voice of their own conscience. In Israel's secular schools, the Hebrew Bible is taught as a history book depicting the early history of the Hebrew people. In fact, some of my teachers did not refer to themselves as Jews but as Hebrews. Jews lived in the Diaspora. Hebrew-speaking Israelis were Hebrews, as was Abraham and all his descendants up to the time of the Babylonian exile in 586 BCE, when the exiled Judeans finally became Jews. The Hebrews had taken time out from history for two thousand years, but they (the pioneering generation of the newly born State of Israel) picked up where the Bible had left off and once again became Hebrews. And yet, miracle of miracles, they failed to convince me that I was a Hebrew rather than a Jew, and that all the prophets heard was the voice of their own consciences. For me the math was very simple. Whose words were more persuasive—the words of a Moses or a Jeremiah, or the words of my grade school teachers?

And yet as I look back on those early years of my life I begin to realize that there was some grain of truth in what my teachers were trying to tell me. The only way a mere mortal can grasp the reality of God is through human understanding and through such a feature of the human brain that traditionally has been referred to as conscience, or to use the Freudian term, the superego. And herein lies the answer as to why God has allowed the Holocaust to happen.

The sages of the Talmud raised the question: Why does the Bible, in referring to God's relation to the biblical patriarchs, use the phrase "God of Abraham, God of Isaac, and God of Jacob"? Why not simply say, "God of Abraham, Isaac and Jacob"? The answer they give is this: The God of Abraham was not quite the same as the God of Abraham's son, Isaac, or Isaac's son, Jacob. To each person God took on a different meaning. While Jews believe in the unity and timelessness of God, they also believe that we, who stand in a relationship to God, are called upon as individuals to form our own personal idea of God, and that we are called as a community to continue to find new meaning in how God's presence is manifested in our particular moment in time. And so there is little point in my answering the question, why did God allow it to happen? Each one of us needs to answer this question for him- or herself. All I can do is try to share my own view in the hope that it may stimulate some thoughts in readers' minds and help in forming some answers, albeit partial, that may shed some light on this issue.

## GOD RECONSIDERED

We are looking for a viable post-Auschwitz God. The first thing we need to come to terms with is that the atrocities of Auschwitz were committed by people like you and me, not by God. But if we are to believe in a loving and caring God, then we have to reconcile this unspeakable evil with the belief that God created a species capable of committing bottomless evil. The common tendency is to ask the question, why did God create such a human race? Why is there so much suffering in the world? Why do innocent children die? People everywhere have been asking these questions for thousands of years, and still do. And many have lost and continue to lose their faith in God when they suffer a personal loss, or when life becomes overwhelming.

What seems to be the ultimate implication of the above questions is the finality of life. Man finds it difficult to accept the reality of death. Life, whether short or long, whether well-lived or a life of misery, is finite. The ultimate question here is: Why did God—if there is a God—create finite beings? Finding this reality to be unbearable, the world's religions created the concept of the afterlife. Whether it is Buddhism with its belief in reincarnation, or the Abrahamic faiths with their belief in heaven and hell, many people, past and present, cling to the notion that after they depart from this life, they will continue to live forever with their individual identity and self-awareness intact.

Christianity was founded on this belief. Islam has embraced it to such a degree that young Muslims in today's world are willing to become martyrs because a much better life is awaiting them. Jews embraced this belief around the time of the birth of Christianity. But when we go back to the teachings of the Hebrew prophets, there is no mention of an afterlife. To the prophets, life is here and now, and when one dies, one's life continues in the lives of one's children and children's children. To this day, Jews live their lives in such a way that the emphasis is always on life here and now, while the belief in heaven and hell is something in the realm of maybe. Maybe there is an afterlife, and maybe there isn't. Reform Jews believe in the immortality of the soul. Orthodox Jews believe in *'olam ha'bah*, the world to come, in which a resurrection of the dead will take place.

Be that as it may, the belief in an afterlife is something no one can prove. Since I cannot prove it, I do not choose to stake my life on it. It seems to me that when God says to Adam, "You are dust, and to dust you shall return" (Gen 3:19), God means exactly that. We are mortal, and we have to accept our mortality. There are reasons why we have to depart from this life, the most obvious being that we have to make room for others to take our place. This is the law of nature, and it applies to all living beings. We must accept it gracefully and make the best of it. It is as good a point of departure as any to begin to come to terms with the possibility of a God we can accept after all that the human race, and particularly the Jews, have been through.

In other words, we have to approach the reality of God by accepting the unbridgeable chasm between the human and the divine. All that we are, God is not, and all that applies to God does not apply to us. God is infinite, yet we are finite. God is all-powerful, yet we are not. God is all-knowing, yet our knowledge is limited. God has answers to questions we cannot answer. And yet, at the same time, as we have seen in the biblical stories of creation, God has endowed us with God-like qualities, such as the ability to think for ourselves, to make the right and the wrong choices, and to go out into the world and fend for ourselves. Perhaps God could have interfered in the Holocaust and stopped the atrocities. And perhaps God did finally interfere. In order for the Holocaust to end before all the Jews of the world

## The Possibility of Faith after the Holocaust

were completely wiped out, the Allies had to first win the war. Nazi Germany and its allies were defeated, and the Jewish people, as has happened several times before since the time of Egyptian bondage, were able to rally and not only survive but also establish a homeland for the first time in two thousand years. Was the hand of God in all this? Is the defeat of evil a sign from God? Were Jewish scientists like Niels Bohr and Robert Oppenheimer who built the atomic bomb that defeated the Japanese guided by the hand of God? And what about the small Jewish community in Palestine that defeated seven Arab armies? How does all this work together, and how are we expected to make any sense out of it? It is what it is, and we must do what Jews have always done, namely, accept the course of events (*tzidduk ha'din*), accept the unfathomable divine justice, and rebuild our lives.

At the same time, we need to understand that we and the entire human race have entered a new phase in human history in regard to the human-divine nexus. God is no longer what God used to be. God is no longer the old man with the white beard (and hasn't been for a very long time) as depicted so beautifully by Michelangelo on the ceiling of the Sistine Chapel in the Vatican. God is no longer Big Daddy who will take us by the hand (as once happened with Adam and Eve) and take care of everything. The time has come for all of us, of all creeds and colors, to turn to one another and at long last accept our global kinship and our global responsibility for one another, and let God take a vacation. God has been too busy for too long, and we have been difficult and unruly children. We need to give God a break, and we need to marshal all of our God-given gifts, particularly our brains and our brawn, to do God's work. Several of the theologians cited earlier—both Jewish and Christian—have derived this conclusion from their thinking about the Holocaust. And as for me, I have felt for years that "God only helps those who help themselves." God may help the helpless in mysterious ways, but it should have long become clear to everyone that man is not supposed to sit on his hands and wait for miracles. In my travels around the world in recent years I have encountered two types of societies. There are those who roll up their sleeves and get the work done, no matter how difficult. And there are those who sit back and find excuses not to make the effort, because "it is too difficult," or "it's useless." Needless to say, the results are there for the whole world to see.

As I mentioned in the beginning of the second part of this book, it has been my experience that there are those who seem to be born with a "God gene," and those who are not. I would take this a step further and suggest that there are those who think they are believers, and those who think they are not. And yet it is not always what one thinks. It is, in effect, what one does. One can act in a godly way, or one can act in an ungodly way. This is precisely what the Hebrew prophets meant when they spoke about ethical action outweighing ritual action. Does God desire offerings or heeding the divine message? the prophet asks. And the question, of course, is rhetorical.

In the book of Deuteronomy we are told that the word of God is not far away from us:

> Now what I am commanding you today is not too difficult for you or beyond your reach. It is not up in heaven, so that you have to ask, "Who will ascend into heaven to get it and proclaim it to us so we may obey it?" Nor is it beyond the sea, so that you have to ask, "Who will cross the sea to get it and proclaim it to us so we may obey it?" No, the word is very near you; it is in your mouth and in your heart so you may obey it. (30:11–14)

We feel the presence of God when we perform an act of kindness, when we feel the pain of others, when we bring joy to others. It is what Martin Buber has taught us: God exists in our relationship with others. When we open our hearts to others, we find God.

Earlier in discussing the language of faith I mentioned the idea of one of the leading Jewish Holocaust theologians of our time, Emil Fackenheim, regarding the 614th commandment. Fackenheim suggested that we add a new commandment to the 613 that appear in the Torah. He wrote that after the Holocaust we need to affirm our Jewish faith so as "not to give Hitler a posthumous victory." I fully agree with him, but I would like to suggest that we also add a 615th commandment, which applies not only to Jews but to the entire world:

*Let us reaffirm the first commandment which says, "I am Adonai your God who brought you out of the land of Egypt" (Exod 20:2), but let us also acknowledge the universality of God as the one who binds the entire human race together, and who commands us to do everything within our power to preserve all human life on this earth.*

Every person, believer and nonbeliever alike, can accept at least the second part of this commandment. The alternative is to continue on the path of hatred and bigotry and genocide which the human race has been pursuing since the beginning of time. Let us, at long last, say *no* to war and wanton killings, which still abound on our planet, and let us begin our journey together on the path of peaceful coexistence. This is precisely what God expects of us, indeed, it is what our humanity expects of us.

# 19

# The Way Back

This book began with the story of the Shanghai Ghetto, where Jewish refugees from Nazi persecution found a haven at the far end of the world. It continued with humankind's history of genocides. It has taken us through the *how* and *why* of the Shoah, and then it turned to the question of divine justice or the absence thereof, and to how humankind can once again find hope in a better future. The moral law in nature operates in such a way that evil carries within itself the seeds of its own destruction, so that good eventually prevails, albeit not instantly, and usually not even within what we might consider a reasonable timeframe.

After the story of the flood, the biblical texts offer us another well-known story, namely, the story of the Tower of Babel. To quote:

> Now the whole world had one language and a common speech. As people moved eastward, they found a plain in Shinar and settled there. They said to each other, "Come, let's make bricks and bake them thoroughly." They used brick instead of stone, and tar for mortar. Then they said, "Come, let us build ourselves a city, with a tower that reaches to the heavens, so that we may make a name for ourselves; otherwise we will be scattered over the face of the whole earth."
>
> But God came down to see the city and the tower the people were building. And God said, "If as one people speaking the same language they have begun to do this, then nothing they plan to do will be impossible for them. Come, let us go down

and confuse their language so they will not understand each other."

So God scattered them from there over all the earth, and they stopped building the city. That is why it was called Babel—because there God confused the language of the whole world. From there God scattered them over the face of the whole earth. (Gen 11:1–9)

This story, like everything else in the Bible, has a multitude of meanings. For one thing, it attempts to provide an answer to the question of why people speak a host of different languages. It also reflects the reaction of a nomadic, desert people to the great temples or ziggurats of Babylonia, which must have overwhelmed them and led them to conclude that the Babylonians were arrogant people who defied the will of God. Jewish tradition tells us that the builders of the Tower of Babel wanted to build a tower so tall that it reached to heaven, and their intent was to dethrone God and become the rulers of the universe. However, the rabbis of the Talmud and the medieval Jewish commentators, such as the great Rashi, found many contradictions in the story, and provided a variety of interpretations. But when we put all those commentaries together, what emerges is the following: Unlike the flood generation, which was utterly wicked and therefore was destroyed, the generation of the Tower of Babel started out as a good generation that had a common language, was united, and worked together in harmony. But by the time it became caught up in the project of building a tower that reached into the heavens, it was carried away by arrogance, became immoral, and provoked the wrath of God. God did not go so far as to destroy that entire generation, as had happened with the generation of the flood, but instead allowed it to survive. So, rather than reaching up to heaven, humankind was scattered around the world, and thus a variety of cultures were created, which, according to some of the commentators, was a positive thing.

The story of the tower of Babel is a metaphor of singular importance for our time. We live in an age of globalization, of the breaking down of barriers among people all over the world, of incredible scientific discoveries and technological advances. English has become a global language used all over the world as a lingua franca in many areas of human endeavor. Man has begun to build tower-of-Babel-like buildings such as the Burj al-Khalifa in Dubai, which dwarfs the Empire State Building, and even taller ones are being planned in other parts of Asia. Nuclear weapons make it possible to wipe out the entire human race. At the same time, nuclear energy holds the promise to solve the world's energy problems. Medicine is making enormous progress, and human life is being prolonged: many more people are reaching the age of one hundred and beyond than ever before. To such progress there is no end in sight. But the question raised by the ancient biblical author remains as valid today as it was thousands of years ago: Is man cognizant of the fact that man is not the master of nature, and that man is bound by the moral law? Will man in the twenty-first century repeat the mistake of the Generation of the Tower of Babel, which thought it was about to become god-like, and in the end was beaten down and scattered? In short, the story of the tower of Babel reminds us that there is a moral law in nature, and that this law emanates from a source beyond human understanding, which is commonly referred to as God. We need to find our way back to the moral law.

How do we find a way back?

Recently an Israeli Orthodox rabbi named Menachem Froman passed away in Israel after a bout with cancer. While he served as a rabbi to settlers on the West Bank, who are considered an obstacle to peace, Froman himself was one of the leading advocates of a two-state solution and of peace with the Palestinians. He and I had attended the same secular high school in Haifa, the Hareali School (he was five years younger), considered by many to be the best high school in Israel to this day. While this school produced more key Israeli military leaders than any school in Israel, I was never taught by my high school teachers to hate the Arabs or look upon them as my enemy. My hometown of Haifa has always been known as a town where Jews and Arabs found a common language. Froman was a product of that environment, and I regret not having known him while he was alive, since I am sure we could have been good friends. Froman knew the top Palestinian leaders, including Yasser Arafat and his successors, and even the leaders of the Hamas, and often met with them, and they all admired him, and told him more than once that with people like him, they could sign a peace agreement in a heartbeat. In an interview in the *Haaretz* newspaper before he died, Froman said something that to me is the answer to how we can make peace in the world and find our way back to the source from which all of us have strayed for so long. He said, and I quote from memory, "Real peace will not be made by politicians. It can only be made by spiritual leaders."[1]

Froman's statement deserves some careful consideration. Faith is man's most intimate experience. It is known to bring out the best in man, but it is also known to bring out the worst. It is common these days to blame all the ills of the world on religion. Books by authors such as Richard Dawkins and Christopher Hitchens, who have been vigorously campaigning against

---

1. Ettinger, "Farewell to a Freedom Fighter."

established religion, have attracted a large readership. Hitchens's book, *God is Not Great*, is a good case in point. The author takes to task each major religion—the three monotheistic faiths, Buddhism, and so on. The trouble with the book is that the late journalist was not exactly an expert on religion. His exposé on Judaism, for example, is far from accurate. He tends to generalize and oversimplify. The subtitle of his book is, *How Religion Poisons Everything*. As a substitute for religion, he and his colleagues offer science and reason. They seem to forget that in the twentieth century science and reason under the guise of several political ideologies failed to bring about a better world, but rather resulted in pseudoscience (eugenics, for instance) and pseudorational regimes, such as National Socialism and Bolshevism, which also tried to substitute science for religion.

The likes of Hitchens and Dawkins also fail to understand that human morality is based on something deeper than human reason, and that natural or physical or even social sciences never produced a moral code to live by. They fail to realize that the Greco-Roman tradition, which gave us reason and philosophy and science, did not provide a moral code that rivals the teachings of Moses and Jesus and Muhammad and the Buddha, and that serves as a substitute for those faiths. Dawkins, Hitchens, and others latch on to ancient myths such as Moses and the burning bush or Muhammad riding his horse to heaven or Jesus walking on water, and present them as the sum and substance of those faiths. They totally ignore the enlightened thinkers of those faiths, and they dwell on the fanatic fringe of each religion as though it represents everyone's thinking. In short, they purposely present a skewed picture that appeals to those who have a gripe against religion, and, to be quite frank about it, they take cheap shots at something they have quite a few mistaken notions about. It is true that religion has not given us utopia. But neither has science or reason. Man went to war in the name of religion, and still does. Even people of the same faith fight each other, and pray to the same God to make them victorious over their coreligionists. But by doing so they do not follow the teachings of their own faith. Quite to the contrary, they violate those teachings. The paraphrased saying is, "religion is the last refuge of the scoundrel."

Throughout time, dictators and villains of all stripes have used religion as a cover-up for their misdeeds and illegitimacy. In the name of love, in the name of patriotism, and in the name of God, man has committed many a crime. This is not to say that love, patriotism, and God are evil. But this seems to be the logic followed by writers like Dawkins and Hitchens. In other words, they put the emphasis on the wrong syll*able*.

It is easy to overlook or simply ignore all the good that the world's religions have done for countless of their followers and communities over the ages, and still do. By ritualizing the lifecycle, believers have been able to sanctify birth, to celebrate life's rites of passage, and to take the edge off the sorrow and pain of bereavement. They have been able to come together on their respective holidays, renew their bond with their heritage, and link up with past generations. By practicing prayer and meditation, they have been able to find solace and inspiration and peace of mind. In our time certain political ideologies have tried to do away with all of this, but have failed. Man continues to find the way back to faith, and faith continues to sustain him. But above all else, it reminds him that there is a higher power that nurtures him, both physically and spiritually.

Rabbi Froman, in making his statement about spiritual leaders rather than politicians (along with politicians we could also include military leaders) bringing peace, did not mean to say that we do not need politicians or military leaders. To the best of my understanding, what he meant was that you cannot leave people's faith out of the equation of bettering the world. Or, for that matter, you cannot leave God out of it. We need God as an anchor for the human condition to find its mooring. Otherwise, we will continue, to follow this metaphor, to toss about on a rocky sea, and our ship will continue to sail aimlessly. We need to find the ultimate God, the one that does not belong to anyone in particular but belongs to everyone. And to do so, all religious leaders need to get together, to begin to talk to one another in the name of their communities, and to find out how they can bring God back into the lives of all their followers.

During my years as a practicing rabbi in several parts of the United States and also in Central America, I have interacted with clergy and scholars of many religious organizations and institutions—whether Jewish, Christian, or of other religions. To this day, long after I have retired from my various careers, I continue to interact with clergy and scholars of other religions. What I keep learning over and over again is that there is a great yearning among all of them—Christian, Jewish, Muslim, Buddhist and others—to reach out to their colleagues in the other faiths and to establish a productive dialogue; to get to know one another better; and to work together for the common good. Quite often they do not know where to begin. Or they are afraid to do so because of political pressure.

Here is one interesting episode I would like to mention, which took place about four years ago: I was invited to participate in a panel on the political situation in the Middle East, which was being taped by an Iranian news agency located in Washington DC for dissemination in the Arabic-speaking world. The Iranians could not—or would not—use an official Jewish or Israeli representative, and since I am not involved in politics they felt I would be a fairly impartial party. The other two panelists were two distinguished professors, one from Georgetown University and one from George Washington University, both of them Arabs living in the United States. In the course of the taping they took the side of Iran's president, Mahmoud Ahmadinejad, while I took the side of Israel. Otherwise, the discussion was quite civil. After the taping ended, one of the two turned to me and said, "You realize, of course, that I had to take the stand I took, as was expected of me in the Arab world. This does not mean that you should take all my remarks literally; how about you and I go out to lunch where I can speak more freely?"

Most people derive their notions of the world and of other human groups and religions from the media—whether from print media or from radio, television, or the Internet. What they fail to realize is that the media hardly ever report incidents such as this one, and many others that I keep experiencing because of my background and credentials. Moreover, the media are busy with stories of human conflict, and neglect to tell us about all the positive things that are happening in our world. I maintain that only by direct contact with many different people and cultures can one begin to obtain an accurate picture of the human condition, and I submit that it has been my great good fortune to travel the globe in recent years and do exactly that.

I would therefore like to expand Rabbi Froman's statement about spiritual leaders rather than politicians being the ones who can bring us closer to a peaceful, godly coexistence. I would like to suggest that spiritual leaders are not only clergy and theologians. They also include inspired political leaders who act not out of self-interest but out of a higher moral conviction—men like Thomas Jefferson and Abraham Lincoln, for example. I would also include social thinkers and reformers like Jean-Jacques Rousseau and John Locke. I would include all the teachers of humanity who were moved by the spirit of something higher than themselves and who gave us a better world. And to the power of the spirit I would like to add the *power of the people*. Spiritual leaders cannot operate in a vacuum. They need to be able to have an impact on their followers. And throughout my lifetime it has been my experience that whenever people are moved by inspired leaders to right the wrongs of society, it is ultimately the power of the people that makes the difference. I have always felt that the saying *vox populi, vox dei*—"the voice of the people is the voice of God"—is where God is to be found. We do not know, and we will never know, the ultimate reality of God. But we can feel the presence of God in human action. Whenever and wherever people overthrow the yoke of tyranny, there God is. Wherever people overcome adversity and want, there God is. Where people live in peace and harmony, there God is.

# Conclusion

We will never know why a loving and caring God told Abraham to sacrifice his only child. We will never know why something as terrible and unspeakable as the Holocaust took place. We have long made our peace with the first question, but we are still struggling with the second. But our children's children will have to come to terms with it. They will have to incorporate it in their Jewish narrative and in their human narrative. They will have to integrate it in their language of faith, not only the Jewish faith but all faith. It will never go away. There is no escaping what had happened. The more you try to distance yourself from it, the more it will come back to haunt you. We, the human race, have been marked with the Sign of Cain. We will find no peace until and unless we begin to learn how to live in peace and harmony with one another. We do not have to clutch everyone to our bosom, but we must treat everyone with respect, with deference, cognizant of our common humanity. We must erase hurtful words from our human vocabulary, and speak no evil. This has been taught by all the major religions, and this has been accepted as the divine will. The ultimate victory over Hitler and his misguided and murderous ideology is the repairing of the world in the image of the kingship of God.

# Bibliography

Arendt, Hannah. *Eichmann in Jerusalem: A Report on the Banality of Evil.* 1963. Reprinted, Penguin Classics. New York: Penguin, 2006.

Baeck, Leo. *This People Israel: The Meaning of Jewish Existence.* Philadelphia: Jewish Publication Society, 1965.

Baldwin, Neil. *Henry Ford and the Jews: The Mass Production of Hate.* New York: Public Affairs, 2001.

Bardakjian, Kevork B. *Hitler and the Armenian Genocide.* Zoryan Institute Special Report 3. Cambridge, MA: Zoryan Institute, 1985.

Bartov, Omer. *Germany's War and the Holocaust: Disputed Histories.* Ithaca: Cornell University Press, 2003.

Bar-Zohar, M. *Beyond Hitler's Grasp: The Heroic Rescue of Bulgaria's Jews.* Avon, MA: Adams Media, 1998.

Bauer, Yehuda. *Rethinking the Holocaust.* Yale Nota Bene. New Haven: Yale University Press, 2002.

Baum, Gregory. "Rethinking the Church's Mission after Auschwitz." In *Auschwitz: Beginning of a New Era?* edited by Eva Fleischner, 113–28. International Symposium of the Holocaust at the Cathedral of Saint John the Divine. New York: Ktav, 1977.

Ben-ami, Shlomo. *Scars of War, Wounds of Peace: The Israeli-Arab Tragedy.* New York: Oxford University Press, 2006.

Berenbaum, Michael, poster. "Jan Karski: Hero, Rescuer, Resistor." Illinois Holocaust Museum. https://www.ilholocaustmuseum.org/jan-karski-hero-rescuer-resistor/.

Berkovitz, Eliezer. *Faith after the Holocaust.* New York: Ktav, 1973.

Brand, Sandra. *I Dared to Live.* Rockville, MD: Shenigold, 2000.

Breitman, Richard. *Architect of Genocide: Himmler and the Final Solution.* New York: Knopf, 1991.

Buber, Martin. *The Eclipse of God: Studies in the Relation between Religion and Philosophy.* Introduction by Robert M. Seltzer. Atlantic Highlands, NJ: Humanity, 1988.

Burg, Avraham. *The Holocaust Is Over; We Must Rise from Its Ashes.* New York: Palgrave Macmillan, 2008.

Cargas, Harry James. *Shadows of Auschwitz: A Christian Response to the Holocaust.* New York: Crossroad, 1990.

# Bibliography

Carroll, James. *Constantine's Sword: The Church and the Jews: A History*. Boston: Houghton Mifflin, 2001.

Cesarani, David. *Becoming Eichmann: Rethinking the Life, Crimes, and Trial of a "Desk Murderer."* Cambridge, MA: Da Capo, 2007.

Charny, Israel W., ed. *Encyclopedia of Genocide*. 2 vols. Santa Barbara, CA: ABC-CLIO, 1999.

Cohen, Arthur. *The Tremendum: A Theological Interpretation of the Holocaust*. New York: Crossroad, 1981.

Cohen-Sherbok, Dan, comp. and ed. *Holocaust Theology: A Reader*. New York: New York University Press, 2002.

Davies, Lizzy. "France Responsible for Sending Jews to Concentration Camps, Court Says." *Guardian*, February 16, 2009. http://www.theguardian.com/world/2009/feb/17/france-admits-deporting-jews/.

Dawidowicz, Lucy S. *The War against the Jews, 1933–1945*. New York: Holt, Reinhart & Winston, 1975.

Dawkins, Richard. *The God Delusion*. Mariner Books. Boston: Houghton Mifflin, 2008.

Dayan, Moshe. *Diary of the Sinai Campaign*. New York: Schocken, 1967.

Des Pres, Terrence. *The Survivor: An Anatomy of Life in the Death Camps*. New York: Oxford University Press, 1980,

Dietrich, Otto. *The Hitler I Knew: The Memoirs of the Third Reich's Press Chief*. New York: Skyhorse, 2010.

Dostoevsky, Fyodor. *The Brothers Karamazov: A Novel in Four Parts with Epilogue*. Translated and annotated by Richard Pevear and Larissa Volokhonsky. New York: Farrar, Straus & Giroux, 2002.

Ettinger, Yair. "Farewell to a Freedom Fighter." *Haaretz*, October 29, 2008. http://www.haaretz.com/weekend/week-s-end/farewell-to-a-freedom-fighter.premium-1.508133/.

Fackenheim, Emil. *To Mend the World: Foundations of Post-Holocaust Jewish Thought*. Bloomington: Indiana University Press, 1994.

Fest, Joachim. *The Face of the Third Reich*. Translated by Michael Bullock. New York: Da Capo, 1999.

Fleischner, Eva, ed. *Auschwitz: Beginning of a New Era?* International Symposium of the Holocaust at the Cathedral of Saint John the Divine. New York: Ktav, 1977.

*Foreign Policy*. "The List: The World's Fastest-Growing Religions," May 14, 2007. http://foreignpolicy.com/2007/05/14/the-list-the-worlds-fastest-growing-religions/.

Friedlander, Albert, ed. *Out of the Whirlwind: A Reader of Holocaust Literature*. Rev. ed. New York: UAHC Press, 1999.

Friedländer, Saul. *Nazi Germany and the Jews: 1933–1945*. Abridged by Orna Kenan. New York: HarperPerennial, 2009.

Friedman, Richard Elliott. *Who Wrote the Bible?* 1987. Reprinted, San Francisco: HarperSanFrancisco, 1997.

Fritz, Stephen G. *Ostkrieg: Hitler's War of Extermination in the East*. Louisville: University Press of Kentucky, 2011.

Fromm, Erich. *Escape from Freedom*. New York: Holt, Rinehart & Winston, 1994.

Gershman, Norman. *Besa*. Documentary available in three parts on YouTube: http://www.youtube.com.

## Bibliography

Gerstenfeld, Manfred. "Wartime and Postwar Dutch Attitudes toward the Jews: Myth and Truth." Jerusalem Letter / Viewpoint. Jerusalem Center for Public Affairs. http://jcpa.org/jl/vp412.htm/.

Gilbert, Martin. "Churchill and the Holocaust." http://www.bbc.co.uk/history/worldwars/genocide/churchill_holocaust_01.shtml/.

———. *Kristallnacht: Prelude to Destruction*. New York: HarperCollins, 2006.

Goebbels, Josef. *The Josef Goebbels Diaries*. New York: Award Books, 1971.

Goldhagen, Daniel. *Hitler's Willing Executioners: Ordinary Germans and the Holocaust*. New York: Vintage, 1997.

Gradowsky, Zalman. *In the Heart of Hell*. Tel Aviv: Yediot Aharonot, 2012 (in Hebrew).

Greenberg, Irving. "Cloud of Smoke, Pillar of Fire: Judaism, Christianity, and Modernity after the Holocaust." In *Auschwitz: Beginning of a New Era?*, edited by Eva Fleischner, 7–55. International Symposium of the Holocaust at the Cathedral of Saint John the Divine. New York: Ktav, 1977.

Hamer, Dean H. *The God Gene: How Faith Is Hardwired into Our Genes*. New York: Doubleday, 2004.

Hecht, Ben. *A Child of the Century*. 1954. Reprinted, New York: Primus, 1985.

Heine, Heinrich. *The Complete Poems of Heinrich Heine: A Modern English Version*, by Hal Draper. Cambridge, MA: Suhrkamp/Insel Boston, 1982.

Hemingway, Ernest. *Green Hills of Africa*. New York: Scribner, 1963.

Heschel, Abraham Joshua. *God in Search of Man: A Philosophy of Judaism*. New York: Farrar, Straus & Giroux, 1976.

———. *Israel: An Echo of Eternity*. New York: Farrar, Straus & Giroux, 1987.

———. *The Prophets: Two Volumes in One*. 1962. Reprinted, Peabody, MA: Hendrickson, 2007.

———. *The Sabbath: Its Meaning for Modern Times*. Noonday Series. New York: Farrar, Straus & Giroux, 1975.

Hilberg, Raul. *The Destruction of the European Jews*. New York: Holmes & Meier, 1984.

Himmler, Katrin. *The Himmler Brothers: A German Family History*. Translated by Michael Mitchell. London: Macmillan, 2007.

The History Place. *The Triumph of Hitler*. "The Burning of Books." http://www.historyplace.com/worldwar2/triumph/tr-bookburn.htm/.

Hitchens, Christopher. *God Is Not Great: How Religion Poisons Everything*. New York: Twelve, 2007.

*The Hitchhiker's Guide to the Galaxy: Earth Edition*. "Josef Mengele—The Angel of Death." http://h2g2.com/approved_entry/A2875368/.

Hitler, Adolf. "The Final Political Testament of Adolf Hitler." http://www.historylearningsite.co.uk/adolf_hitler_political_testament.htm/

———. *Mein Kampf*. Translated by Ralph Manheim. Boston: Houghton Mifflin, 1971.

———. "On the Jewish Question." http://www.jewishvirtuallibrary.org/jsource/Holocaust/hitjew.html/.

International Holocaust Remembrance Alliance. "Hungary." https://www.holocaustremembrance.com/member-countries/holocaust-education-remembrance-and-research-hungary/.

Irving, David. "Revelations from Goebbels' Diary: Bringing to Light Secrets of Hitler's Propaganda Minister." Institute for Historical Review. http://www.ihr.org/jhr/v15/v15n1p-2_Irving.html/.

## Bibliography

Isaac, Jules. *The Teaching of Contempt: Christian Roots of Anti-Semitism*. New York: Holt, Rinehart & Winston, 1964.

"Jan Karski (1914–2000); Humanity's Hero." http://www.google.com/culturalinstitute/exhibit/jan-karski-humanity-s-hero/QR_UaCtP.

Jewish Library. "Chiune Sugihara." http://www.jewishvirtuallibrary.org/jsource/Holocaust/sugihara.html/.

Joyce, James. *Ulysses*. New York: The Modern Library, 1946.

Karski, Jan. *Story of a Secret State*. Boston: Houghton Mifflin, 1944.

Katsh, Abraham I., trans. and ed. *The Warsaw Diary of Chaim A. Kaplan*. Rev. ed. New York: Collier, 1973.

Katz, Jacob, *Exclusiveness and Tolerance: Studies of Jewish-Gentile Relations in Medieval and Modern Times*. New York: Behrman House, 1983.

Kershaw, Ian. *Hitler: A Biography*. New York: Norton. 2008.

Lemkin, Raphael. "Genocide." *American Scholar* 15 (1946) 227–30. http://www.preventgenocide.org/lemkin/americanscholar1946.htm/.

Levi, Primo. "Primo Levi's Heartbreaking, Heroic Answers to the Most Common Questions He Was Asked about 'Survival in Auschwitz.'" 100 Years, 100 Stories. *New Republic*, October 23, 2014. http://www.newrepublic.com/article/119959/interview-primo-levi-survival-auschwitz/.

Levine. Hillel. *In Search of Sugihara: The Elusive Japanese Diplomat Who Risked His Life to Rescue 10,000 Jews from the Holocaust*. Kindle ed. New York: Free Press, 1996.

Lita'i, Chaim Lazar. *Masada of Warsaw*. Tel Aviv: Machon Jabotinski, 2014 (in Hebrew).

*London Times*. Unsigned editorial, July 16, 1938.

Maduro, Otto, ed. *Judaism, Christianity, and Liberation: An Agenda for Dialogue*. 1991. Reprinted, Eugene, OR: Wipf & Stock, 2009.

Manvell, Roger, and Heinrich Fraenkel. *Doctor Goebbels, His Life and Death*. 1960. Reprinted, New York: Skyhorse, 2010.

Maybaum, Ignaz. *The Face of God after Auschwitz*. Amsterdam: Polak & Van Gennep, 1965.

Mayer, Arno J. *Why Did the Heavens Not Darken? The "Final Solution" in History*. 1988. Reprinted, New York: Verso, 2012.

McGarry, Michael B. *Christology after Auschwitz*. An Exploration Book. New York: Paulist, 1977.

McGarty, Craig. *Categorization in Social Psychology*. Thousand Oaks, CA: Sage, 1999.

Meir, Golda. *My Life*. London: Weidenfeld & Nicolson, 1975.

Metz, Johann Baptist. *The Emergent Church: The Future of Christianity in a Postbourgeois World*. Translated by Peter Mann. London: SCM, 1981.

Mondale, Walter. "Geneva and Evian." *New York Times*, n.p. July 28, 1979.

Morse, Arthur D. *While Six Million Died: A Chronicle of American Apathy*. New York: Overlook, 1998

Nagorski, Andrew. *Hitlerland: American Eyewitnesses to the Nazi Rise to Power*. New York: Simon & Schuster, 2012.

National Council of Churches, and the National Conference of Catholic Bishops. "A Statement to Our Fellow Christians." Issued by the Study Group on Christian-Jewish Relations. http://www.bc.edu/content/dam/files/research_sites/cjl/sites/partners/csg/csg1973.htm/.

Nietzsche, Friedrich. *Thus Spoke Zarathustra*. New York: Viking, 1960.

# Bibliography

The Nizkor Project. "Joseph Goebbels' Diaries: Excerpts, 1942–43; Part 2 of 2." http://www.nizkor.org/hweb/people/g/goebbels-joseph/goebbels-1948-excerpts-02.html.
Orwell, George. *1984*. New York: Signet, 1950.
Paldiel, Mordecai. *Saving the Jews: Amazing Stories of Men and Women Who Defied the "Final Solution."* Rockville, MD: Schreiber, 2000.
Peck, Abraham J., ed. *Jews and Christians after the Holocaust*. Philadelphia: Fortress, 1982.
Porat, Dina. *The Blue and the Yellow Stars of David: The Zionist Leadership in Palestine and the Holocaust, 1939–1945*. Cambridge: Harvard University Press, 1990.
Posner, Gerald. *Mengele: The Complete Story*. New York: Cooper Square, 2000.
Raphael, Melissa. *The Female Face of God in Auschwitz: A Jewish Feminist Theology of the Holocaust*. Religion and Gender. London: Routledge, 2003.
Read, Anthony. *The Devil's Disciples: Hitler's Inner Circle*. New York: Norton, 2004.
Remarque, Erich Maria. *All Quiet on the Western Front*. New York: Random House Trade Paperbacks, 2013.
Rosenbaum, Ron. *Explaining Hitler: The Search for the Origins of His Evil*. New York: Da Capo, 2014.
Rosenberg, Stuart, dir. *Voyage of the Damned*. ITC Entertainment. 1976.
Roth, Philip. *The Plot against America*. New York: Vintage, 2005.
Rousseau, Jean-Jacques. *The Social Contract, and The Discourses*. Everyman's Library 162. New York: Knopf, 1993.
Rubenstein, Richard L. *After Auschwitz: History, Theology, and Contemporary Judaism*. 2nd ed. Johns Hopkins Jewish Studies. Baltimore: Johns Hopkins University Press, 1992.
Santa Ana, Julio de. "The Holocaust and Liberation." In *Judaism, Christianity, and Liberation: An Agenda for Dialogue*, edited by Otto Maduro, 40–52. 1991. Reprinted, Eugene, OR: Wipf & Stock, 2009.
Schoenberner, Gerhard. *The Yellow Star: The Persecution of the Jews in Europe, 1933–1945*. Translated by Susan Sweet. New York: Fordham University Press, 2004.
Schüssler Fiorenza, Elisabeth, and David Tracy, eds. *The Holocaust as Interruption*. Conciliuim 175. Norwich, UK: SCM, 1984.
Sereny, Gitta. *Into That Darkness: From Mercy Killing to Mass Murder*. New York: McGraw-Hill, 1974.
Shirer, William L. *The Rise and Fall of the Third Reich: A History of Nazi Germany*. New York: Simon & Schuster, 2011.
Speer, Albert. *Inside the Third Reich: Memoirs*. Translated by Richard and Clara Winston. New York: Simon & Schuster, 1997.
Steiner, George. *The Portage to San Cristobal of A. H.* Phoenix Fiction. Chicago: University of Chicago Press, 1999.
Steiner, Jean-François. *Treblinka*. Translated by Helen Weaver. New York: Meridian, 1994.
Sudetic, Charles. "World War II." In "Historical Setting" (chapter 1), 40–42. In *Romania: A Country Study*. Edited by Ronald D. Bachman. 2nd ed. Washington DC: Federal Research Division, Library of Congress, 1991. http://www.countrystudies.us/romania/22.htm/.
Swain, K. W. *A Great Silence in the Land*. New York: AuthorHouse, 2010.
Thomas, Dylan. *Collected Poems of Dylan Thomas*. Introduction by Paul Muldoon. New York: New Directions, 2010.

## Bibliography

Thomas, Gordon, and Max, Morgan-Witt. *Voyage of the Damned*. London: Hodder & Stoughton, 1974.

Tracy, David. "Religious Views after the Holocaust: A Catholic View." In *Jews and Christians after the Holocaust*, edited by Abraham J. Peck, 87–107. Philadelphia: Fortress, 1982.

Trunk, Isaiah. *Judenrat: The Jewish Councils in Eastern Europe under Nazi Occupation*. Lincoln: University of Nebraska Press, 1996.

Tuchman, Barbara. *The Guns of August*. New York: Presidio, 2004.

Van Buren, Paul. *Discerning the Way: A Theology of Jewish-Christian Reality*. New York: Seabury, 1980.

*Völkischer Beobachter*. Unsigned editorial. July 1938.

Wells, H. G. *Outline of History: Being a Plain History of Life and Mankind*. Garden City, NY: Garden City Books, 1956.

Wiesel, Elie. *Night*. New York: Hill & Wang, 1960.

Wikipedia. "Obersalzberg Speech." http://en.wikipedia.org/wiki/Obersalzberg_Speech.

Wikipedia. "Balfour Declaration." http://en.wikipedia.org/wiki/Balfour_Declaration.

Woeste, Victoria Saker. *Henry Ford's War on Jews and the Legal Battle against Hate Speech*. Stanford: Stanford University Press, 2012.

Wright, Clyde J. *Protocols of The Meetings of The Learned Elders of Zion*. Whitefish, MT: Literary Licensing, 2013.

Yanklowitz, Schmuly. "Genocide in the Torah: The Existential Threat of Amalek." My Jewish Learning. http://www.myjewishlearning.com/beliefs/Issues/War_and_Peace/Combat_and_Conflict/Types_of_War/Genocide.shtml.

Zygielbojm, Szmul. "The Last Letter From Szmul Zygielbojm, The Bund Representative with The Polish National Council in Exile." http://yad-vashem.org.il/about_holocaust/documents/part2/doc154.html/.

www.ingramcontent.com/pod-product-compliance
Lightning Source LLC
Chambersburg PA
CBHW031358230426
43670CB00006B/587